The Indian Hundi

James F. Frayne

MONTANA PUBLISHERS

First Printing: 2017

Montana Publishers

ISBN: 978-1-326-87077-5

Ordering information:
Special discounts are available on quantity purchases by corporations, associations, educators, and others.
For details, contact the publisher at the e-mail address detailed below.

U.S. trade bookstores and wholesalers:
Please contact publishers at: e-mail at TGTG2014@hotmail.com

By the same author:
Easy as you Go! A Mathematical Companion (Volume 1: A – L)
Easy as you Go! A Mathematical Companion (Volume 2: M- Z)
A-Star Mathematics Question Bank (Without Solutions)
A-Star Mathematics Question Bank (With Solutions)
Selected Biology Advance Level Topics Volume 1 (A to J)
Selected Biology Advance Level Topics Volume 1 (K to Z))
Tall Grows the Grass (Full Adventure Novel)
Tall Grows the Grass (Books 1 – 3)
Past and Future Present (Novel)
Hell Bank Notes (Catalogue of Contemporary Issues)
Romancing the Wood (Wooden Nickel 'Flats' of the USA)
Jenny Two-tails and her Friends (Children's Story Book)

For more details, please visit author's website at:
http://jamesfrayne.net

Contents

Jammu &
Kashmir
Himachal
Pradesh
Punjab
Uttarakhand
Sikkim
Rajasthan
Uttar Pradesh
Assam
Nagaland
Meghalaya
Bihar
Manipur
Tripura
Mizoram
Jharkhand
Gujarat
Madhya Pradesh
West
Bengal
Odisha
(Orissa)
Andhra Pradesh
Goa
Karnataka
Tamil Nadu

INDIA

Hundi (Indian Bill of Exchange)

Bombay, India, late 19th century ADA note with a special, coded message

A bill of exchange is a written note given by one person to another, instructing a third person to pay whoever presents it to them a sum of money. The Indian name for a bill of exchange is a *hundi*. This one contains a request by a Bombay merchant for the payment of 300 *rupees*, and bears a revenue stamp of Queen Victoria (empress of India 1876-1901) for one *anna* (1/16th of a *rupee*).

.Preface

The peculiar and somewhat unique nature of the Indian Hundi places it in a dubious category and were it not for its latter day application, it would have been difficult to regard it in any way a paper money. Yet the introduction of the Khadi Hundis in the mid 20th century has necessarily raised the status of hundis, in general, much nearer to money than to that of scrip.

Firstly then, what are hundis? Hundis refer to financial instruments which evolved on the Indian sub-continent. They were used in trade and credit transactions and, as such, were used as remittance instruments for the purpose of transfer of funds from one place to another. In the days of the Princely States and the British Raj these hundis served as Travellers Cheques. They were also used as credit instruments for borrowing and as bills of exchange for trade transactions.

Technically, a hundi is an unconditional order in writing made by a person directing another to pay a certain sum of money to a person named in the order. Being a part of an informal system, however, hundis now have no legal status and were not covered under the Negotiable Instruments Act, 1881.

Hundis appear to have been in use in India from at least the sixteenth century. Banarasi Das, an Indian merchant born in 1586, records that his father gave him a hundi for 200 rupees to enable him to borrow money in another city and start trading there (*ref: British Museum*).

What makes hundis so interesting is the sheer variety of them and the uses to which they were put. As a safety precaution, moreover, they were usually written in an elaborate script which only bankers knew how to read and write. They are still used in India today, even though the resources of modern banking are available for most commercial transactions.

Types of Hundi

Sahyog Hundi: This is drawn by one merchant on another, asking the latter to pay the amount to a third merchant. In this case the merchant on whom the hundi is drawn is of some 'credit worthiness' in the market and is known in the bazaar. A *sahyog hundi* passes from one hand to another till it reaches the final recipient, who, after reasonable enquiries, presents it to the drawee for acceptance of the payment. *Sahyog* means co-operation in Hindi and Gujrati, the predominant languages of traders. The hundi is so named because it required the co-operation of multiple parties to ensure that the hundi has an acceptable risk and fairly good likelihood of being paid, in the absence of a formalized credit monitoring and reporting framework.

Darshani Hundi: This is a hundi payable on sight. It must be presented for payment within a reasonable time after its receipt by the holder. Thus, it is similar to a demand bill.

Muddati Hundi: A *muddati* or *miadi hundi* is payable after a specified period of time. This is similar to a time bill.

There are few other varieties; the Nam-jog hundi, Furman-jog hundi, Dhani-jog hundi, Jokhim hundi, Jawabi hundi, etc.:

Nam-jog hundi: Such a hundi is payable only to the person whose name is mentioned on the Hundi. Such a hundi cannot be endorsed in favour of any other person and is akin to a bill on which a restrictive endorsement has been made.

Furman-jog Hundi: Such a hundi can be paid either to the person whose name is mentioned in the hundi or to any person so ordered by him. Such a hundi is similar to a cheque payable on order and no endorsement is required on such a hundi.

Dhani-jog Hundi: When the hundi is payable to the holder or bearer, it is known as a *dhani-jog hundi*. It is similar to an instrument payable to bearer.

Jokhim Hundi: Normally a hundi is unconditional but a *jokhim hundi* is conditional in the sense that the drawer promises to pay the amount of the hundi only on the satisfaction of a certain condition. Such a hundi is not negotiable, and the prevalence of such hundis is very rare these days because banks and insurance companies refuse to accept such hundis.

Jawabi Hundi: If money is transferred from one place to another through the hundi and the person receiving the payment on is to give an acknowledgement (jawab) for same, then such a hundi is known as a *jawabi hundi*.

Khaka Hundi: A hundi which has already been paid is known as a *khaka hundi*.

Khoti Hundi: In case there is any kind of defect in the hundi or in case the hundi has been forged, then such a hundi is known as a *khoti hundi*.

Khadi Hundi: *Khādī* refers to Indian cloth spun and woven by hand. The raw materials may be cotton, silk, or wool, which are spun into threads on a spinning wheel called a charkha

Khadi Hundis (1955-58) were issued as a local currency and were used as an exchange medium for khadi cloth. They could only be redeemed at a KHADI BHANDAR (hand woven cloth outlet). These issues also commemorate Mahatma Ghandi for his dedication to poor women who spun Khadi cloth to improve their lives.

In India, Khadi is therefore not just a cloth, it is a whole movement started by Mohandas Karamchand Gandhi. The Khadi movement promoted an ideology, an idea that Indians could be self-reliant on cotton and be free from foreign cloth and clothing.

During the time of the British Raj, the British were selling to them at very high cost cloths. The British would buy cotton from India at cheap prices and export it to Britain where it was woven to make clothes. These clothes were then brought back to India to be sold at hefty prices. The khadi movement aimed at boycotting foreign goods including cotton and promoting Indian goods, thereby improving India's economy.

Mahatma Gandhi began promoting the spinning of khādī for rural self-employment and self-reliance (instead of using cloth manufactured industrially in Britain) in 1920's India, thus making khadi an integral part and icon of the Swadeshi movement.

The freedom struggle revolved around the use of khādī fabrics and the dumping of foreign-made clothes. When some people complained about the costliness of khadi to Mahatma Gandhi, he started wearing only dhoti.

Various state governments and the Government of India have been appealing to citizens to promote the usage of Khadi.

Regular Hundi Issues

Agra (Uttar Pradesh State)
आगरा
آگره

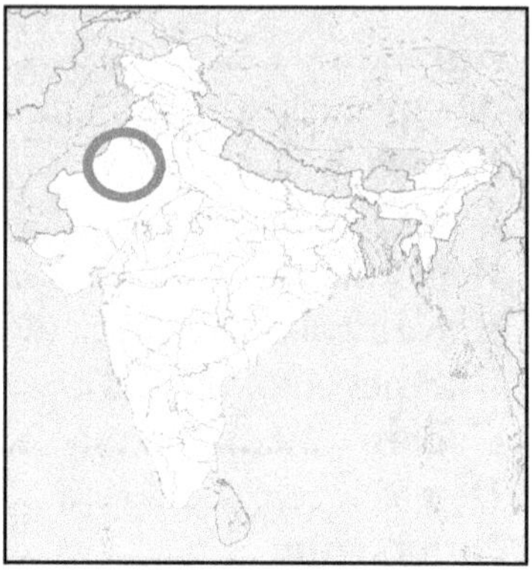

Agra is a city on the banks of the river Yamuna in the northern state of Uttar Pradesh. It is 378 kilometres west of the state capital, Lucknow, 206 kilometres south of the national capital New Delhi and 125 kilometres north of Gwalior.

Legend ascribes the founding of the city to Raja Badal Singh, a Sikarwar Rajput king (circa 1475). However, the 11th century Persian poet Mas'ūd Sa'd Salmān writes of a desperate assault on the fortress of Agra, then held by the Shāhī King Jayapala, by Sultan Mahmud of Ghazni. It was mentioned for the first time in 1080 AD when a Ghaznavide force captured it. Sultan Sikandar Lodī (1488–1517) was the first to move his capital from Delhi to Agra in 1506. He died in 1517 and his son, Ibrāhīm Lodī, remained in power there for nine more years and several palaces, wells and a mosque were built by him in the fort during his period, finally being defeated at the Battle of Panipat in 1526.

Between 1540 and 1556, Afghans, beginning with Sher Shah Suri ruled the area. It achieved fame as the capital of the Mughal Empire from 1556 to 1658.

Taj Mahal

Agra Fort

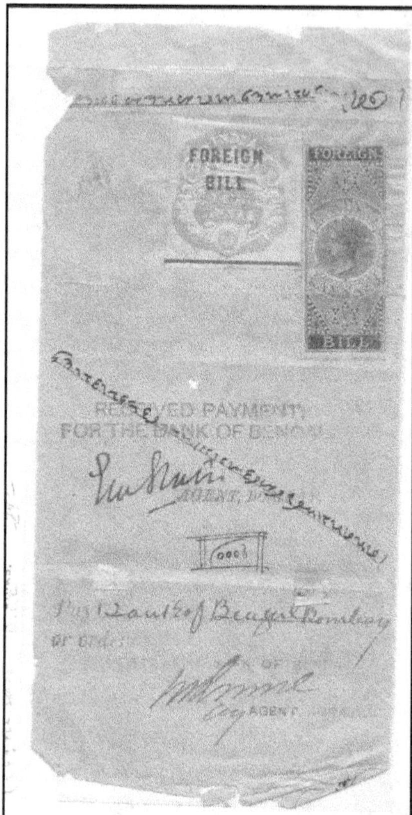
FOREIGN BILL
FOREIGN
BILL
RECEIVED PAYMENT
FOR THE BANK OF BENGAL
AGENT

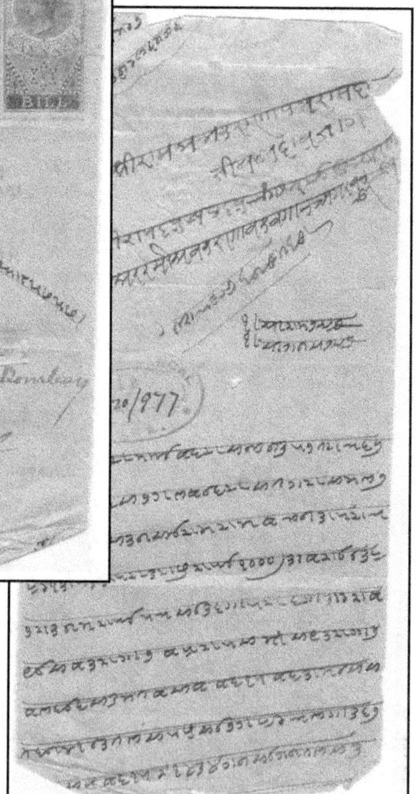

Alwar (Rajasthan State)
अलवर

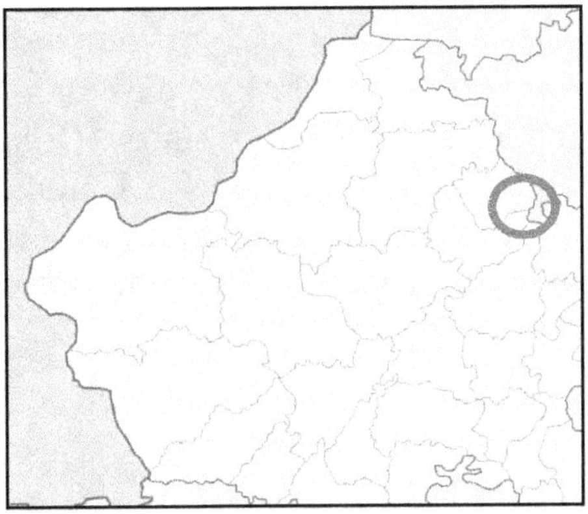

Alwar is a city in the Indian state of Rajasthan.

It was formerly the capital of the princely state of **Alwar** which was ruled by Kachwaha (Naruka) Rajputs. It was formerly spelt as "Ulwar" in British India. This placed it in last position in alphabetically ordered lists, so a king changed the spelling to "Alwar" to bring it to the top. Alwar is also known by the name "Matsya Nagar"

Alwar dates back to 1000 AD. The king of Amer (old seat of Jaipur state) ruled the area in the 11th century and his territory extended up to the present city of Alwar.

He founded the city of Alpur in 1106 Vikrami Samvat (1049 AD) after his own name which eventually became Alwar. From time to time, different sub-clans of Rajputs ruled Alwar. Nikumbh Rajputs, Badgujar Rajputs and last was Naruka (Kachwaha) Rajputs who took the control over this area. Marathas and Jats of Bharatpur also ruled this region for very short period.

A brave Rajput Partap Singh took the Alawar Fort from Jat Raja of Bharatpur on an agreement and laid down the foundation for modern Alwar.

On 18th March 1948, the state merged with three neighbouring princely states (Bharatpur, Dholpur and Karauli) to form the Matsya Union. On 15th May 1949, it was united with neighbouring princely states and the territory of Ajmer to form the present-day Indian state of Rajasthan.

Neemrana
(A district in Alwar)

25P.
HUNDI
25 PAISE
SPECIAL ADHESIVE
SPECIAL ADHESIVE
SPECIAL ADHESIVE
SPECIAL ADHESIVE
Authorised Signatory

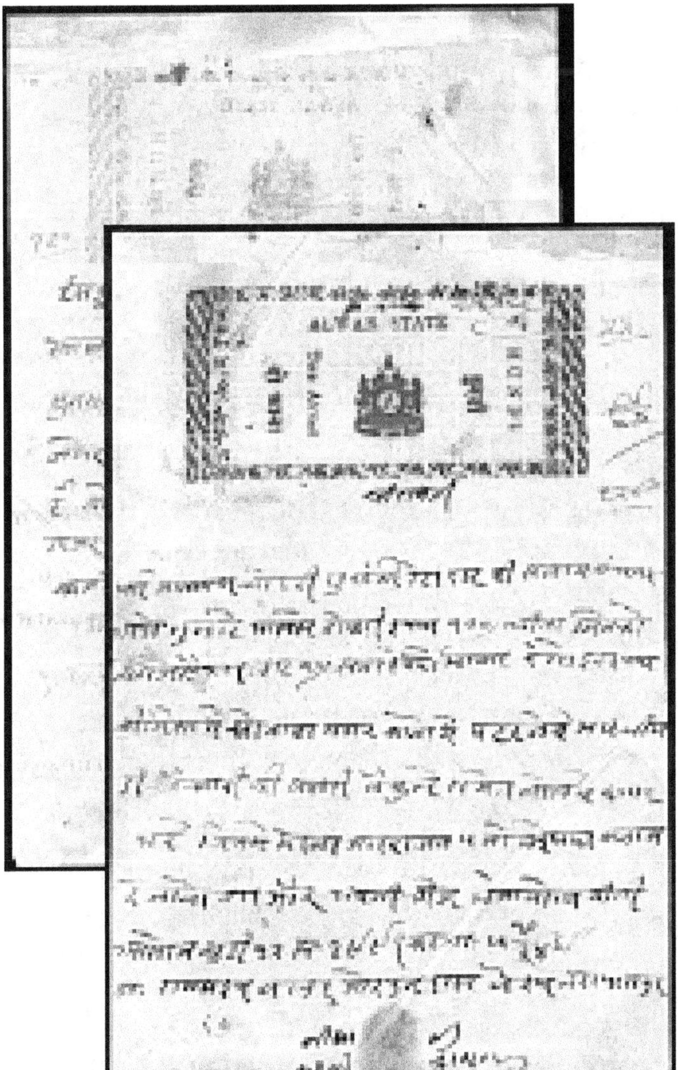
ALWAR STATE

Bamra (State)
बामरा रियासत

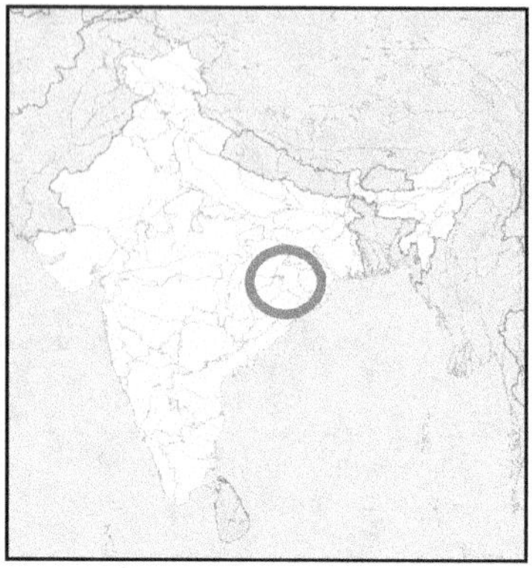

Bamra State or **Bamanda State**, was one of the Princely states of India during the period of the British Raj, its capital was in Debagarh (Deogarh). Bamra State acceded to India in 1948.

A legend states that the Raja of Bamra belonged to the Gangabasi Rajput dynasty of Patna. He is believed to have been stolen as a child and was made the ruler of the state of Bamra by the Bhuiya and Khond people around 1545.

The Bengal-Nagpur Railway passed through the northeastern part of Bamra, with two stations in the state: Bamra Road and Garpos. The state was under the political control of the Commissioner of the Chhattisgarh Division of the Central Provinces until 1905, under the Bengal Presidency until 1912, under the Bihar and Orissa Province until 1936 and under Orissa Province until it ceased to be a princely state. On 1st January 1948 Bamra's last princely ruler signed the accession to the Indian Union.

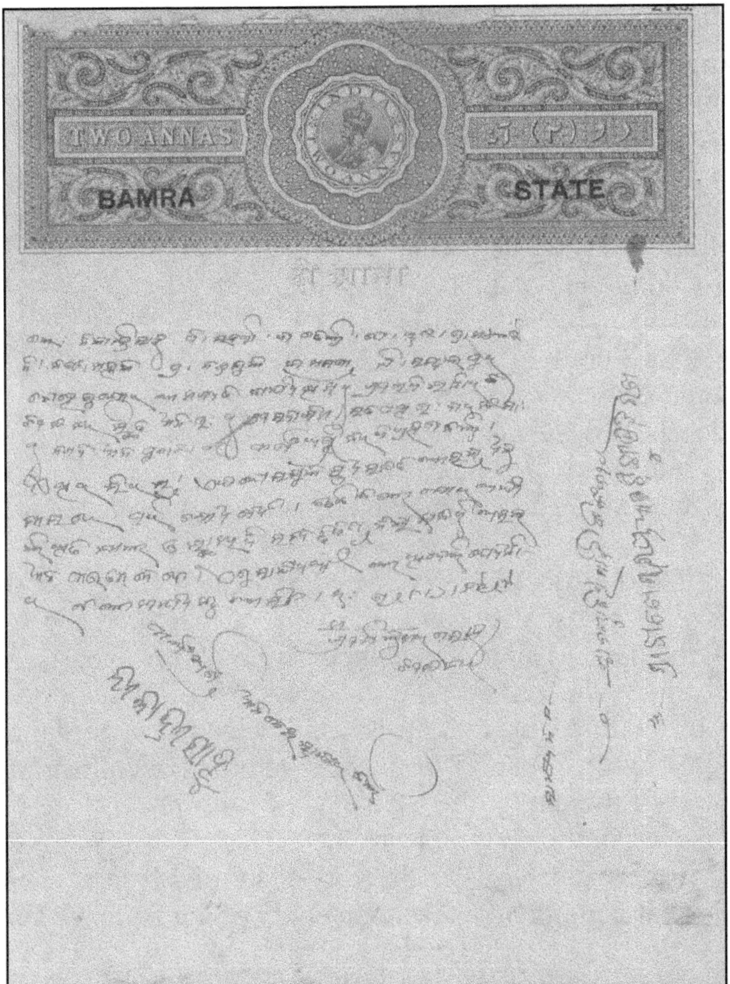
TWO ANNAS
BAMRA
STATE

Bangalore (Karnataka State)
ಬೆಂಗಳೂರು

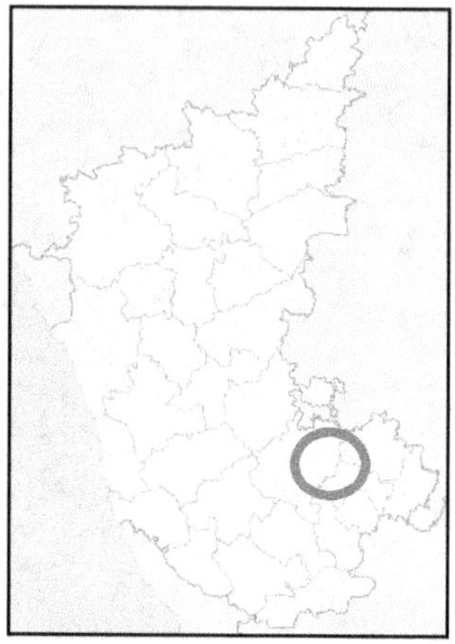

Bangalore, officially known as **Bengaluru**, is the capital of the Indian state of Karnataka.

A succession of South Indian dynasties, the Western Gangas, the Cholas and the Hoysalas, ruled the present region of Bangalore until in 1537 BCE, Kempé Gowdā – a feudal ruler under the Vijayanagara Empire – established a mud fort considered to be the foundation of modern Bangalore.

In 1638, the Marāthās conquered and ruled Bangalore for almost 50 years, after which the Mughals captured and sold the city to the Mysore Kingdom of the Wadiyar dynasty.

It was captured by the British after victory in the Fourth Anglo-Mysore War (1799), who returned administrative control of the city to the Maharaja of Mysore. The old city developed in the dominions of the Maharaja of Mysore and was made capital of the Princely State of Mysore, which existed as a nominally sovereign entity of the British Raj.

In 1809, the British shifted their cantonment to Bangalore, outside the old city, and a town grew up around it, which was governed as part of British India.

Following India's independence in 1947, Bangalore became the capital of Mysore State, and remained capital when the new Indian state of Karnataka was formed in 1956.

The two urban settlements of Bangalore – city and cantonment – which had developed as independent entities merged into a single urban centre in 1949. The existing Kannada name, *Bengalūru*, was declared the official name of the city in 2006.

Shiva Statue, Bangalore

The Begur Nageshwara Temple was built in Bangalore around circa 860, during the reign of the Wester Ganga Dynasty.

Bangalore Palace, built in 1887 in Tudor architectural style was modelled on the Windsor Castle in England.

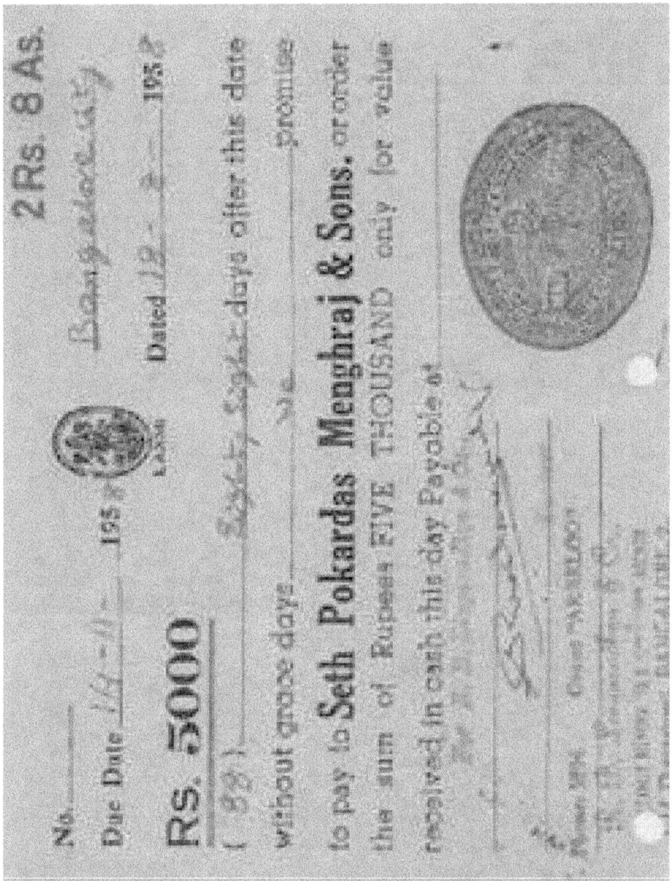

2Rs. 8 As.

No.

Due Date 14-11- 195

Bangalore City

Dated 12-8- 195

Rs. 5000

(88) Eighty Eight days after this date

without grace days We promise

to pay to Seth Pokardas Menghraj & Sons, or order

the sum of Rupees FIVE THOUSAND only for value

received in cash this day Payable at

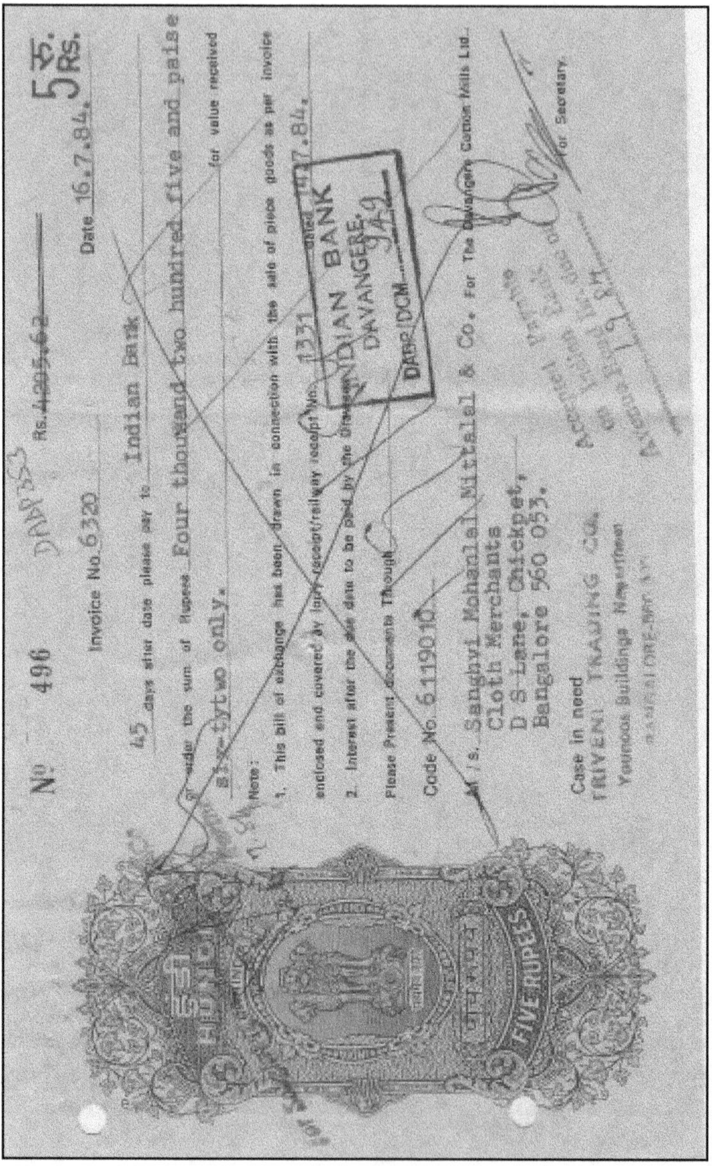

Nº 496 DABP353 Rs. ~~4205.62~~

5 रु. Rs.

Invoice No. 6320 Date 16.7.84.

45 days after date please pay to Indian Bank

or order the sum of Rupees Four thousand two hundred five and paise six-tytwo only. for value received

Note:

1. This bill of exchange has been drawn in connection with the sale of piece goods as per invoice enclosed and covered by lorry receipt/railway receipt No. 1331 dated 14.7.84.

2. Interest after the due date to be paid by the Drawees.

Please Present documents Through

Code No. 6119010

M/s. Sanghvi Mohanlal Mittalal & Co.
Cloth Merchants
D S Lane, Chickpet,
Bangalore 560 053.

For The Davangere Cotton Mills Ltd.

For Secretary.

Case in need
TRIVENI TRADING CO.
Younoos Buildings Nagarthpet
[illegible]

INDIAN BANK
DAVANGERE.
DABP/DCM 949

Accepted Payable on Indian Bank Avenue Road Br. due on 1.9.84

Beja (State)

The Princely State of Beja was a semi-sovereign kingdom of India (Himachal Pradesh) from the 18th century till 15th April 1948. It was ruled by a cadet branch of the Tomara dynasty (*Tunwar*) with the title of *Thakur*.

It is one of the eighteen Simla Hill States, situated just below Kasauli to the west and is bordered by Mahlog, Patiala State, Kuthar and the Bharauli tract of Simla District around Sabathu.

Beja included 45 villages, over an area of 13 km^2 (or 5 m^2) with 1,131 subjects.

Beja is one of the original constituent members of the Chamber of Princes, a number of smaller states indirectly represented by twelve princes whom they periodically elected.

Sh. Laxmi Chand last emperor of Beja Hill State along with his wife, Himachal Prades

Palace cum Fort of Beja Princely State, Simla Hill States, Himachal Pradesh

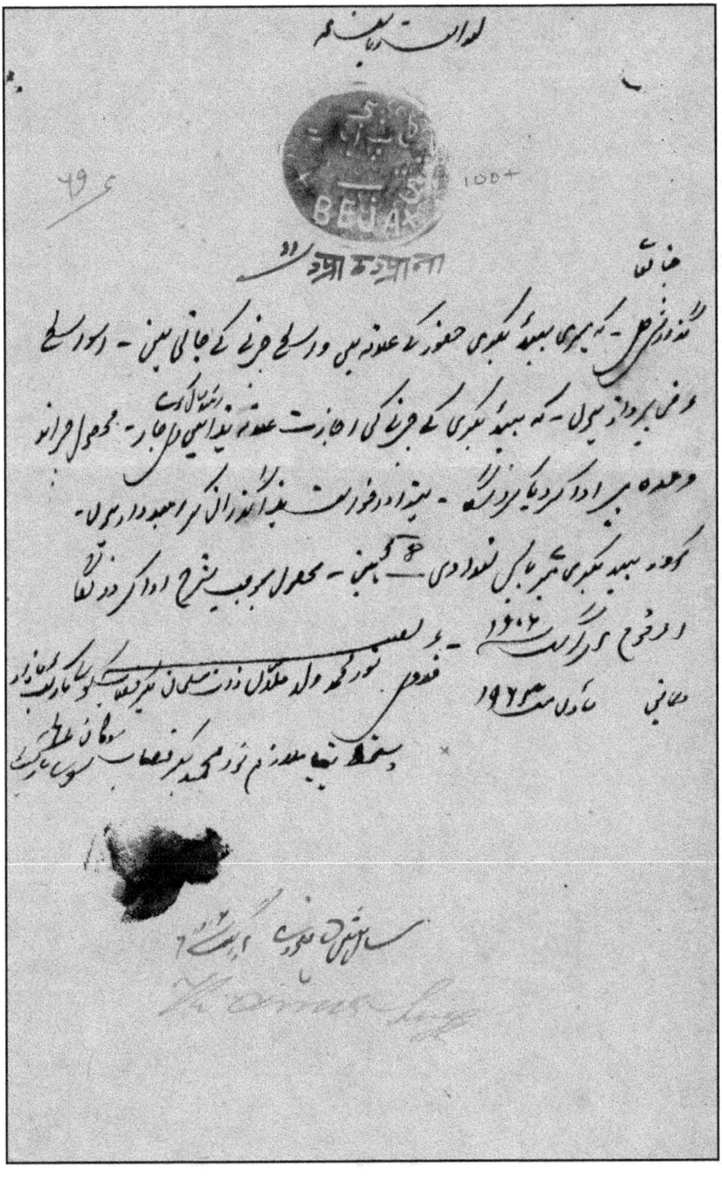

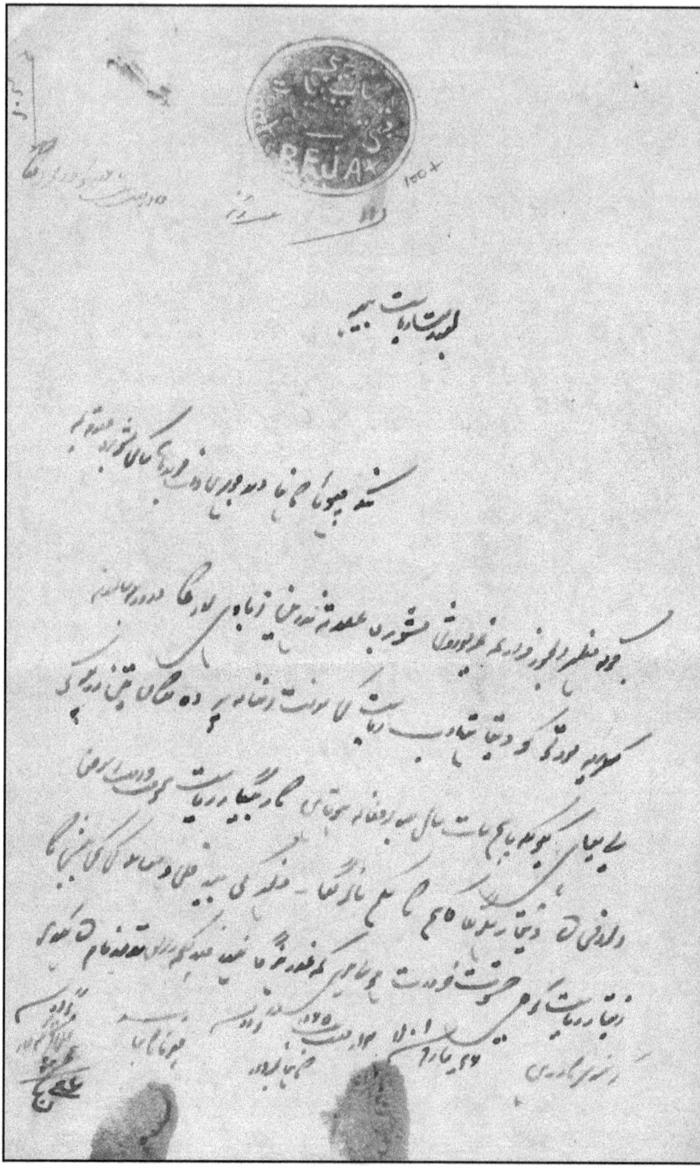

Bewar (Town)

बेवर بیور

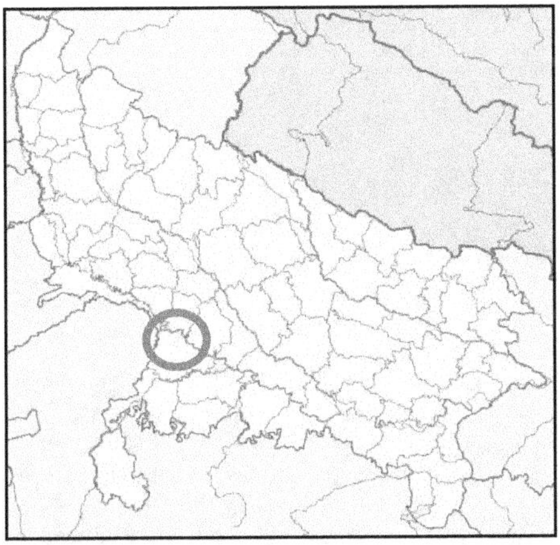

Bewar is a town and urban municipality in Mainpuri district in the state of Uttar Pradesh, India.

It is believed that the city of Bewar was established by Vidura of the Mahabharata. The town later contributed to India's fight for independence. The name Bewar originated during the Mutiny of 1857, the English placed warning banners on all the entrances of the town saying "BEWARE". Gradually, with time, the letter "E" was omitted and the town became known as "BEWAR".

Every year, a 16-days special exhibition, *Shaheed Mela*, takes place. The exhibition was founded by Shri Jagdish Narayan Tripathi who contributed greatly in the development of this town. He also founded Shaheed Smarak and Shaheed Mandir at the place where Shaheed Krishna Kumar (aged 14 yrs.), Shaheed Jamuna Prasad Tripathi (aged 40 yrs.) and 'Shaheed Sita Ram Gupta (aged 42 yrs.), lost their lives while fighting the British on 15th August, 1942

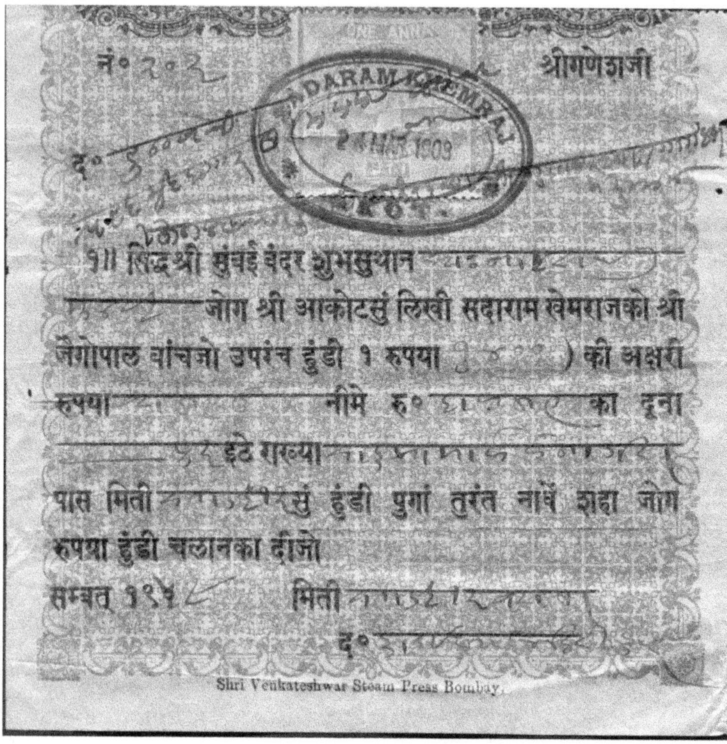
ONE ANNA

नं०

श्रीगणेशजी

द०

॥ सिद्धश्री मुंबई बंदर शुभसुथान
जोग श्री आकोटसुं लिखी सदाराम खेमराजको श्री
जैगोपाल वांचजो। उपरंच हुंडी १ रुपया ( ) की अक्षरी
रुपया नीमे रु० का दूना
इठे राख्या
पास मिती सुं हुंडी पुगां तुरंत नांवें शहा जोग
रुपया हुंडी चलानका दीजो।

सम्बत १९ मिती

द०

Shri Venkateshwar Steam Press Bombay.

Bikaner (State)
बीकानेर
ਬਿਕਾਨੇਰ

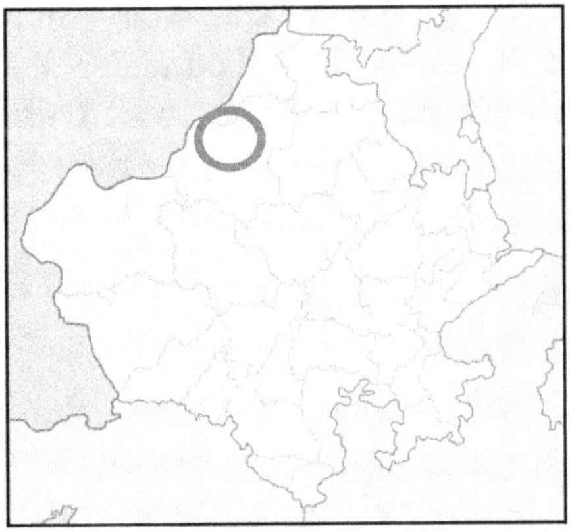

Formerly the capital of the princely state of Bikaner, the city was founded by Rao Bika in 1486 and from its small origins it has developed into the fourth largest city in Rajasthan.

Prior to the mid 15th century, the region that is now Bikaner was a barren wilderness called Jangladesh. Rao Bika established the city of Bikaner in 1488. He was the first son of Maharaja Rao Jodha of the Rathor clan, the founder of Jodhpur and conquered the largely arid country in the north of Rajasthan. As the first son of Jodha he wanted to have his own kingdom, not inheriting Jodhpur from his father or the title of Maharaja. He therefore decided to build his own kingdom in what is now the state of Bikaner in the area of Jangladesh. Though it was in the Thar Desert, Bikaner was considered an oasis on the trade route between Central Asia and the Gujarat coast as it had adequate spring water. Bika's name was attached to the city he built and to the state of Bikaner ("the settlement of Bika") that he established.
Bika built a fort in 1478, which is now in ruins, and a hundred years later a new fort was built about 1.5 km from the city centre, known as the Junagarh Fort.

Around a century after Rao Bika founded Bikaner, the state's fortunes flourished under the sixth Raja, Rai Singhji, who ruled from 1571 to 1611. During the Mughal Empire's rule in the country, Raja Rai Singh accepted the suzerainty of the Mughals and held a high rank as an army general at the court of the Emperor Akbar and his son the Emperor Jahangir.

General Maharaja Ganga Singh, who ruled from 1887 to 1943, was the best-known of the Rajasthan princes and was a favourite of the British Viceroys of India. He was appointed a Knight Commander of the Order of the Star of India, served as a member of the Imperial War Cabinet, represented India at the Imperial Conferences during the First World War and the British Empire at the Versailles Peace Conference.

Ganga Singh's son, Lieutenant-General Sir Sadul Singh, the Yuvaraja of Bikaner, succeeded his father as Maharaja in 1943, but acceded his state to the Union of India in 1949.

Junagarh Fort

Laxmi Niwas Palace

Lalgarh Palace

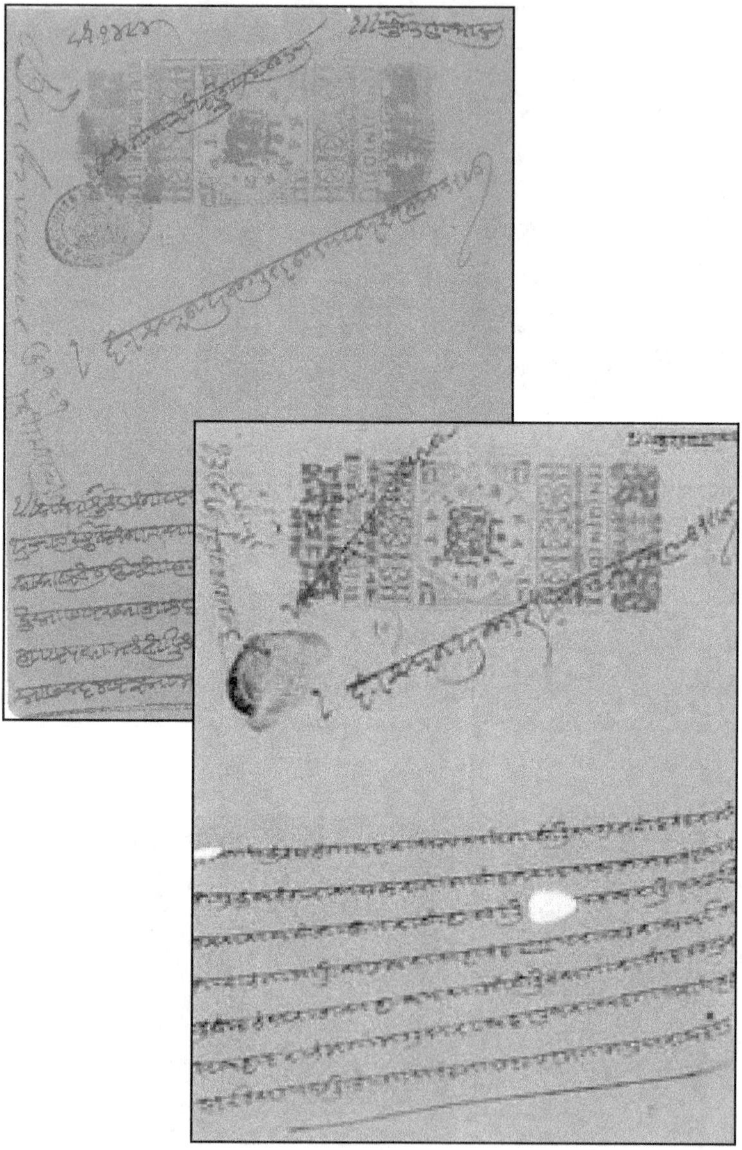

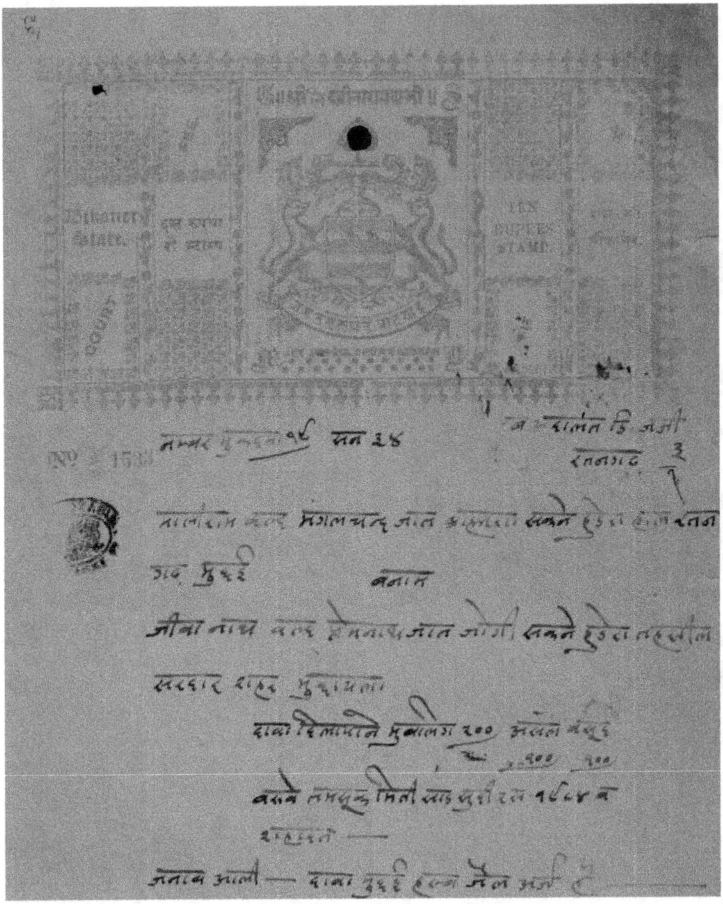

Bikaner State

दस रुपया

TEN RUPEES STAMP

COURT

अदालत डि॰ जजी

रतनगढ़

नम्बर मुकदमा ९६ सन ३४

No. 1533

तालाराम वल्द मंगलचन्द जात कलाल सकूने हुडेरा तहसील रतनगढ़ मुद्दई

बनाम

जीवानाथ वल्द हेमनाथ जात जोगी सकूने हुडेरा तहसील सरदारशहर मुद्दायला

दावा दिलापाने मुबलिगा २०० असल मय सूद

[illegible] १०० १००

बाबत तमस्सुक मिती [illegible] १९८४ का

शहादत —

जनाब आली — दावा मुद्दई हस्ब जैल अर्ज है —

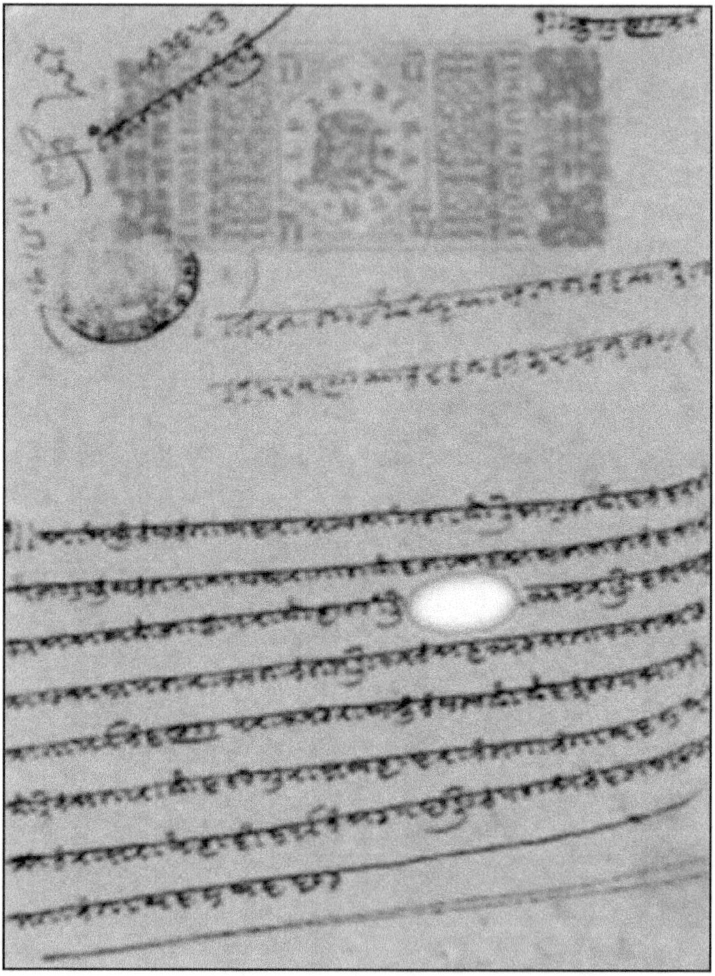

Cochin (Kerala State)

കൊച്ചി

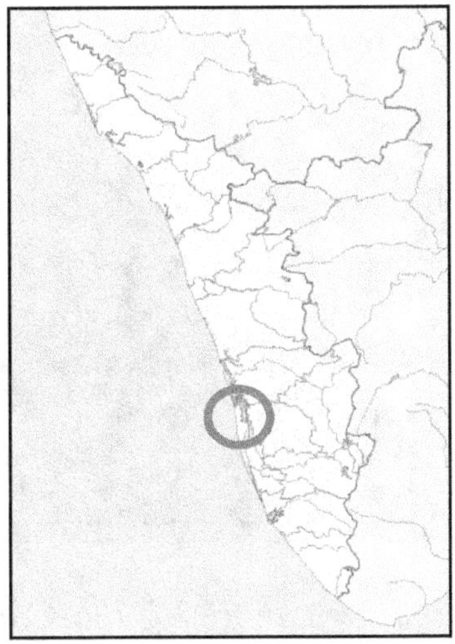

Cochin also known as **Kochi**, is a major port city on the south-west coast of India by the Arabian Sea and the Laccadive Sea and is part of the district of Ernakulam in the state of Kerala. It is often called Ernakulam, which refers to the mainland part of the city. Kochi city is also a part of the Greater Cochin region.

In 1947, when India gained independence from the British colonial rule, Cochin was the first princely state to join the Indian Union willingly. In 1949, Travancore-Cochin state came into being with the merger of Cochin and Travancore.

The King of Travancore was the Rajpramukh of the Travancore-Cochin Union from 1949 to 1956. Travancore-Cochin, was in turn merged with the Malabar district of the Madras State. Finally, the Government of India's States Reorganisation Act (1956) inaugurated a new state - Kerala - incorporating Travancore-Cochin (excluding the four southern Taluks which were merged with Tamil Nadu), Malabar District, and the taluk of Kasargod, South Kanara.

Established in 1926, the Cochin Port Trust overlooks the activities of Cochin Port

St. Francis Church built in 1503, is the oldest European church in India

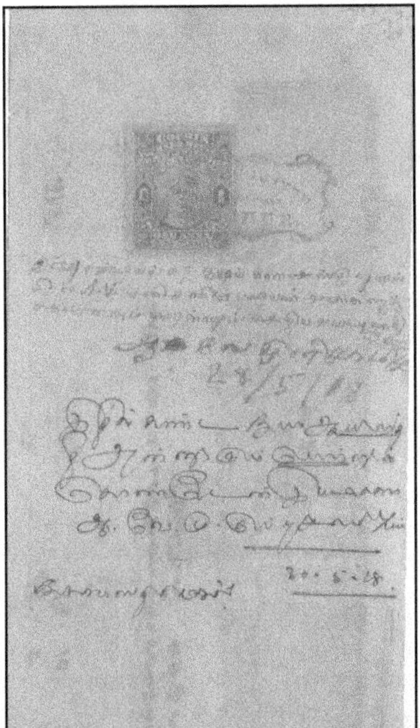

28/5/18

30.5.18

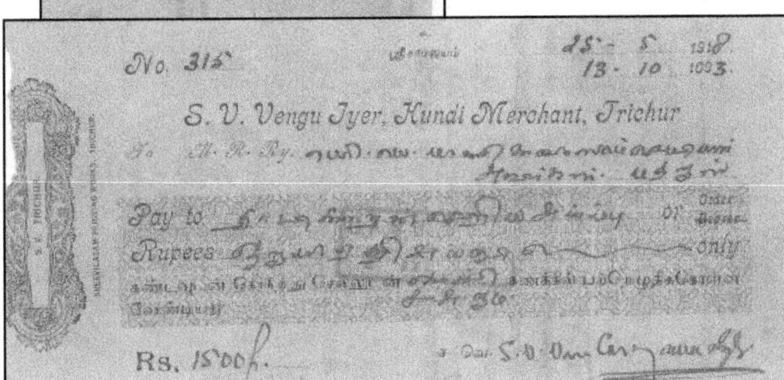

No. 315 — 25-5-1918 / 13-10-1093

S. V. Vengu Iyer, Hundi Merchant, Trichur

To M. R. Ry.

Pay to ... or Order

Rupees ... only

Rs. 1500/-

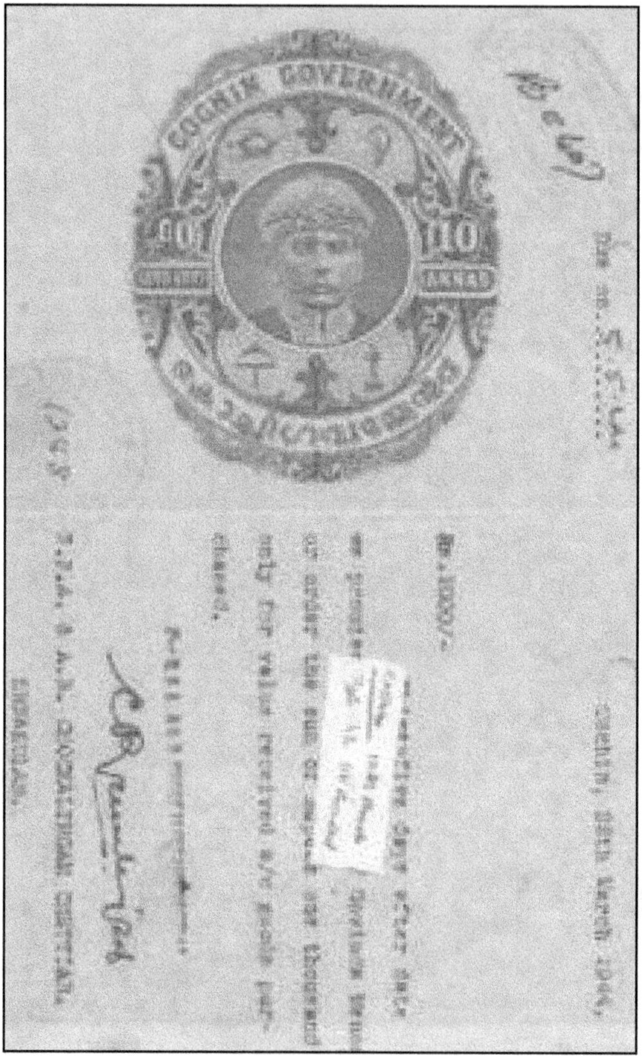
COCHIN GOVERNMENT
ANNAS

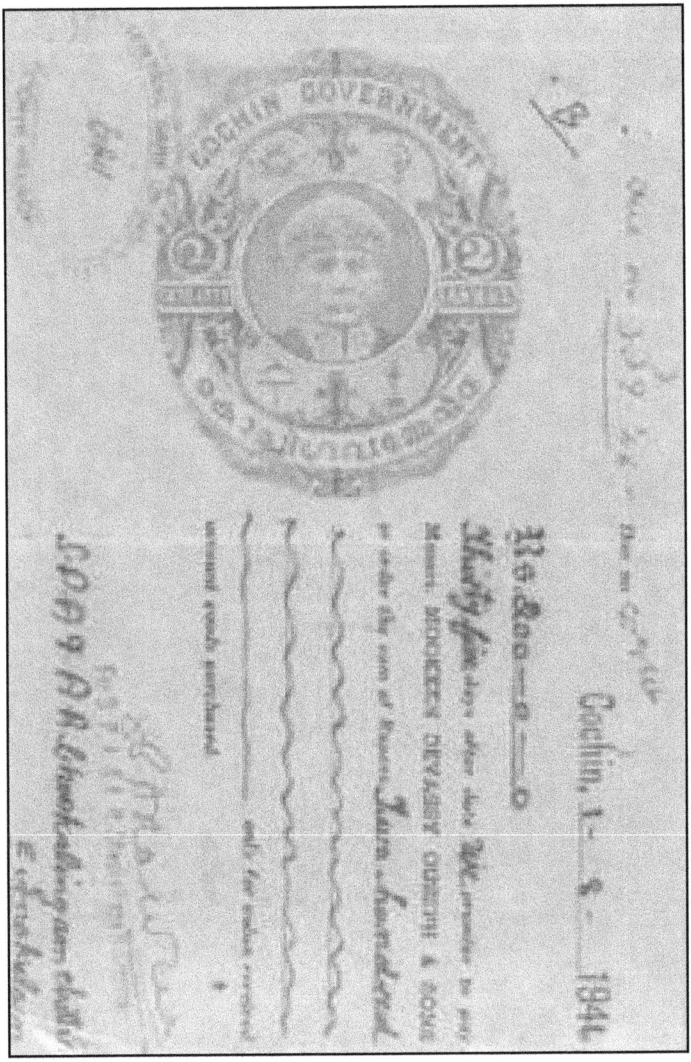
COCHIN GOVERNMENT
Cochin, 1— 8 — 1946
Rs. 200—0—0

COCHIN GOVERNMENT
ANNAS
Proprietor,
Pharmacy,

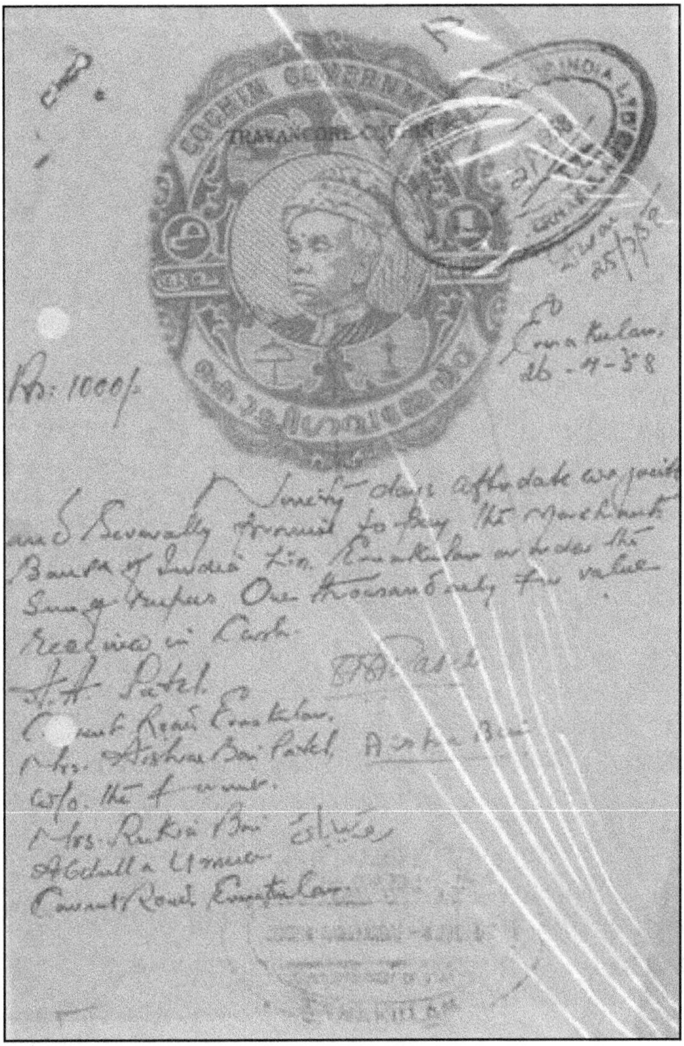
COCHIN GOVERNMENT
TRAVANCORE-COCHIN

Rs: 1000/-

Ernakulam,
26-11-58

Ninety days after date we jointly and severally promise to pay the Merchants Bank of India Ltd. Ernakulam or order the sum of rupees One thousand only for value received in cash.

A.A. Patel.
Convent Road Ernakulam.
Mrs. Aishabai Patel
W/o. the former.
Mrs. Rukia Bai
Abdulla Umar
Convent Road, Ernakulam

Dewas (State)
देवास रियासत

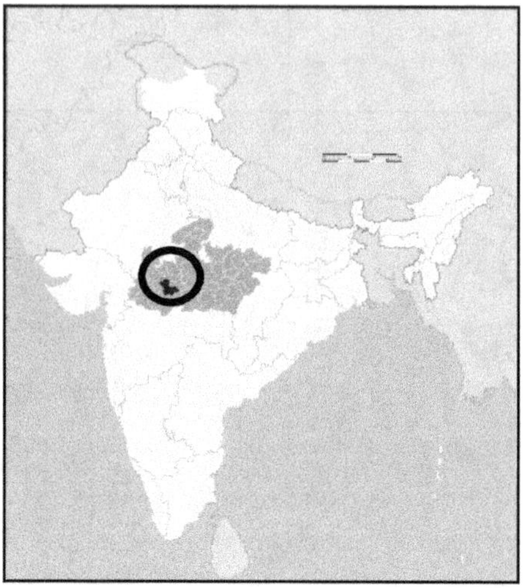

The name Dewas is derived from the *Devi Vaishini* hill in the city, commonly known as *Tekri*. The hill has a temple of deity Devi Tulja Bhawani, Chamunda Mata and Kalika Mata. The word Dewas is also believed to be a sandhi of words Dev deity and Vas Marathi for abode, thus Dewas means *abode of the deity or god.*

Dewas State was a territory within Western India, which was the seat of two Maratha princely states during the British Raj: 'Dewas Junior' - Jivaji Rao ('Dada Saheb') and Dewas Senior - Tukoji Rao ('Baba Saheb'). On 12th December 1818 Dewas State became a British protectorate.

The seats were established in 1728 by two brothers from the Puar clan, who advanced into Malwa with the Maratha Peshwa Baji Rao, and divided the territory among themselves after the Maratha conquest.

The two Rajas heading Dewas states both lived in separate residences in the town of Dewas, and ruled over separate areas.

The brothers divided the territory among themselves; their descendants ruled as the senior and junior branches of the family. After 1841, each branch ruled his own portion as a separate state, though the lands belonging to each were so intimately entangled, that even in Dewas, the capital town, the two sides of the main street were under different administrations and had different arrangements for water supply and lighting.

Maharaja Tukoji Rao III Puar also known as Kesho Rao Bapu Saheb. (**Dewas** *Senior*)
1888 - 1937

Maharaja Vikramsinharao Tukojirao Nana Saheb Puar, 7th Maharaja (Dewas-Senior) 1937 - 1948

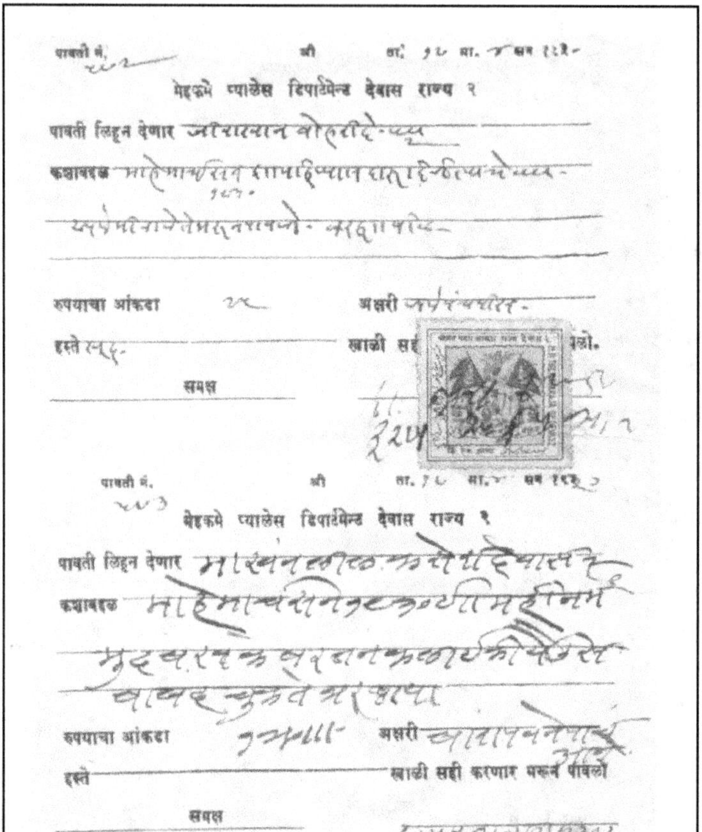
पावती नं. श्री ता. मा. सन

मेहकमे प्यालेस डिपार्टमेन्ट देवास राज्य २

पावती लिहून देणार

कशाबदल

रुपयाचा आंकडा अक्षरी

हस्ते खाली सही ... ली.

समक्ष

पावती नं. श्री ता. मा. सन

मेहकमे प्यालेस डिपार्टमेन्ट देवास राज्य १

पावती लिहून देणार

कशाबदल

रुपयाचा आंकडा अक्षरी

हस्ते खाली सही करणार भरून पावलो

समक्ष

Dungarpur (City)

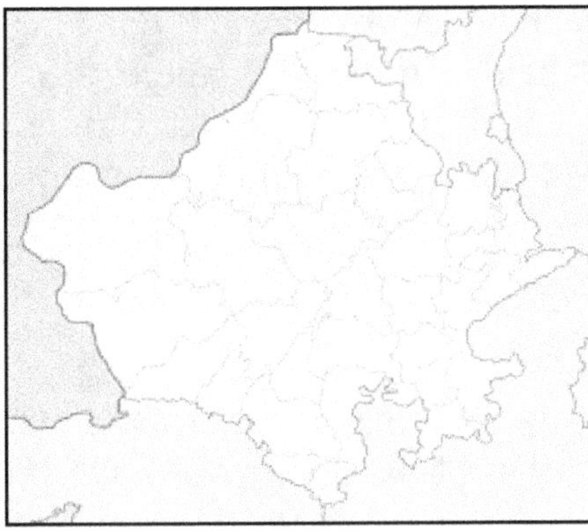

Dungarpur is a city in the southernmost part of Rajasthan state of India.

It was founded in 1358 A.D. by Rawal Veer Singh, the eldest son of the ruler of Mewar, Karan Singh. They are descendants of Bappa Rawal, eighth ruler of the Guhilot Dynasty and founder of the Mewar Dynasty (734-753).

The chiefs of Dungarpur, who bear the title of Maharawal, are descended from Mahup, the eldest son of Karan Singh, a chief of Mewar in the 12th century, and claim the honours of the elder line of Mewar. Mahup, disinherited by his father, took refuge with his mother's family, the Chauhans of Bagar, and made himself lord of that country at the expense of the Bhil chiefs.

The town of Dungarpur, the capital of the state, was founded towards the end of the 14th century by his descendant, Rawal Bir Singh, the Sixth descendant of Sawant Singh of Mewar, who named it after Dungaria, an independent Bhil chieftain whom he had ordered assassinated.

After the death of Rawal Udai Singh of Bagar at the Battle of Khanwa in 1527, where he fought alongside Rana Sanga against Babar, his territories were divided into the states of Dungarpur and Banswara.

Successively under Mughal, Maratha, and British Raj control by treaty in 1818, it remained a 15-gun salute state.

In 1901 the total population of Dungarpur was 100,103, while that of the town was 6,094. The last princely ruler of Dungarpur was HH Rai-i-Rayan Maharawal Shri Lakshman Singh Bahadur (1918–1989).

Haveli Juna Mahal

Dev Somnath Temple

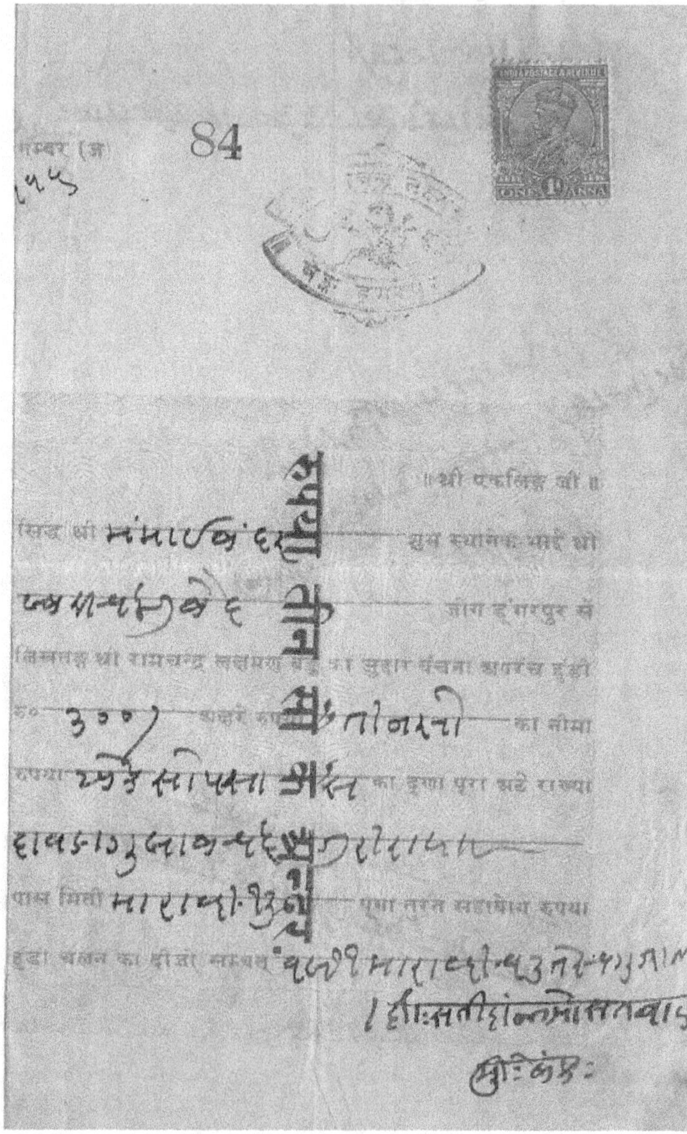

नम्बर (अ 84

॥श्री एकलिङ्ग जी॥

सिद्ध श्री शुभ स्थाने भाई श्री

जोग डूंगरपुर में

लिखतङ्ग श्री रामचन्द्र लक्ष्मण का जुहार बंचना अपरंच हुंडी

रु० ३०० अक्षरे तीनसौ का नीमा

रुपया का दूणा पूरा अठे राख्या

पास मिती पूगा तुरत सहाजोग रुपया

हुंडी चलन का दीजो मरजाद

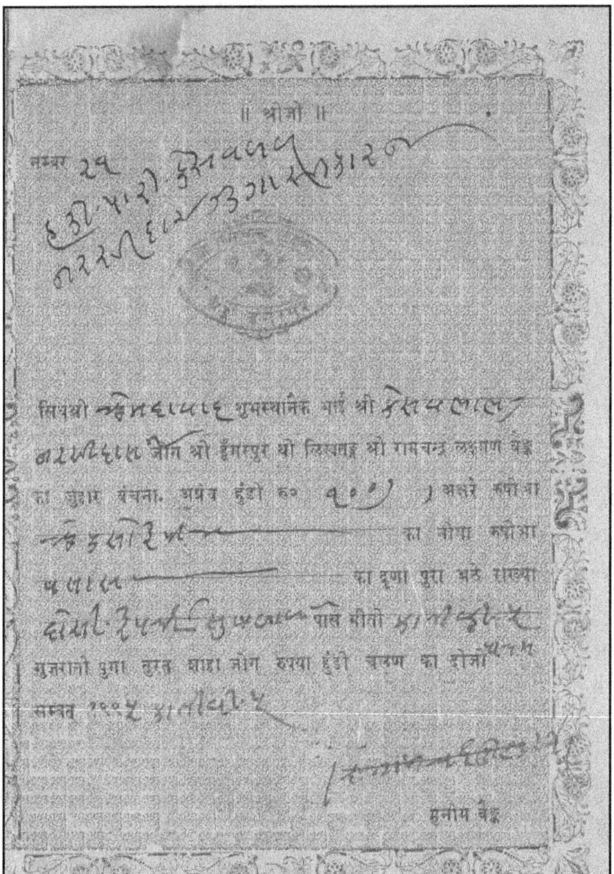

॥ श्रीजी ॥

नम्बर २९ [illegible]

सिधश्री [illegible] शुभस्थानिक भाई श्री [illegible]

[illegible] जोग श्री डूंगरपुर थी लिखतङ्ग श्री रामचन्द्र लक्ष्मण वैद्य

का जुहार बंचना. अप्रंच हुंडी रु० [illegible]) अक्षरे रुपीआ

[illegible] का नीमा रुपीआ

[illegible] का दूणा पूरा अठे राख्या

[illegible] पास मीती [illegible]

मुजरानो पुगा तुरत शाहा जोग रुपया हुंडी चलण का दीजो

सम्वत १९०५ [illegible]

[illegible]

मुनीम वैद्य

Gugarat (State)
ગુજરાત

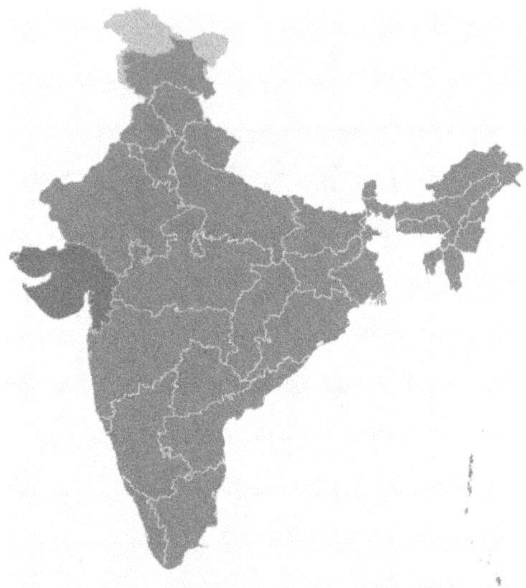

Gujarat is a state in Western India, sometimes referred to as the "Jewel of Western India".

In the 1600's, the Dutch, French, English and Portuguese all established bases along the western coast of the region. Portugal was the first European power to arrive in Gujarat, and after the Battle of Diu and Treaty of Bassein, acquired several enclaves along the Gujarati coast, including Daman and Diu as well as Dadra and Nagar Haveli. These enclaves were administered by Portuguese India under a single union territory for over 450 years, only to be later incorporated into the Republic of India on 19th December 1961 by military conquest.

The British East India Company established a factory in Surat in 1614 following the commercial treaty made with Mughal Emperor Nuruddin Salim Jahangir, which formed their first base in India, but it was eclipsed by Bombay after the English received it from Portugal in 1668 as part of the marriage treaty of Charles II of England and

Catherine of Braganza, daughter of King John IV of Portugal. The state was an early point of contact with the west, and the first British commercial outpost in India was in Gujarat.

17th century French explorer François Pyrard de Laval, who is remembered for his 10-year sojourn in South Asia, bears witness accounts that the Gujaratis were always prepared to learn workmanship from the Portuguese, also in turn imparting skills to the Portuguese:

"I have never seen men of wit so fine and polished as are these Indians: they have nothing barbarous or savage about them, as we are apt to suppose. They are unwilling indeed to adopt the manners and customs of the *Portuguese*; yet do they regularly learn their manufactures and workmanship, being all very curious and desirous of learning. In fact the *Portuguese* take and learn more from them than they from the *Portuguese*."

Later in the 17th century, Gujarat came under control of the Hindu Maratha Empire that rose defeating the Muslim Mughals and who dominated the politics of India. Most notably, from 1705 to 1716, Senapati Khanderao Dabhade led the Maratha Empire forces in Baroda. Pilaji Gaekwad, first ruler of Gaekwad dynasty, established the control over Baroda and other parts of Gujarat.

The British East India Company wrested control of much of Gujarat from the Marathas during the Second Anglo-Maratha War in 1802–1803. Many local rulers, notably the Rajput Maratha Gaekwad Maharajas of Baroda (Vadodara), made a separate peace with the British and acknowledged British sovereignty in return for retaining local self-rule.

Mahatma Gandhi picked salt at Dandi beach, South Gujarat ending the Salt Satyagraha on 5th April 1930.

Gujarat was placed under the political authority of the Bombay Presidency, with the exception of Baroda state, which had a direct relationship with the Governor General of India. From 1818 to 1947, most of present day Gujarat, including Kathiawar, Kutch and northern and eastern Gujarat were divided into hundreds of princely states, but several districts in central and southern Gujarat, namely Ahmedabad, Broach (Bharuch), Kaira (Kheda), Panchmahal and Surat, were governed directly by British officials.

Rani ki vav 11th century

Taranga Jain Temple constructed by Kumarapala (1143–1172 CE)

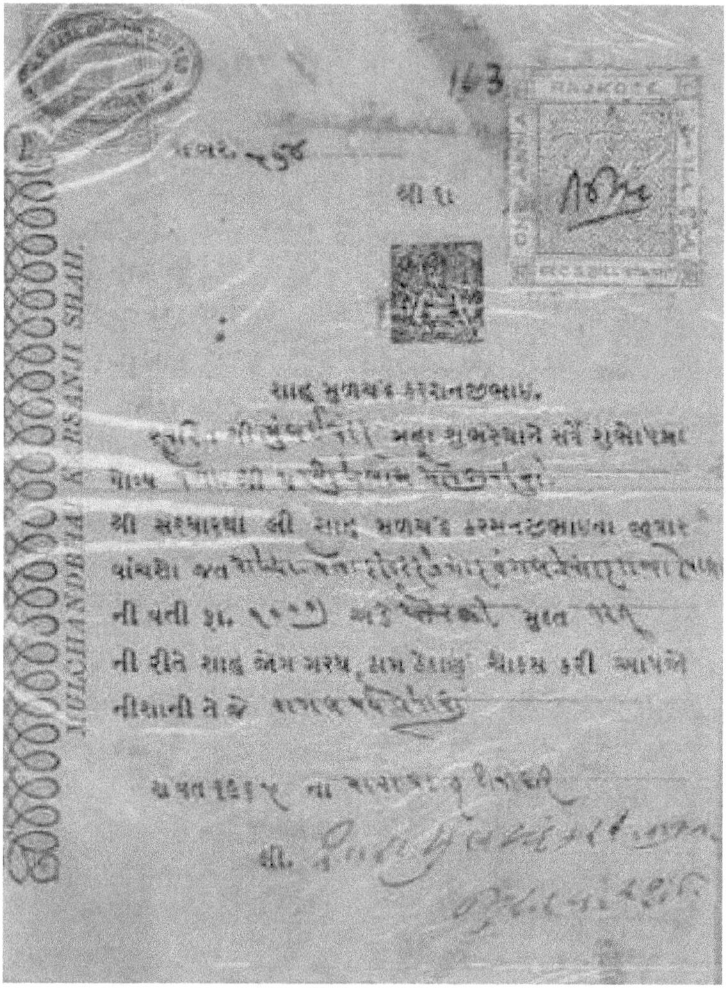
163

RAJKOTE

Holkar (State)

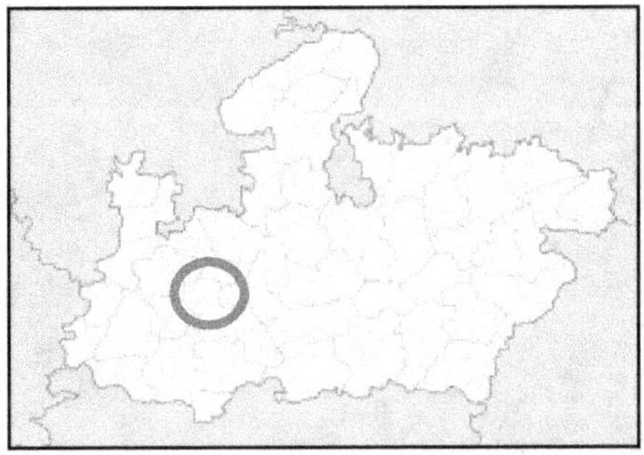

In 1733, the Peshwa assumed the full control of Malwa, and appointed his commander Malhar Rao Holkar as the Subhedar (Governor) of the province. Nandlal Chaudhary accepted the suzerainty of the Marathas.

On 29th July 1732, Bajirao Peshwa-I granted Holkar State by merging 28 and half parganas to Malhar Rao Holkar, the founder ruler of Holkar dynasty. His daughter-in-law Ahilyabai Holkar moved the state's capital to Maheshwar in 1767, but Indore remained an important commercial and military centre.

In 1818, the Holkars were defeated by the British during the Third Anglo-Maratha War, in the Battle of Mahidpur by virtue of which the capital was again moved from Maheshwar to Indore. A residency with British resident was established at Indore, but Holkars continued to rule Indore State as a princely state mainly due to efforts of their Dewan Tatya Jog. After India's independence in 1947, Holkar State, along with a number of neighbouring princely states, acceded to Indian Union. In 1948, with the formation of Madhya Bharat, Indore became the summer capital of the state. On 1st November 1956, when Madhya Bharat was merged into Madhya Pradesh, the state capital was moved to Bhopal.

Tookajee Rao Holkar II, Indore, from a drawing by Mr. W. Carpenter, Jun.," from the Illustrated London News, 1857

HH Tukoji Rao Holkar III, The Maharaja of Indore (1890-1978) by Lauder, London

Rajwada Palace

Daly College

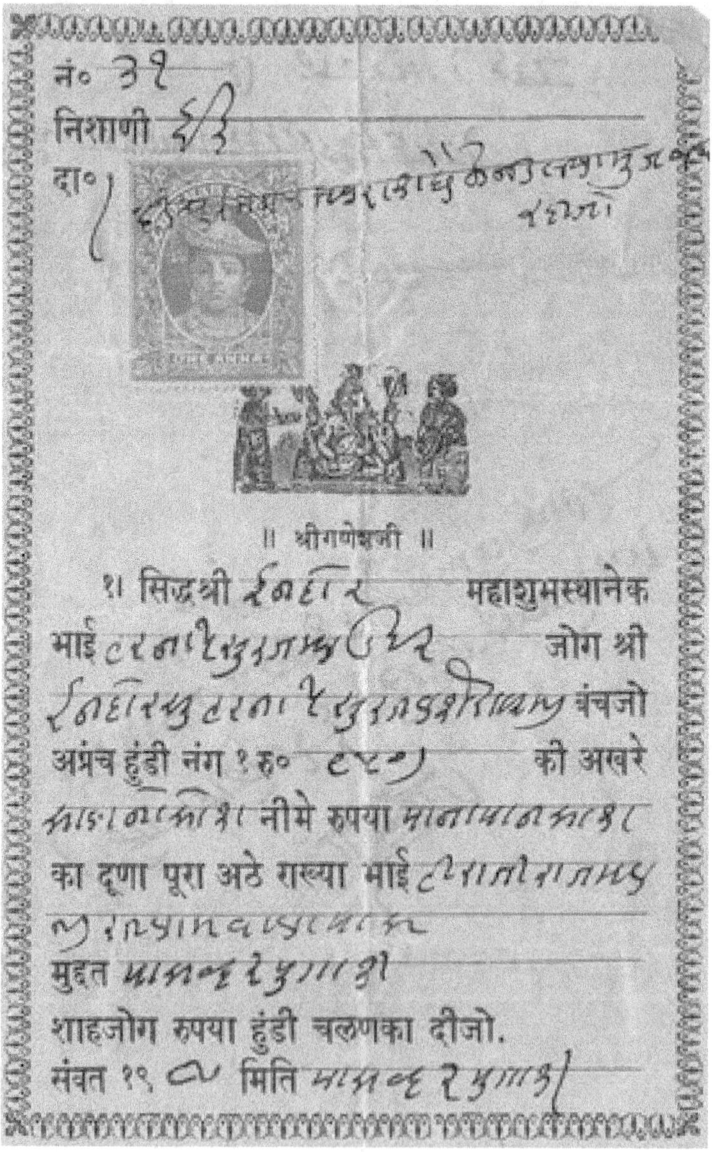

नं० ३१

निशाणी [illegible]

दा० [illegible]

॥ श्रीगणेशजी ॥

१। सिद्धश्री [illegible] महाशुभस्थानेक

भाई [illegible] जोग श्री

[illegible] बंचजो

अप्रंच हुंडी नंग १ रु० [illegible] की अखरे

[illegible] नीमे रुपया [illegible]

का दूणा पूरा अठे राख्या भाई [illegible]

[illegible]

मुदत [illegible]

शाहजोग रुपया हुंडी चलणका दीजो.

संवत १९ [illegible] मिति [illegible]

Hyderabad (Telangana State)

హైదరాబాద్

حیدرآباد

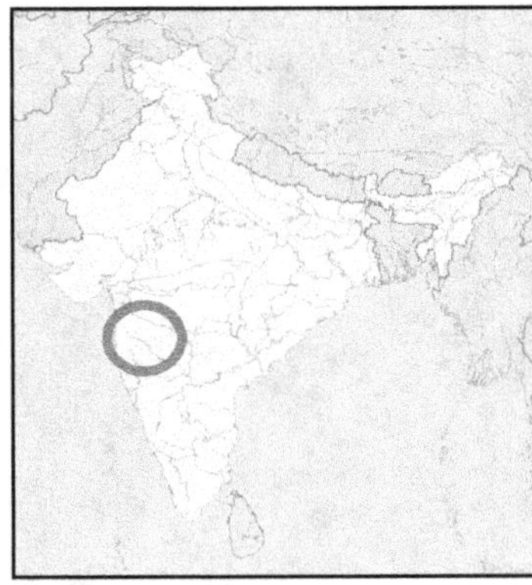

Hyderabad is the capital of the southern Indian state of Telangana and *de jure* capital of Andhra Pradesh.

Established in 1591 by Muhammad Quli Qutb Shah, Hyderabad remained under the rule of the Qutb Shahi dynasty for nearly a century before the Mughals captured the region. In 1724, Mughal viceroy Asif Jah I declared his sovereignty and created his own dynasty, known as the Nizams of Hyderabad.

The Nizam's dominions became a princely state during the British Raj, and remained so for 150 years, with the city serving as its capital. The city continued as the capital of Hyderabad State after it was brought into the Indian Union in 1948, and became the capital of Andhra Pradesh after the States Reorganisation Act, 1956.

The Qutb Shahi Tombs at Ibrahim Bagh are the tombs of the seven Qutb Shahi rulers.

The Telangana and Andhra Pradesh legislatures are housed in the State Assembly Building.

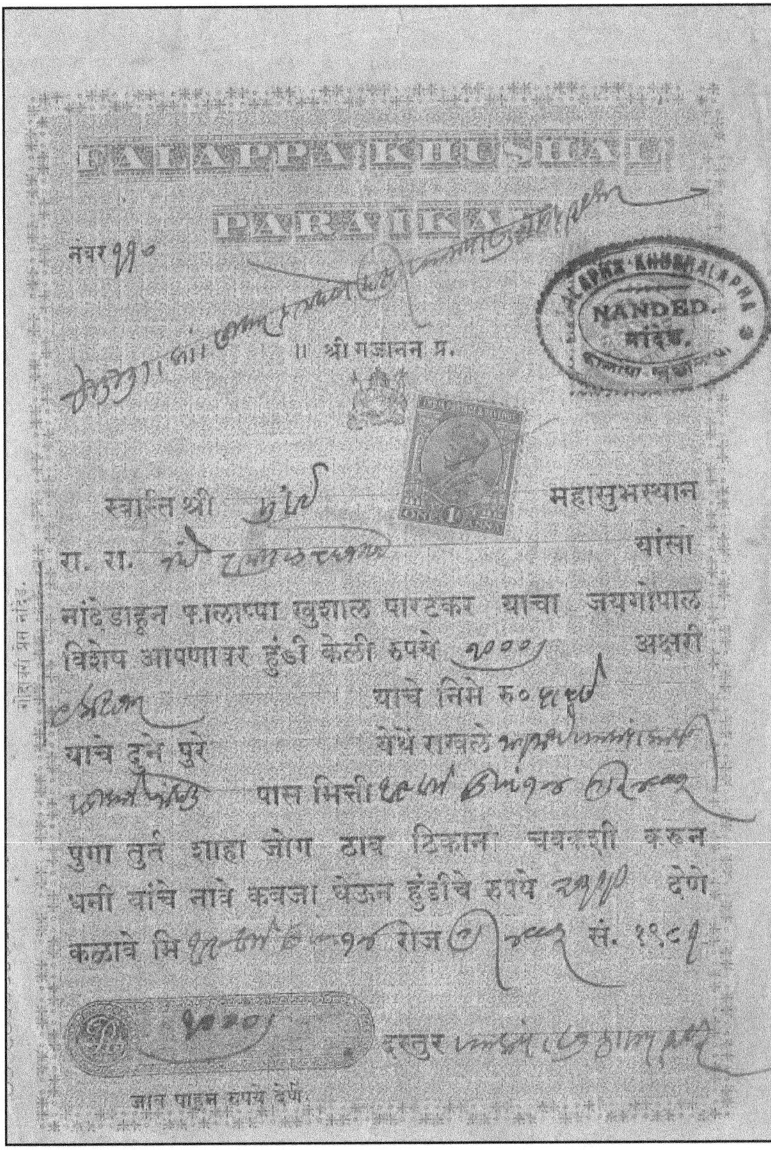

DALAPPA KHUSHAL

PARATKAR

नंबर ११०

NANDED. नांदेड.

॥ श्री गजानन प्र.

स्वस्ति श्री महासुभस्थान

रा. रा. यांसी

नांदेडाहून दालाप्पा खुशाल पारटकर यांचा जयगोपाल

विशेष आपणावर हुंडी केली रुपये १००० अक्षरी

याचे निमे रु०

याचे दुने पुरे येथें राखले

पास मिती

पुगा तुर्त शाहा जोग ठाव ठिकाना चवकशी करुन

धनी यांचे नांवे कबजा घेऊन हुंडीचे रुपये देणे

कळावे मि रोज सं. १९८१

दस्तुर

जान पाहून रुपये देणे.

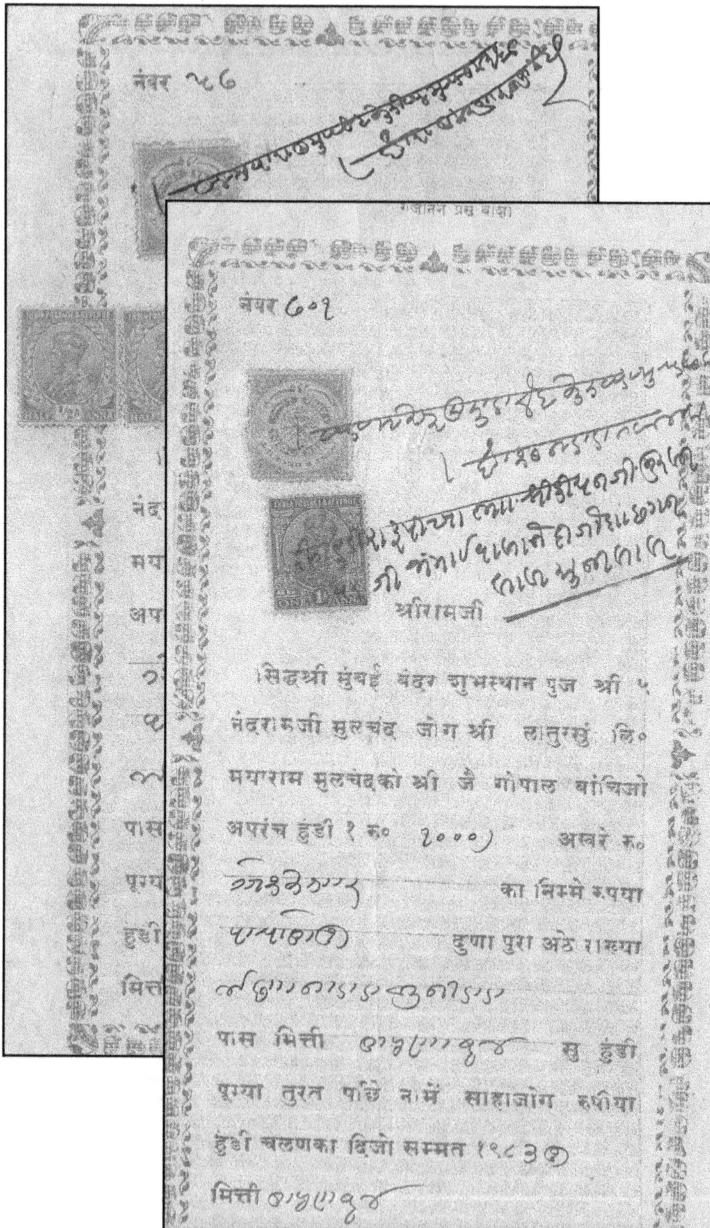

नंबर ६०१

श्रीरामजी

सिद्धश्री मुंबई बंदर शुभस्थान पुज श्री ५
नंदराकजी मुरचंद जोग श्री लातुरसुं लि०
मयाराम मुलचंदको श्री जै गोपाल बांचिजो
अपरंच हुंडी १ रु० २०००) अखरे रु०
का निम्मे रुपया
दुणा पुरा अठे राख्या
पास मित्ती सु हुंडी
पुग्या तुरत पांछे नामें साहाजोग रुपीया
हुंडी चलणका दिजो सम्मत १९८३

मित्ती

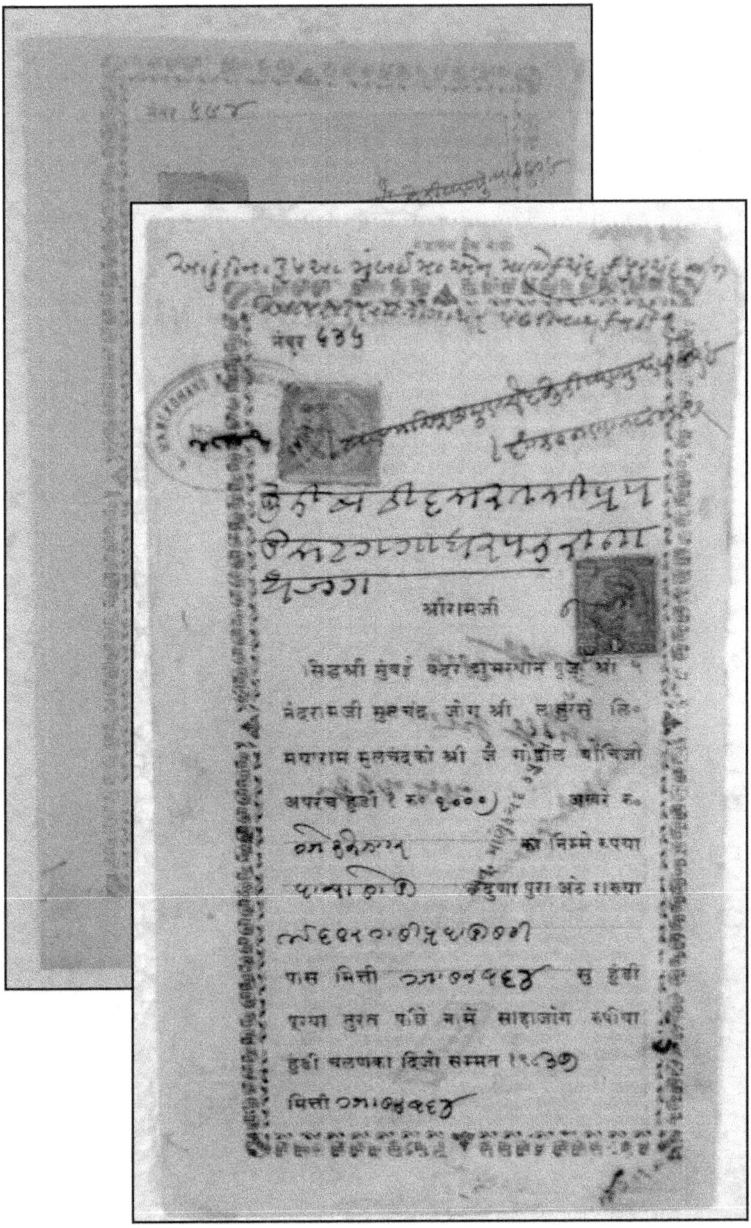
नंबर ६३५

श्रीरामजी

सिद्धश्री मुंबई बंदरे शुभस्थाने पूज्य श्री
नेंदरामजी मुलचंद जोग श्री लाहोरसे लि०
मयाराम मुलचंदको श्री जे गोपाल वाँचिजो
अपरंच हुंडी १ रु० १०००) अंकरे रु०
का निम्मे रुपया
कहुंणा पुरा अंठे राखया
पास मिती सु हुंडी
रुपया तुरत पछे नामे साहाजोग रुपीया
हुंडी चलणका दिजो सम्मत १९८३
मिती

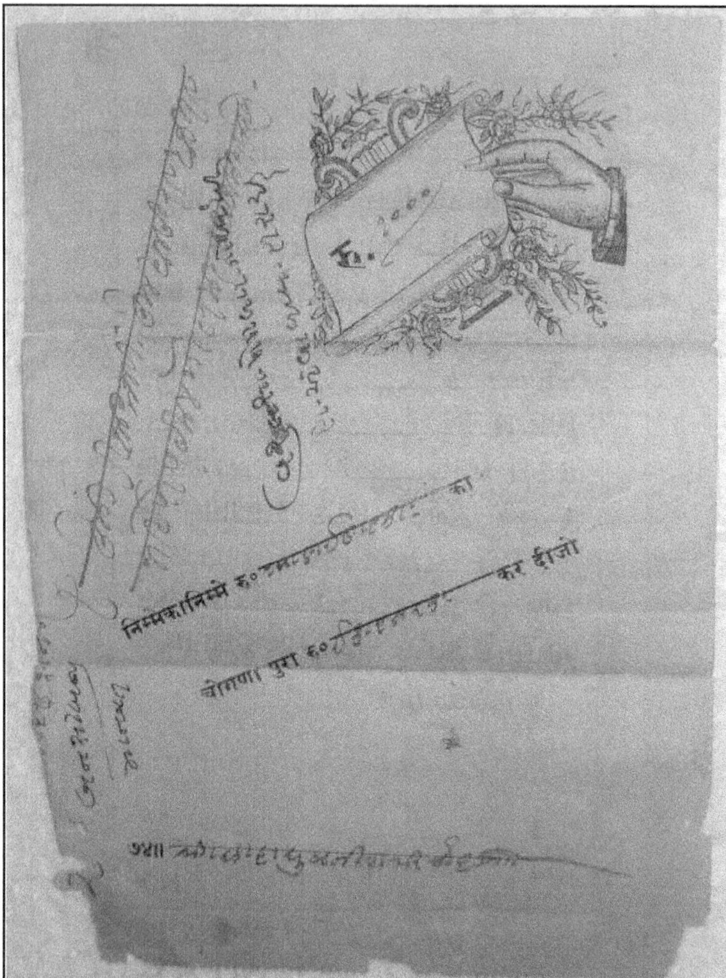

Indore State/ Holkar (State)
इंदौर रियासत

Indore State, also known as **Holkar State** was a Maratha princely state in India during the British Raj. Its rulers belonged to the Holkar dynasty and the state was under the Central India Agency. Indore was a 19-Gun Salute (21 locally) princely state (a rare high rank). Indore princely state was located in the present-day Indian state of Madhya Pradesh. The capital of the state was the city of Indore.

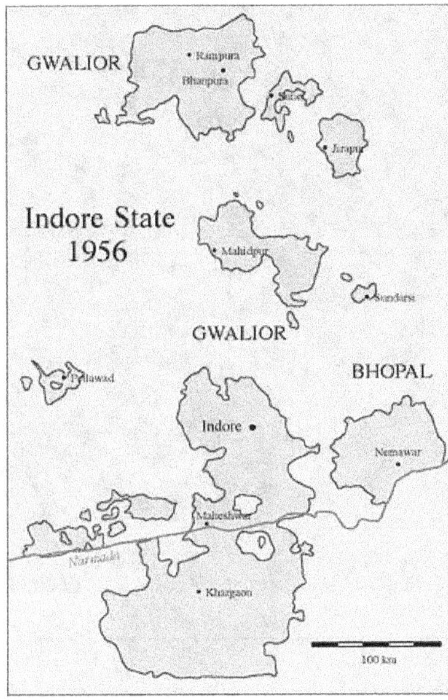

On 29th July 1732, Bajirao Peshwa-I granted Holkar State by merging 28 and half parganas to Malhar Rao Holkar, the founder ruler of Holkar dynasty. His daughter-in-law Ahilyabai Holkar moved the state's capital to Maheshwar in 1767, but Indore remained an important commercial and military centre. After the defeat of the Holkar rulers in the Third Anglo-Maratha War, an agreement was signed on 6th January 1818 with the British and Indore State became a British protectorate. The Holkar dynasty was able to continue to rule Indore as a princely state mainly owing to the efforts of their Dewan (Chief Minister) Tatya Jog.

The Rajawada (Old Palace) of Indore

The Sukhnivas Palace.

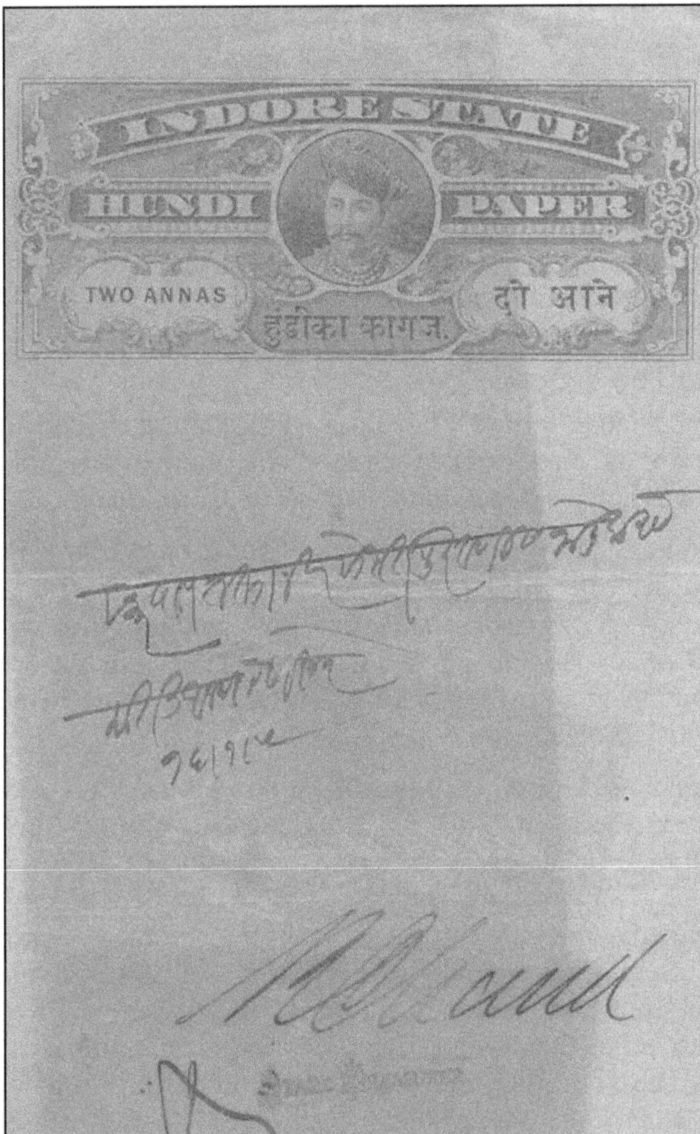
INDORE STATE
HUNDI PAPER
TWO ANNAS
दो आने
हुंडीका कागज.

Jafrabad (State)
જાફરાબાદ રિયાસત

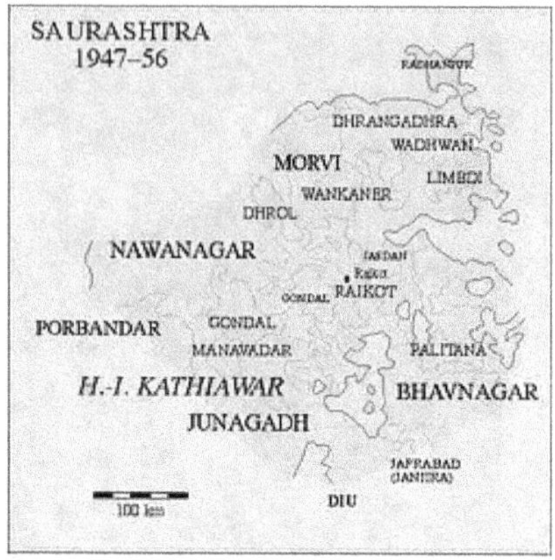

Jafarabad or **Jafrabad State** was a tributary princely state in India during the British Raj. It was located in the Kathiawar Peninsula on the Gujarat coast.

The state had formerly been part of the Baroda Agency and later of the Kathiawar Agency of the Bombay Presidency and was a dependency of the Nawab of Janjira State.

Jafarabad State was founded around 1650. On 6th December 1733 the ruler of Jafarabad State signed a defensive and offensive treaty with the British East India Company. In 1759, the Jafarabad and Janjira states entered into a personal union. Finally in 1834 Jafarabad State became a British protectorate.

Around 1731 when the Mughal Empire rule was relaxed in Gujarat, the local *Thanedar* (ruler) who was an ally in the Muslim Mughal garrison became independent. Thereafter the *Thanedar* and the local Kolis were devoted to piracy, repeatedly attacking ships and disturbing commercial traffic from Surat. Sidi Hilal, the prince of the dynasty of Janjira which was then ruling Surat, attacked the Kolis, destroyed their boats and captured them demanding a hefty fine. The Thanedar of Jafarabad could not afford to pay the fine and hence Jafarabad town was sold to Sidi Hilal in 1759.

Sidi Hilal soon realized that he could not keep the city given the situation of lawlessness in the Kathiawar peninsula and in 1762 he transferred Jafarabad to the Nawab of Janjira, who paid the debts and appointed him governor.

Under British protectorate the Nawabs of Janjira were considered separate second class rulers among the rulers of Kathiawar, but they were later promoted to first class. In the nineteenth century the rulers maintained a military force of 123 men. Jafarabad State acceded to the Indian Union on 8th March 1948.

Janjira ruins

Janjira Fort

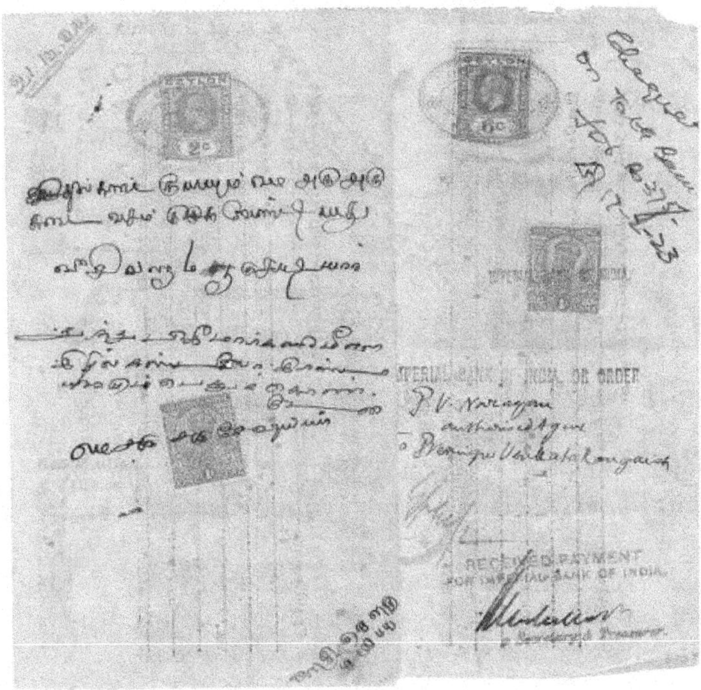

RECEIVED PAYMENT
FOR IMPERIAL BANK OF INDIA

Jaipur (Rajasthan State)
जयपुर

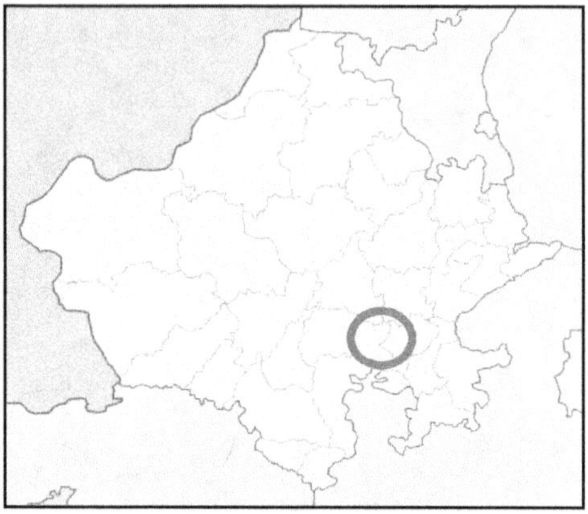

Jaipur is the capital of the Indian state of Rajasthan in Northern India. It was founded on 18th November 1726 by Maharaja Jai Singh II, the ruler of Amer after whom the city is named.

The city of Jaipur was founded in 1726 by Jai Singh II, the Raja of Amer who ruled from 1688 to 1758. He planned to shift his capital from Amer, 11km (7m) to Jaipur to accommodate the growing population and increasing scarcity of water. Jai Singh consulted several books on architecture and architects while planning the layout of Jaipur.

Under the architectural guidance of Vidyadhar Bhattacharya, Jaipur was planned based on the principles of Vastu Shastra and Shilpa Shastra. The construction of the city began in 1726 and took four years to complete the major roads, offices and palaces. The city was divided into nine blocks, two of which contained the state buildings and palaces, with the remaining seven allotted to the public. Huge ramparts were built, pierced by seven fortified gates.

Ganesha Pol of *Amer Fort*

Birla Mandir, Jaipur

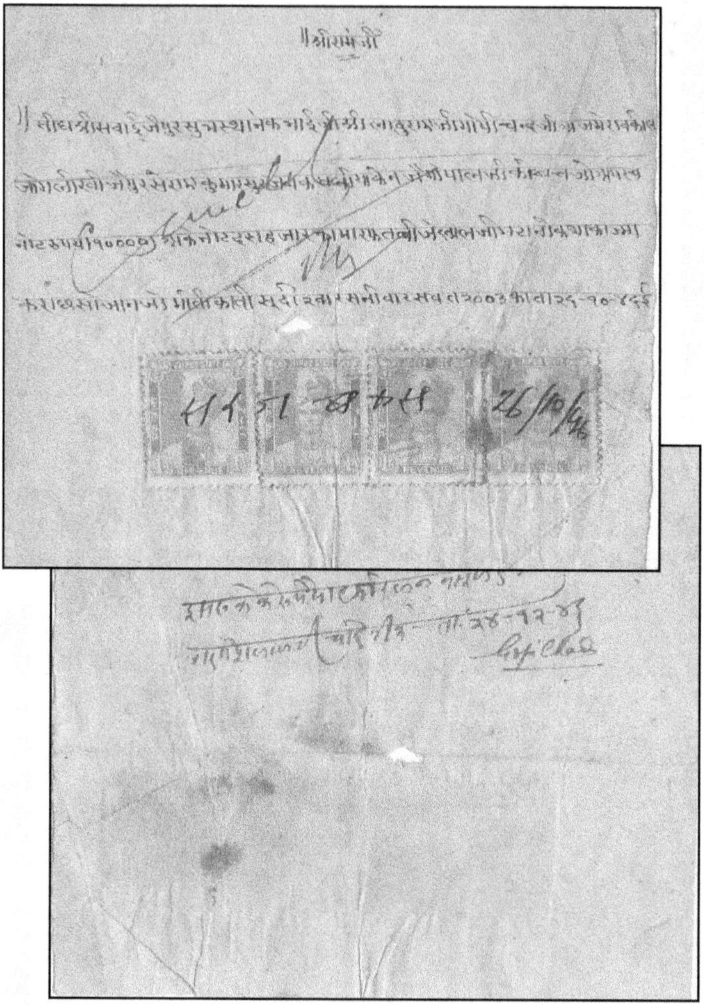
॥श्रीरामजी

26/10/46

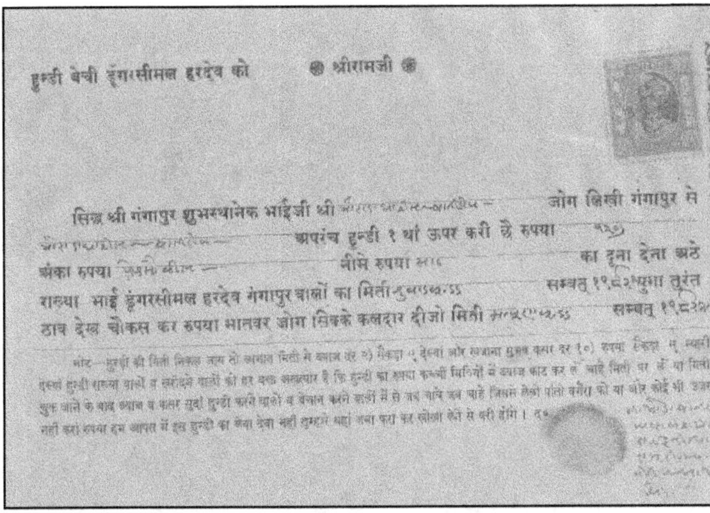

हुन्डी बेची डूंगरसीमल हरदेव को ॐ श्रीरामजी ॐ

सिद्ध श्री गंगापुर शुभस्थानेक भाईजी श्री ______ जोग लिखी गंगापुर से ______ अपरंच हुन्डी १ थां ऊपर करी छे रुपया ______ अंका रुपया ______ नीमे रुपया ______ का दूना देना अठे राख्या भाई डूंगरसीमल हरदेव गंगापुर वालों का मिती ______ सम्बत् १९८२ पुगा तुरंत ठाव देख चौकस कर रुपया भातवर जोग सिक्के कलदार दीजो मिती ______ सम्बत् १९८२

नोट—हुन्डी की मिती निकल जाय तो अगाड़ी मिती से ब्याज दर ५) सैकड़ा ५ देस्यां और खजाना मुजब कसर दर १०) रुपया सैकड़ा सू ज्यादी देस्यां हुन्डी राख्यां वालों व खरीदने वालों को हर वक्त अख्त्यार है कि हुन्डी का रुपया कच्ची मितियों में ब्याज काट कर लें चाहे मिती पर लें या मिती चुक जाने के बाद ब्याज व कसर सुदां हुन्डी करने वालों व बेचान करने वालों में से जब चाहे जब चाहे जिससे लेवो पांती वगैरा की या और कोई भी उजर नहीं करां रुपया हम आपस में इस हुन्डी का लेना देना नहीं तुम्हारे यहां जमा करा कर खोला लेने से बरी होंगे। द०

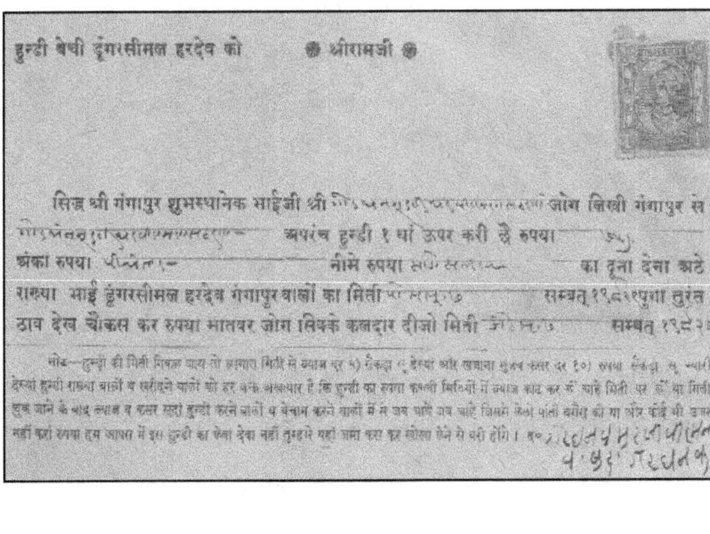

हुन्डी बेची डूंगरसीमल हरदेव को ॐ श्रीरामजी ॐ

सिद्ध श्री गंगापुर शुभस्थानेक भाईजी श्री ______ जोग लिखी गंगापुर से ______ अपरंच हुन्डी १ थां ऊपर करी छे रुपया ______ अंका रुपया ______ नीमे रुपया ______ का दूना देना अठे राख्या भाई डूंगरसीमल हरदेव गंगापुर वालों का मिती ______ सम्बत् १९८२ पुगा तुरंत ठाव देख चौकस कर रुपया भातवर जोग सिक्के कलदार दीजो मिती ______ सम्बत् १९८२

नोट—हुन्डी की मिती निकल जाय तो अगाड़ी मिती से ब्याज दर ५) सैकड़ा ५ देस्यां और खजाना मुजब कसर दर १०) रुपया सैकड़ा सू ज्यादी देस्यां हुन्डी राख्यां वालों व खरीदने वालों को हर वक्त अख्त्यार है कि हुन्डी का रुपया कच्ची मितियों में ब्याज काट कर लें चाहे मिती पर लें या मिती चुक जाने के बाद ब्याज व कसर सुदां हुन्डी करने वालों व बेचान करने वालों में से जब चाहे जब चाहे जिससे लेवो पांती वगैरा की या और कोई भी उजर नहीं करां रुपया हम आपस में इस हुन्डी का लेना देना नहीं तुम्हारे यहां जमा करा कर खोला लेने से बरी होंगे। द०

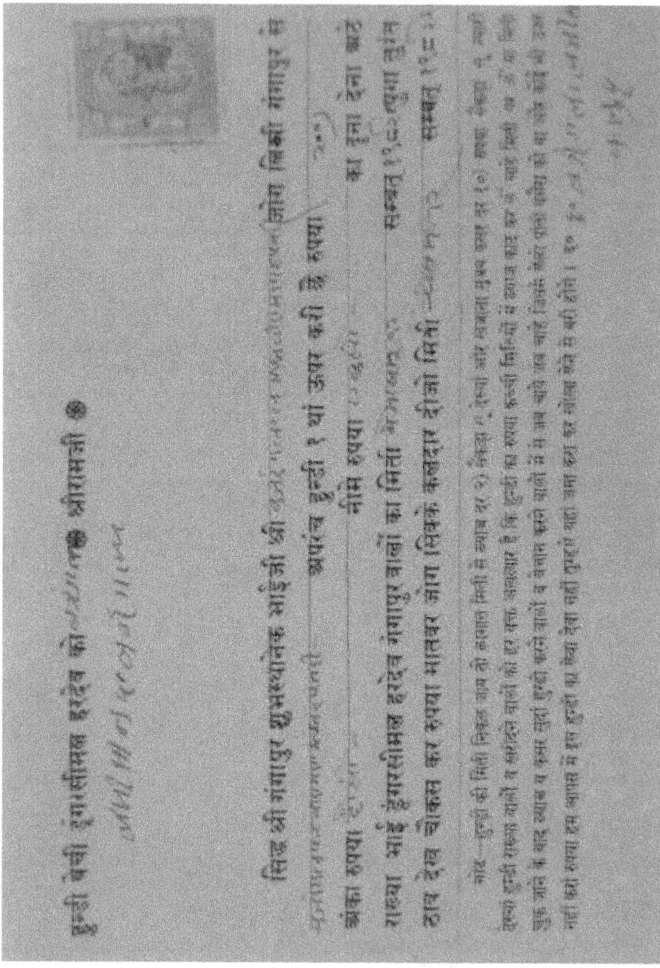

हुन्डी बेची डूंगरसीमल हरदेव को ॐ श्रीरामजी ॐ

सिद्ध श्री गंगापुर शुभस्थानेक भाईजी श्री जोग लिखी गंगापुर से

अपरंच हुन्डी १ थां ऊपर करी छै रुपया

अंका रुपया नीमे रुपया का दूना देना अठे

राख्या भाई डूंगरसीमल हरदेव गंगापुर वालों का मिती सम्वत् १९८ पूगा तुरंत

ठाव देख चौकस कर रुपया मातबर जोग सिकें कलदार दीजो मिती सम्वत् १९८

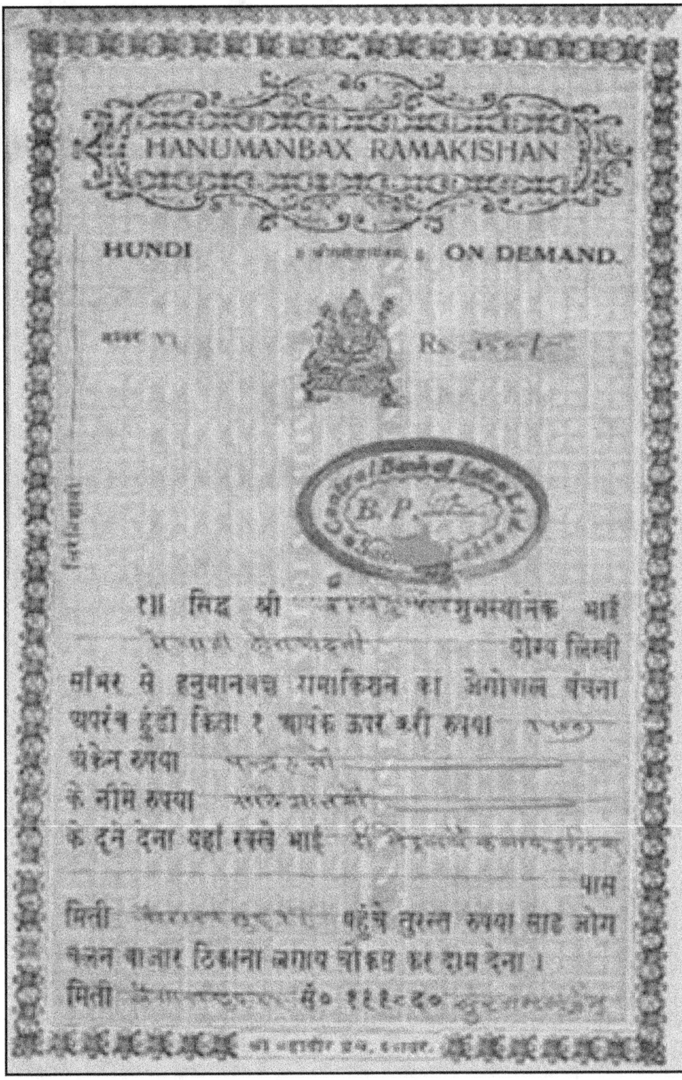
HANUMANBAX RAMAKISHAN

HUNDI ON DEMAND.

Rs.

B.P.

॥ सिद्ध श्री ... शुभस्थानेक भाई

जोग लिखी

सांभर से हनुमानबक्स रामकिसन का जेगोपाल बंचना

अपरंच हुंडी किता १ आपके ऊपर करी रुपया

अंकेन रुपया

के नीमे रुपया

के दूने देना यहाँ रक्खे भाई

पास

मिती ... पहुँचे तुरन्त रुपया साह जोग

चलन बाजार ठिकाना लगाय चौकस कर दाम देना।

मिती ... सं० १९९८०

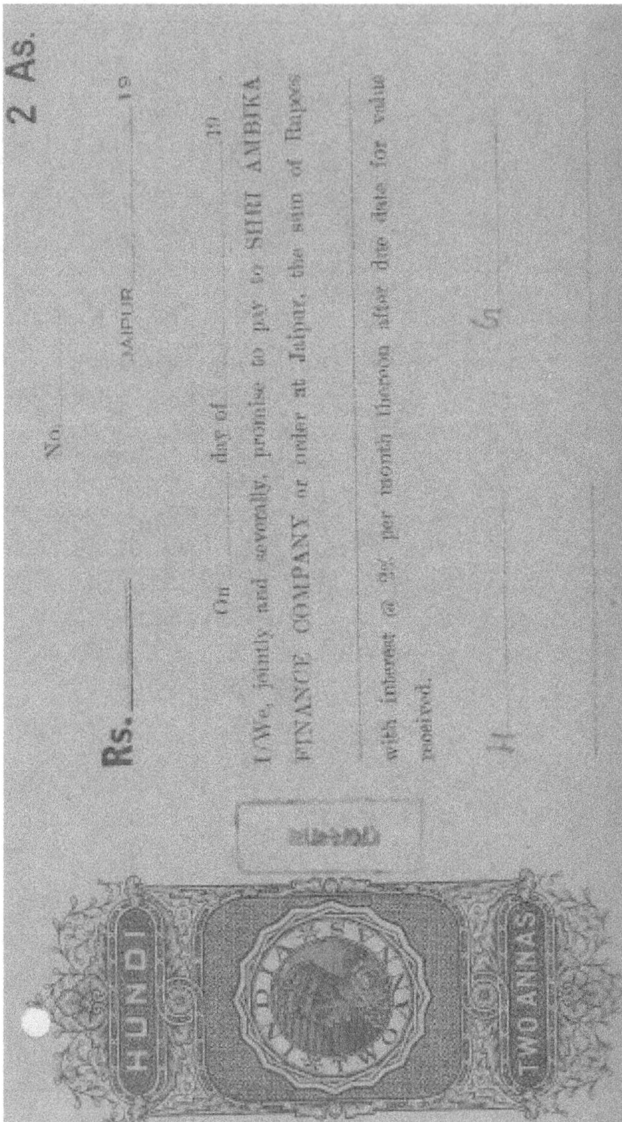
2 As.
HUNDI
TWO ANNAS
INDIA STAMP TWO ANNAS
No.
Rs.
JAIPUR 19
On day of 19
I/We, jointly and severally, promise to pay to SHRI AMBIKA FINANCE COMPANY or order at Jaipur, the sum of Rupees
with interest @ 2% per month thereon after due date for value received.

Jammu and Kashmir (State)
جموں و کشمیر

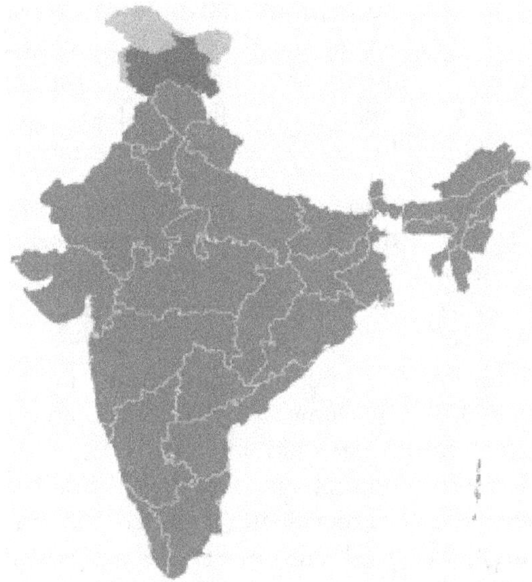

Jammu and Kashmir is located mostly in the Himalayan mountains, and shares borders with the states of Himachal Pradesh and Punjab to the south.

Maharaja Hari Singh became the ruler of the princely state of Jammu and Kashmir in 1925, and he was the reigning monarch at the conclusion of the British rule in the subcontinent in 1947. With the impending independence of India, the British announced that the British Paramountcy over the princely states would end, and the states were free to choose between the new Dominions of India and Pakistan or to remain independent. It was emphasised that independence was only a `theoretical possibility' because, during the long rule of the British in India, the states had come to depend on British Indian government for a variety of their needs including their internal and external security.

Jammu and Kashmir had a Muslim majority (77% Muslim by the previous census in 1941). Following the logic of Partition, many people in Pakistan expected that Kashmir would join Pakistan. However, the predominant political movement in the Valley of Kashmir (Jammu and Kashmir National Conference) was secular, and was allied with the Indian National Congress since the 1930's; so many in India too had expectations that Kashmir would join India. The Maharaja was faced with indecision.

On 22nd October 1947, rebellious citizens from the western districts of the State and Pushtoon tribesmen from the Northwest Frontier Province of Pakistan invaded the State, backed by Pakistan. The Maharaja initially fought back but appealed for assistance to the Indian Government, who agreed on the condition that the ruler accede to India. Maharaja Hari Singh signed the Instrument of Accession on 26th October 1947 in return for military aid and assistance, which was accepted by the Governor General the next day. While the Government of India accepted the accession, it added the proviso that it would be submitted to a "reference to the people" after the state is cleared of the invaders, since "only the people, not the Maharaja, could decide where Kashmiris wanted to live." It was a provisional accession.

Once the Instrument of Accession was signed, Indian soldiers entered Kashmir with orders to evict the raiders. The resulting Indo-Pakistani War of 1947 lasted until the end of 1948. At the beginning of 1948, India took the matter to the United Nations Security Council. The Security Council passed a resolution asking Pakistan to withdraw its forces as well as the Pakistani nationals from the territory of Jammu and Kashmir, and India to withdraw the majority of its forces leaving only a sufficient number to maintain law and order, following which a Plebiscite would be held. A ceasefire was agreed on 1st January 1949, supervised by UN observers.

A special United Nations Commission for India and Pakistan (UNCIP) was set up to negotiate the withdrawal arrangements as per the Security Council resolution.

The UNCIP made three visits to the subcontinent between 1948 and 1949, trying to find a solution agreeable to both India and Pakistan. It passed a resolution in August 1948 proposing a three-part process. It was accepted by India but effectively rejected by Pakistan. In the end, no withdrawal was ever carried out, India insisting that Pakistan had to withdraw first, and Pakistan contending that there was no guarantee that India would withdraw afterwards. No agreement could be reached between the two countries on the process of demilitarisation.

India and Pakistan fought two further wars in 1965 and 1971. Following the latter war, the countries reached the Simla Agreement, agreeing on a Line of Control between their respective regions and committing to a peaceful resolution of the dispute through bilateral negotiations.

Shalimar Gardens

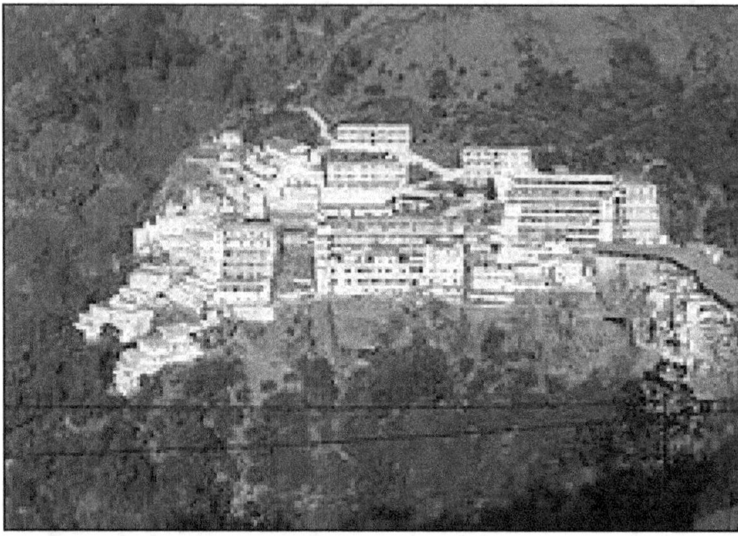

Vaishno Devi

A mosque in Srinagar

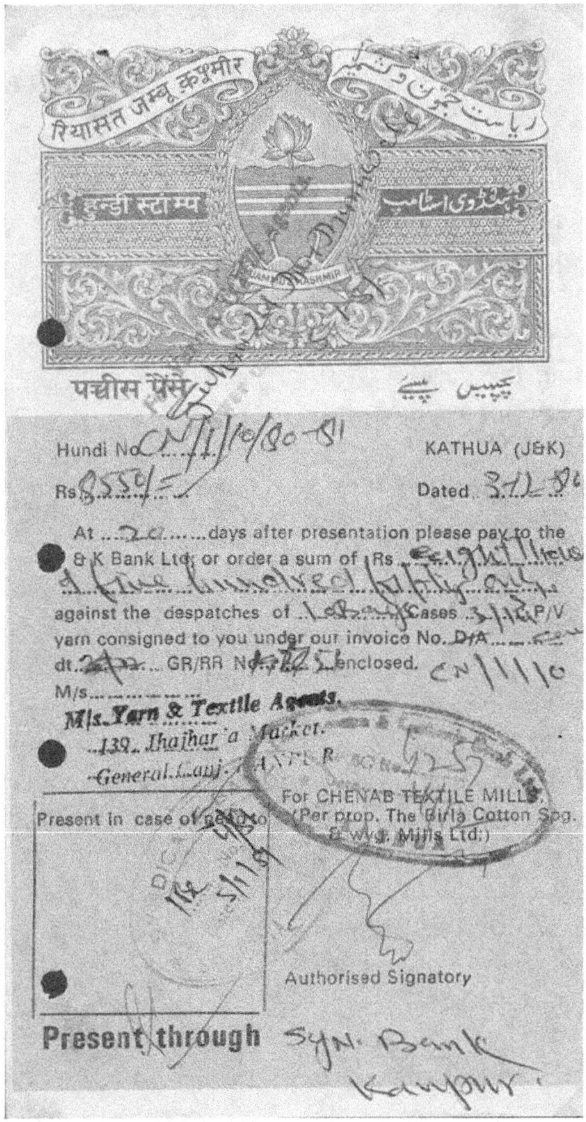

रियासत जम्मू कश्मीर

ریاست جموں و کشمیر

हुन्डी स्टाम्प

ہنڈوی اسٹامپ

JAMMU & KASHMIR

पच्चीस पैसे

پچیس پیسے

Hundi No. CN/11/10/80-81 KATHUA (J&K)

Rs. 8554/- Dated 3.11.80

At ..20.. days after presentation please pay to the J & K Bank Ltd. or order a sum of Rs. eight thousand five hundred fifty four only against the despatches of ...... Cases ...... P/V yarn consigned to you under our invoice No. D/A ...... dt. ...... GR/RR No. ...... enclosed. CN/11/10

M/s ......

M/s. Yarn & Textile Agents.

139, Jhajhar'a Market.

General Ganj. KANPUR

For CHENAB TEXTILE MILLS

(Per prop. The Birla Cotton Spg. & Wvg. Mills Ltd.)

Present in case of need to

Authorised Signatory

Present through Syn. Bank Kanpur.

Jodhpur (Rajasthan State)
जोधपुर

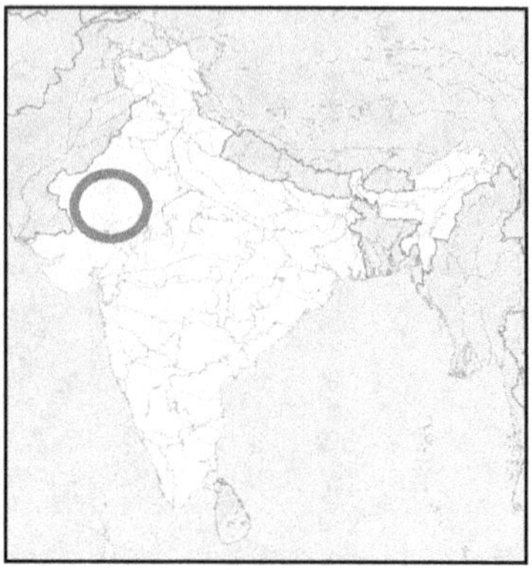

Jodhpur is the second largest city in the Indian state of Rajasthan. It was formerly the seat of a princely state of the same name, the capital of the kingdom known as Marwar.

According to the Rajasthan District Gazetteer's of Jodhpur and the Hindu epic *Ramayana* (composed up to the 4th century AD), Abhiras (Ahirs) were the original inhabitants of Jodhpur and later Aryans spread to this region.

Jodhpur was also part of the Gurjara–Pratihara Empire and until 1100 AD was ruled by a powerful Gurjar King. Jodhpur was founded in 1459 by Rao Jodha, a Rajput chief of the Rathore clan. Jodha succeeded in conquering the surrounding territory and thus founded a state which came to be known as Marwar. As, Jodha hailed from the nearby town of Mandore, that town initially served as the capital of this state. However, Jodhpur soon took over that role, even during the lifetime of Jodha.

Jaswant Thada cenotaph in Jodhpur

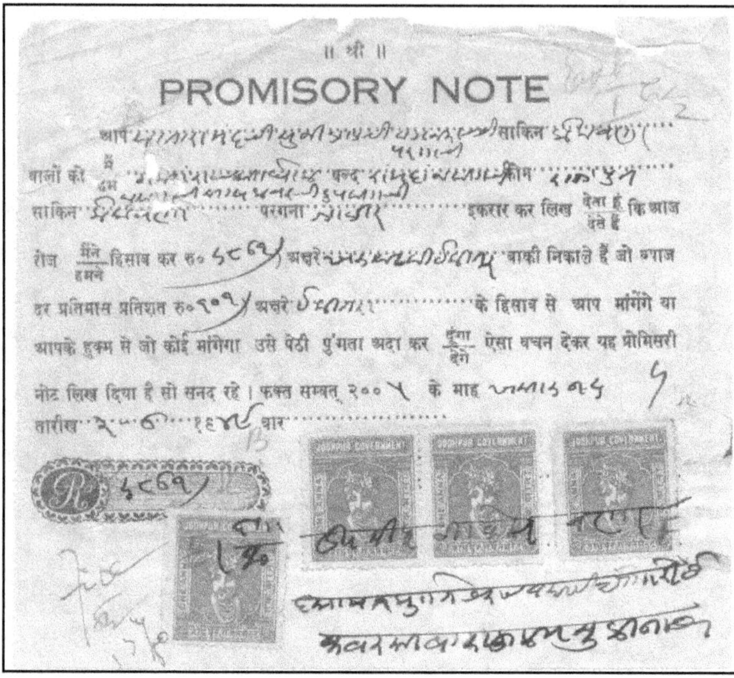

॥ श्री ॥

PROMISORY NOTE

आप ...... साकिन ......

वालों को मैं/हम ...... साकिन ...... परगना ...... इकरार कर लिख देता हूँ/देते हैं कि आज

रोज मैंने/हमने हिसाब कर रु० ...... अक्षरे ...... बाकी निकाले हैं जो ब्याज

दर प्रतिमास प्रतिशत रु० ...... अक्षरे ...... के हिसाब से आप मांगेंगे या

आपके हुक्म से जो कोई मांगेगा उसे पेठी पुंमता अदा कर दूंगा/देंगे ऐसा वचन देकर यह प्रोमिसरी

नोट लिख दिया है सो सनद रहे। फक्त सम्वत् २००५ के माह ......

तारीख ...... वार ......

JODHPUR GOVERNMENT

Karnataka (State)

ಕರ್ನಾಟಕ

ಕರುನಾಡು

Karnataka is a state in south western region of India. It was formed on 1st November 1956, with the passage of the States Reorganisation Act. Originally known as the **State of Mysore**, it was renamed *Karnataka* in 1973. The capital and largest city is Bangalore (Bengaluru).

After India's independence, the Maharaja, Jayachamarajendra Wodeyar, allowed his kingdom's accession to India. In 1950, Mysore became an Indian state of the same name; the former Maharaja served as its *Rajpramukh* (head of state) until 1975.

Following the long-standing demand of the Ekikarana Movement, Kodagu- and Kannada-speaking regions from the adjoining states of Madras, Hyderabad and Bombay were incorporated into the Mysore state, under the States Reorganisation Act of 1956. The thus expanded state was renamed Karnataka, seventeen years later, in 1973.

Statue of Ugranarasimha at Hampi

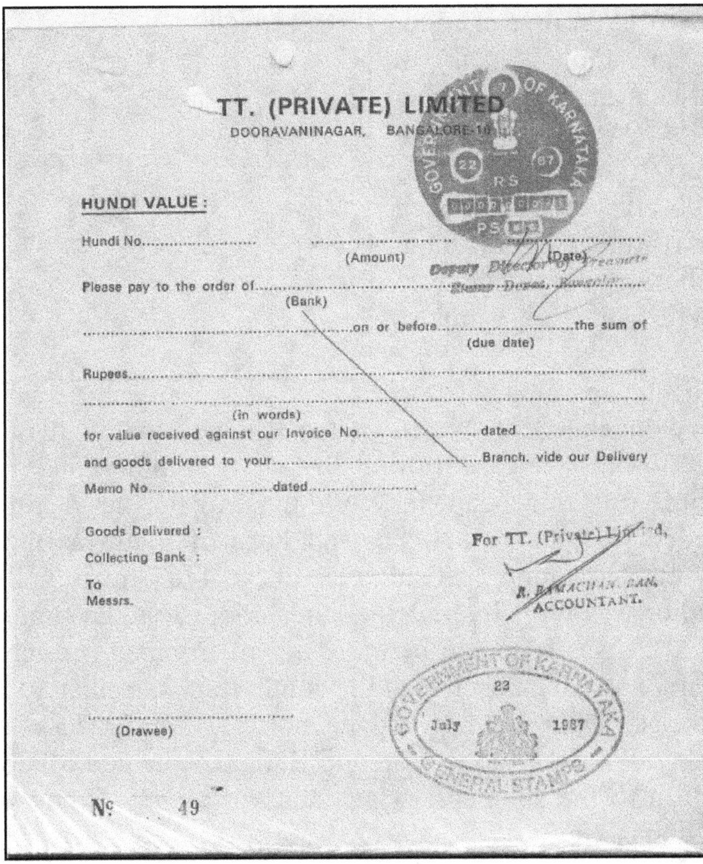

TT. (PRIVATE) LIMITED

DOORAVANINAGAR, BANGALORE-16

HUNDI VALUE :

Hundi No.......................... ....

(Amount) (Date)

Please pay to the order of..

(Bank)

....on or before..............................the sum of

(due date)

Rupees..

....

(in words)

for value received against our Invoice No.............................dated ....

and goods delivered to your...Branch, vide our Delivery

Memo No..........................dated..........................

Goods Delivered :

Collecting Bank :

To

Messrs.

....

(Drawee)

For TT. (Private) Limited,

ACCOUNTANT.

GOVERNMENT OF KARNATAKA

22

RS

PS

GOVERNMENT OF KARNATAKA

22

July 1987

GENERAL STAMPS

№ 49

Madhya Bharat (State)
मध्य भारत

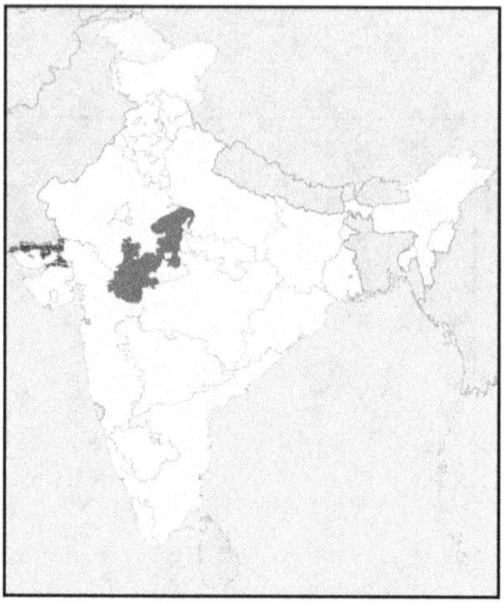

Madhya Bharat also known as **Malwa Union**, was an Indian state in west-central India, created on 28th May 1948 from twenty-five princely states which until 1947 had been part of the Central India Agency, with Jivaji Rao Scindia as its Rajpramukh.

With the passing of the Indian Independent Act 1947, the Princely States of India had all been released from British suzerainty and had become fully independent. While most of the states' rulers acceded to India or to Pakistan, those of Madhya Bharat delayed.The union had an area of 46,478 square miles. Gwalior was the winter capital and Indore was the summer capital. It was bordered by the states of Bombay (presently Gujarat and Maharashtra) to the southwest, Rajasthan to the northeast, Uttar Pradesh to the north, Uttar Pradesh and Vindhya Pradesh to the east, and Bhopal State and Madhya Pradesh to the southeast. The state was mostly Hindu and Hindi-speaking.

On 1st November 1956, Madhya Bharat, together with the states of Vindhya Pradesh and Bhopal State, was merged into Madhya Pradesh.

Jai Vilas Palace, Gwalior

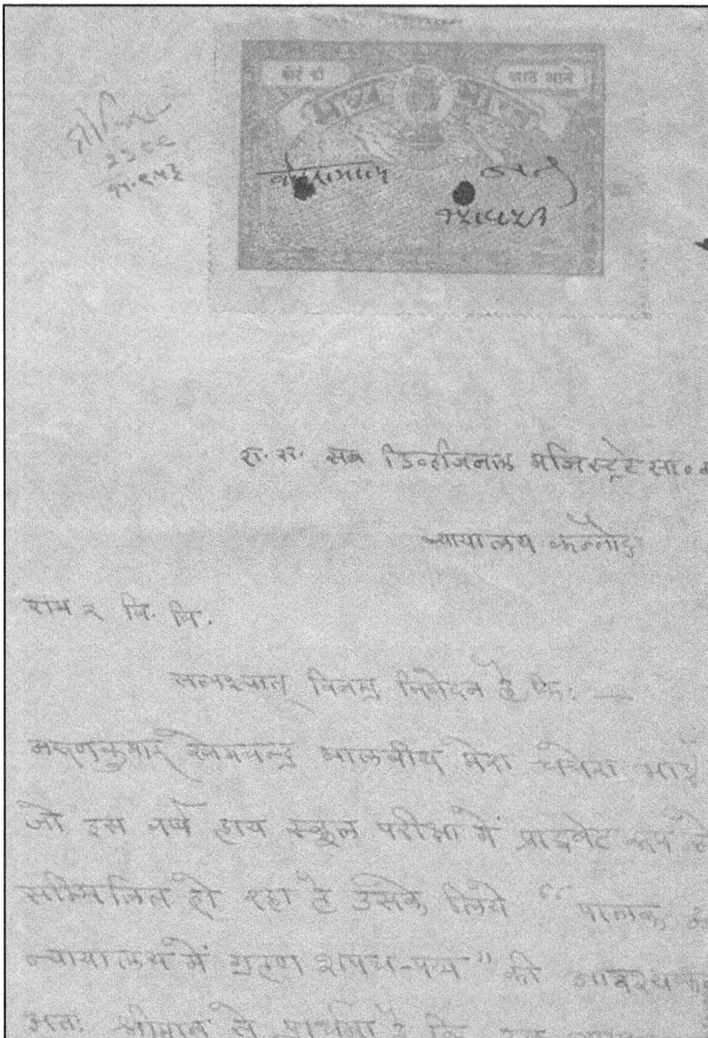

रा. रा. सब डिव्हिजनल मजिस्ट्रेट सा. [illegible]

न्यायालय कन्नौद

राम २ वि. वि.

सनम्रभाव विनम्र निवेदन है कि: —

अरुणकुमार रामचन्द्र मालवीय मेरा चचेरा भाई [illegible]

जो इस वर्ष हाय स्कूल परीक्षा में प्राइवेट रूप से

सम्मिलित हो रहा है उसके लिये "पालक [illegible]

न्यायालय में शुद्ध शपथ-पत्र" की आवश्यकता [illegible]

अतः श्रीमान से प्रार्थना है कि उक्त शपथ पत्र [illegible]

Mumbai (Bombay)

मुंबई

Mumbai (also known as Bombay, the official name until 1995) is the capital city of the Indian state of Maharashtra.

The Mughal Empire, founded in 1526, was the dominant power in the Indian subcontinent during the mid-16th century. Growing apprehensive of the power of the Mughal emperor Humayun, Sultan Bahadur Shah of the Gujarat Sultanate was obliged to sign the Treaty of Bassein with the Portuguese Empire on 23rd December 1534. According to the treaty, the seven islands of Bombay, the nearby strategic town of Bassein and its dependencies were offered to the Portuguese. The territories were later surrendered on 25th October 1535.

The Portuguese were actively involved in the foundation and growth of their Roman Catholic religious orders in Bombay. They called the islands by various names, which finally took the written form *Bombaim*. The islands were leased to several Portuguese officers during their regime.

Apart from several prominent churches, the Portuguese also built several fortifications around the city like the Bombay Castle, *Castellan de Aguada* (Castelo da Aguada or Bandra Fort), and Madh Fort.

The English were in constant struggle with the Portuguese vying for hegemony over Bombay, as they recognised its strategic natural harbour and its natural isolation from land-attacks.

By the middle of the 17th century the growing power of the Dutch Empire forced the English to acquire a station in western India. On 11th May 1661, the marriage treaty of Charles II of England and Catherine of Braganza, daughter of King John IV of Portugal, placed the islands in possession of the English Empire, as part of Catherine's dowry to Charles.

In accordance with the Royal Charter of 27th March 1668, England leased these islands to the English East India Company in 1668 for a sum of £10 per annum.

In 1687, the English East India Company transferred its headquarters from Surat to Bombay.

The Portuguese presence ended in Bombay when the Marathas under *Peshwa* Baji Rao I captured Salsette in 1737, and Bassein in 1739.

From 1782 onwards, the city was reshaped with large-scale civil engineering projects aimed at merging all the seven islands into a single amalgamated mass. This project, known as Hornby Vellard, was completed by 1784. In 1817, the British East India Company under Mountstuart Elphinstone defeated Baji Rao II, the last of the Maratha *Peshwa* in the Battle of Khadki.

Following his defeat, almost the whole of the Deccan came under British suzerainty, and was incorporated into the Bombay Presidency.

The success of the British campaign in the Deccan marked the end of all attacks by native powers.

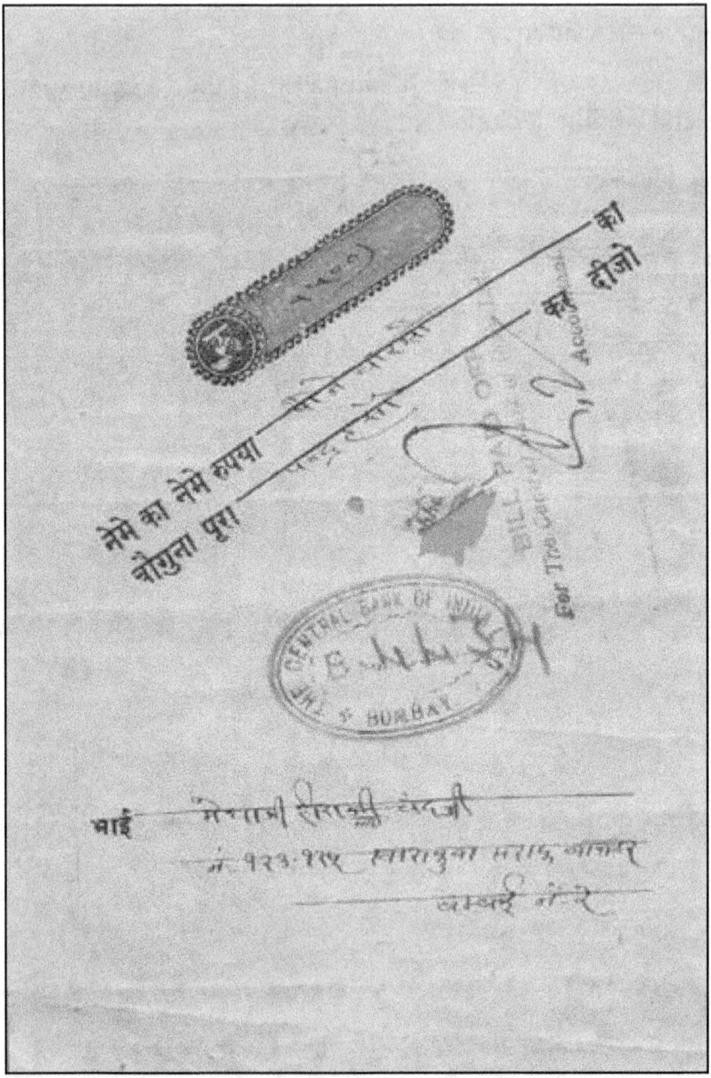

नेमे का नेमे रुपया का

चौगुना पूरा का दीजो

THE CENTRAL BANK OF INDIA

BOMBAY

For The Central ... Account

भाई

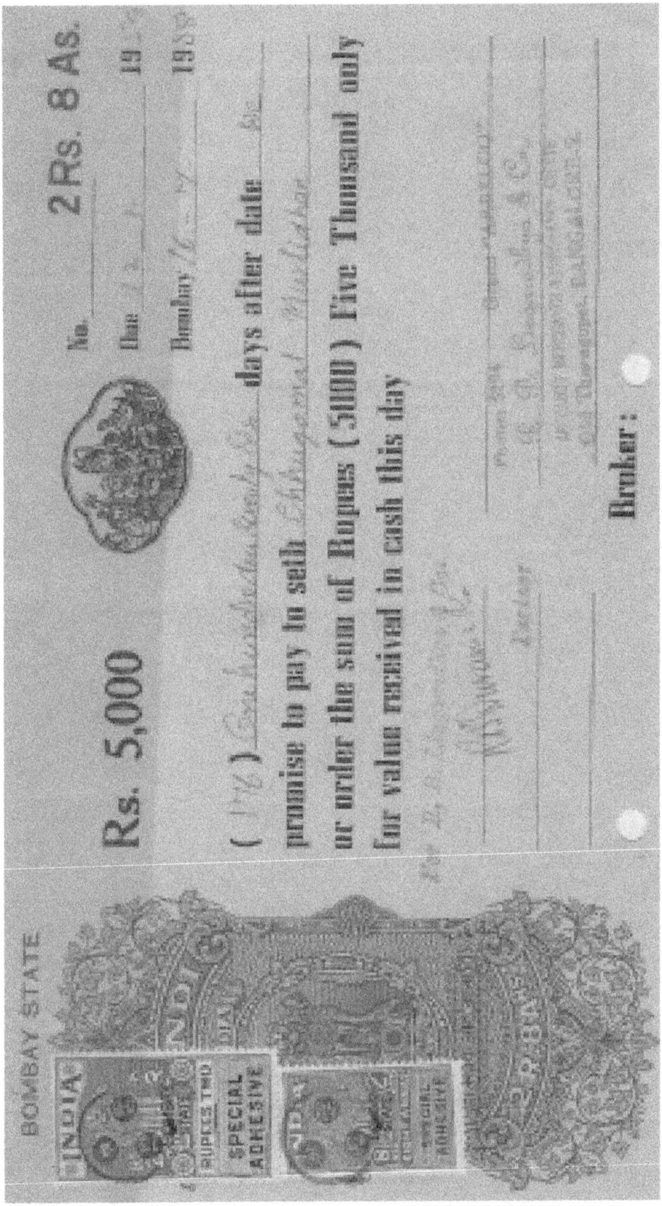

BOMBAY STATE

Rs. 5,000

2Rs. 8 As.

No.

Due 19

Bombay 19

( ) days after date
promise to pay to seth
or order the sum of Rupees (5000) Five Thousand only
for value received in cash this day

Broker:

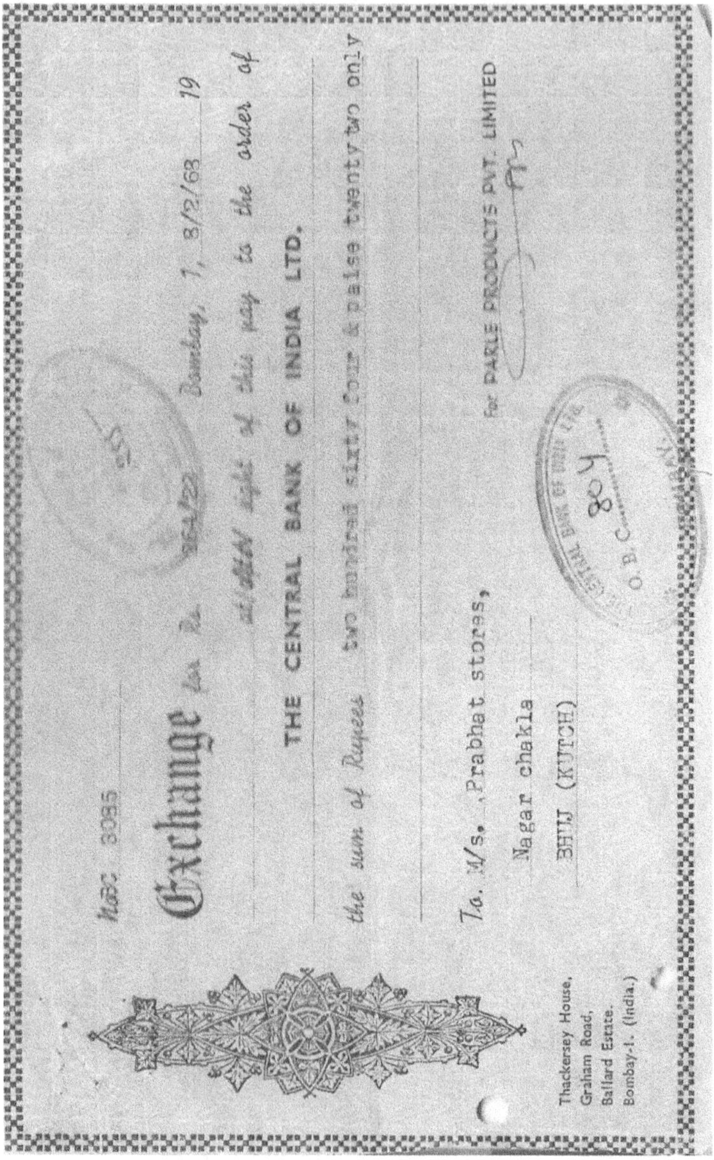
No. 3085
Exchange for Rs.
Bombay, 1, 8/2/68 19
at sight of this pay to the order of
THE CENTRAL BANK OF INDIA LTD.
the sum of Rupees two hundred sixty four & paise twenty two only
To. M/s. Prabhat stores,
Nagar chakla
BHUJ (KUTCH)
For PARLE PRODUCTS PVT. LIMITED
Thackersey House,
Graham Road,
Ballard Estate,
Bombay-1. (India.)
O.B.C. 804

Mysore (Kingdom/State)

ಮೈಸೂರು

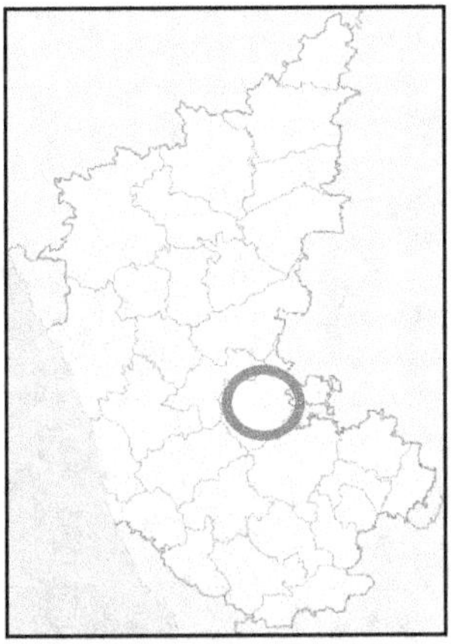

Mysore, officially renamed as **Mysuru**, is the third most populous city in the state of Karnataka, India.

The Mysore Kingdom, governed by the Wodeyar family, initially served as a vassal state of the Vijayanagara Empire. With the decline of the Vijayanagara Empire after the Battle of Talikota in 1565, the Mysore Kingdom gradually achieved independence, and by the time of King Narasaraja Wodeyar (1637) it had become a sovereign state.

Seringapatam (modern-day Srirangapatna), near Mysore, was the capital of the kingdom from 1610. The 17th century saw a steady expansion of its territory and, under Narasaraja Wodeyar I and Chikka Devaraja Wodeyar, the kingdom annexed large expanses of what is now southern Karnataka and parts of Tamil Nadu, to become a powerful state in the southern Deccan.

After Indian independence, Mysore city remained as part of the Mysore State, now known as Karnataka. Jayachamarajendra Wodeyar, then king of Mysore, was allowed to retain his titles and was nominated as the *Rajapramukh* (appointed governor) of the state.

Mysore Palace

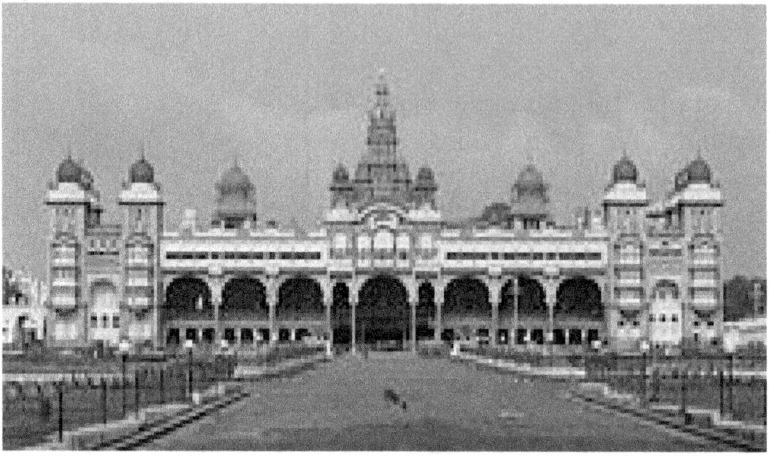

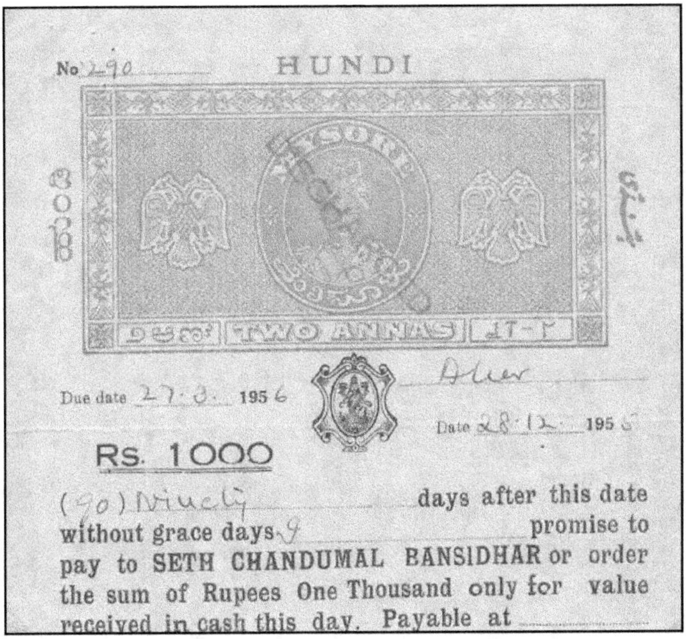

No 290 HUNDI

MYSORE

TWO ANNAS

Due date 27.3. 1956

Date 28.12. 1955

Rs. 1000

(90) Ninety days after this date without grace days 9 promise to pay to SETH CHANDUMAL BANSIDHAR or order the sum of Rupees One Thousand only for value received in cash this day. Payable at

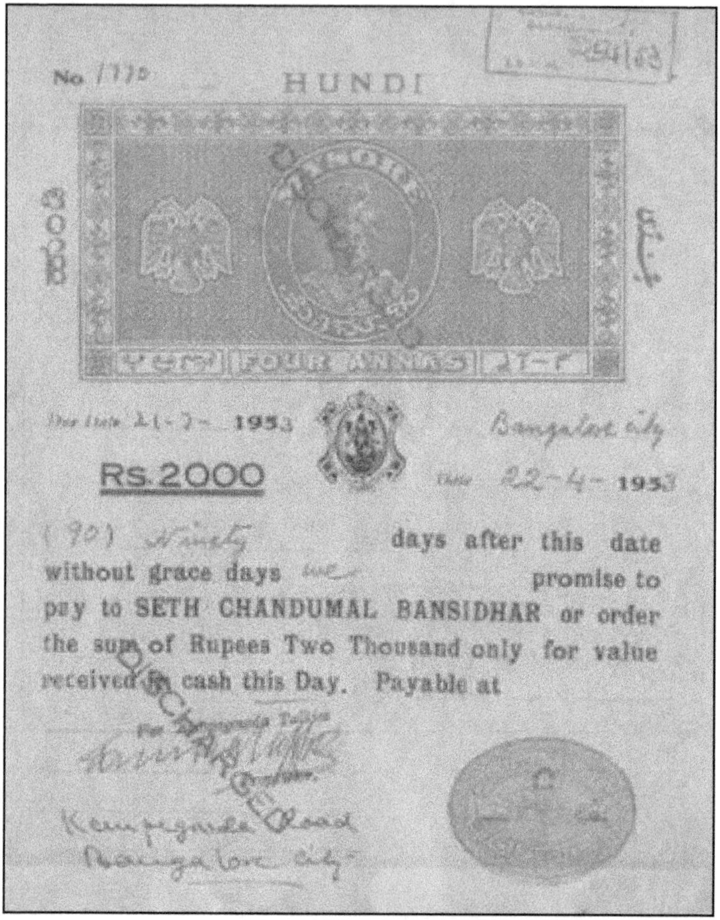
No 1770 HUNDI

FOUR ANNAS

Due date 21-7-1953

Bangalore City

Rs.2000

Date 22-4-1953

(90) Ninety days after this date without grace days we promise to pay to SETH CHANDUMAL BANSIDHAR or order the sum of Rupees Two Thousand only for value received in cash this Day. Payable at

DISCHARGED

Kempegowda Road
Bangalore City

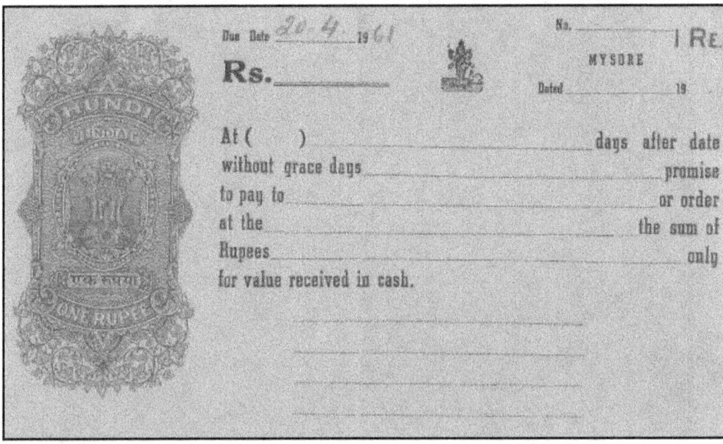

HUNDI INDIA एक रुपया ONE RUPEE

Due Date 20-4-1961 No. ______ 1 RE.

Rs. ______ MYSORE

Dated ______ 19

At ( ) ______ days after date without grace days ______ promise to pay to ______ or order at the ______ the sum of Rupees ______ only for value received in cash.

HUNDI INDIA 2R. 8A.

2 Rs. 8 As.

No. ______

Due Date 14-11-1958 LAXMI Bangalore city

Dated 18-8-1958

Rs. 5000

(88) Eighty Eight days after this date without grace days We promise to pay to **Seth Pokardas Menghraj & Sons.** or order the sum of Rupees FIVE THOUSAND only for value received in cash this day Payable at ______

BANGALORE-2

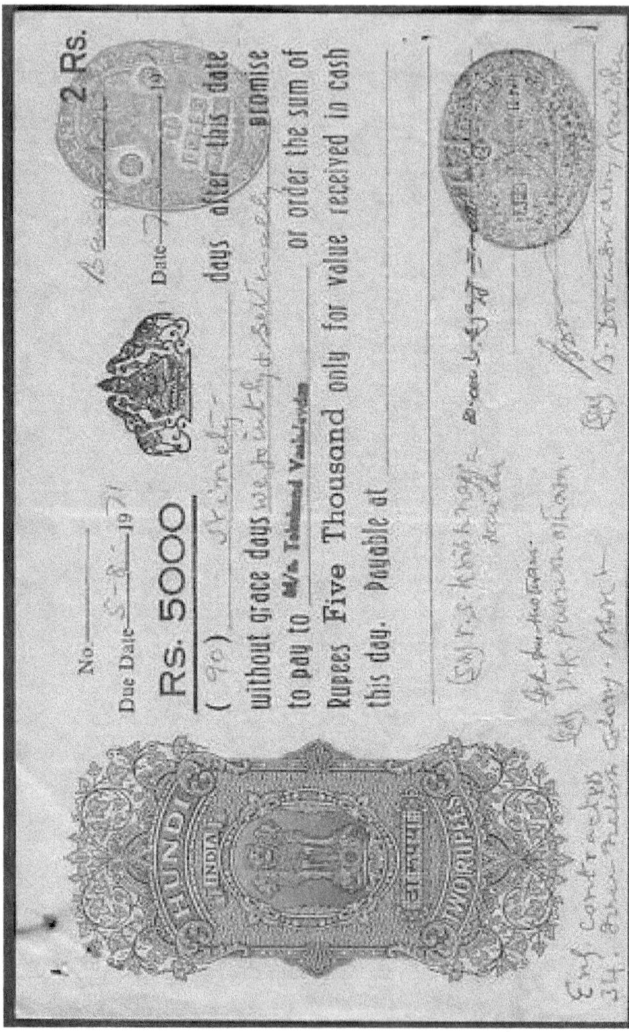

No.

Due Date 5-8-1971

Date

Rs. 5000

(90) Ninety days after this date without grace days we jointly & severally promise to pay to M/s. Tolchand Vashdevdas or order the sum of Rupees Five Thousand only for value received in cash this day. Payable at

Nabha (State)

ਨਾਭਾ ਰਜ਼ਿਆਸਤ/ नाभा रियासत

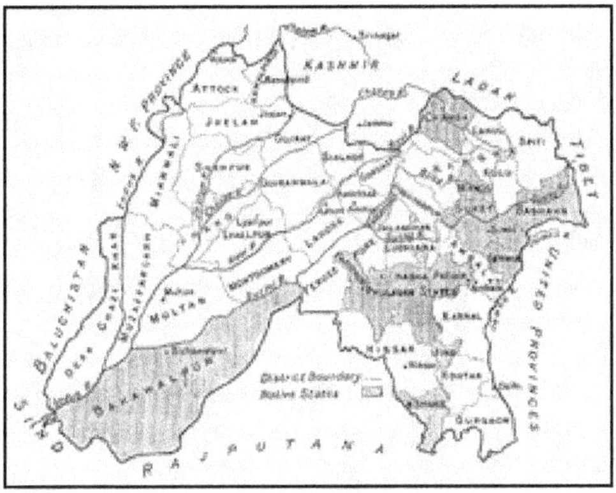

Nabha State in a 1911 map of Punjab

Nabha State, with its capital at Nabha, was one of the Phulkian princely states of Punjab during the British Raj in India.

The family claims descent from the Bhatti founder of Jaisalmer, Jaisal. His third son, Rai Hem, left the family domains after the usual quarrel and carved out a small principality for himself around Bhatinda and Bhatner. His successor in the fourth degree, Khiwa, fell on hard times and was forced to move to Kot Ladwa, where he married a girl from the Jat Basehra caste, against the clan traditions of the Rajputs. Thereafter many quarrels ensued between his descendants at the Bhattis.

The Mughals appointed his descendant Mehraj in 1526. This office became hereditary amongst his descendants until Phul, the Sikh ancestor of the dynasty, who came to rule over Patiala, Jind and Nabha.

The state was established in 1763 after the capture of Sirhind by the Sikh Confederacy. With the capture of Sirhind, most of the old imperial province was divided amongst the Phulkian chiefs. The area around Amloh was taken by the chief of the Nabha, Hamir Singh.

In 1809, with the power of Ranjit Singh expanding, Nabha State fell under the protection of the East India Company. During the Indian rebellion of 1857 the state was loyal to itssubsidiary alliance with the British and was granted territory as a reward. The state entered a period of prosperity under the rule of Hira Singh.

In 1947, with the British departure from India, the subsidiary alliance was dissolved and Nabha was briefly fully independent. Its ruler soon decided to sign an instrument of accession, acceding to the new Dominion of India, when the state was combined with other princely states into the Patiala and East Punjab States Union. It later became part of the Indian state of Punjab.

Sir Hira Singh, Raja of Nabha
(circa. 1843-1911)

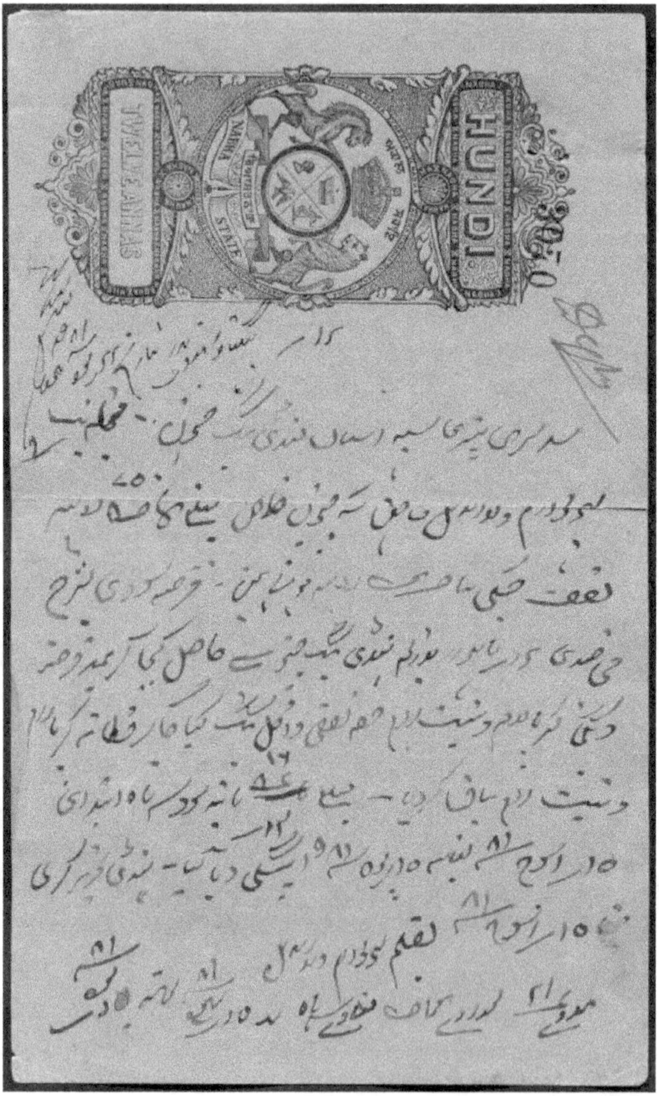
HUNDI
TWELVE ANNAS
NABHA STATE
3050

Nawanagar (State)

નવાનગરરિયાસત
नवानगर रियासत

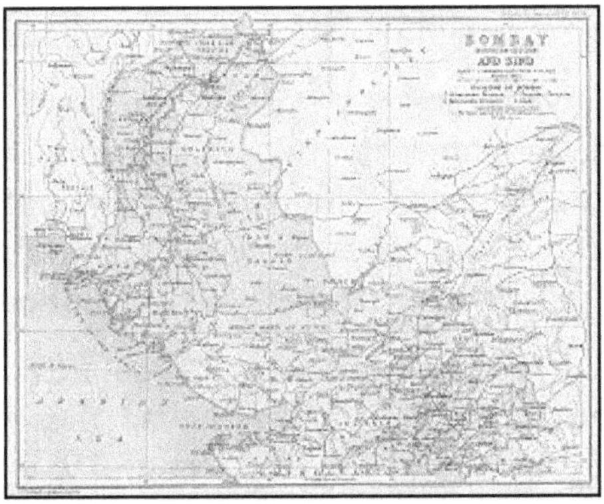

Navanagar, part of Bombay Presidency, 1909

Nawanagar was an Indian princely state in the historical Halar region, located on the southern shores of the Gulf of Kutch. It was ruled by the Jadeja dynasty from its formation in about 1540 until 1948 when it became a part of newly formed India. The city is now known as Jamnagar.

Its rulers, who used the title of "Jam Saheb", were Hindu Rajput of the same clan as the Rao of Kutch. They were entitled to a 15-gun salute. The state was part of the Kathiawad Agency, within the Gujarat Division of Bombay Presidency.

Nawanagar was founded in 1540 by Jam Sri Rawalji, a descendant of the Jadeja ruler of Kutch, and was thereafter in an almost constant state of war with its neighbours and with the Mughal Empire. Two such major wars were the Battle of Mithoi and Battle of Bhuchar Mori fought in 1591. The "Walker Treaty of 1807" brought peace to the Kathiawar states for the first time in several generations.

Nawanagar came under British protection on 22nd February, 1812.

Jam Saheb Shri Sir Ranjitsinhji remained the Chancellor of the Chamber of Princes (1931–1933). After his death, in 1933, he was succeeded by his nephew Jam Saheb Shri Sir Digvijaysinhji, who became its Chancellor (1937–1944).

Nawanagar was one of the first princely states to sign the Instrument of Accession in 1948 after Indian independence. Afterwards, the former ruler, Digvijaysinhji, served as the first Rajpramukh of Kathiawad then represented his country at the United Nations.

In 1949, the former princely states of Nawanagar and Dhrol, Jalia Dewani in Kathiawar merged into the new state of Saurashtra. On 19th June, 1959, the boundaries of the district were enlarged by the inclusion of the adjoining Okhamandal, and the district was renamed Jamnagar. This district became part of the new State of Gujarat on the division of the State of Bombay on 1st May, 1960.

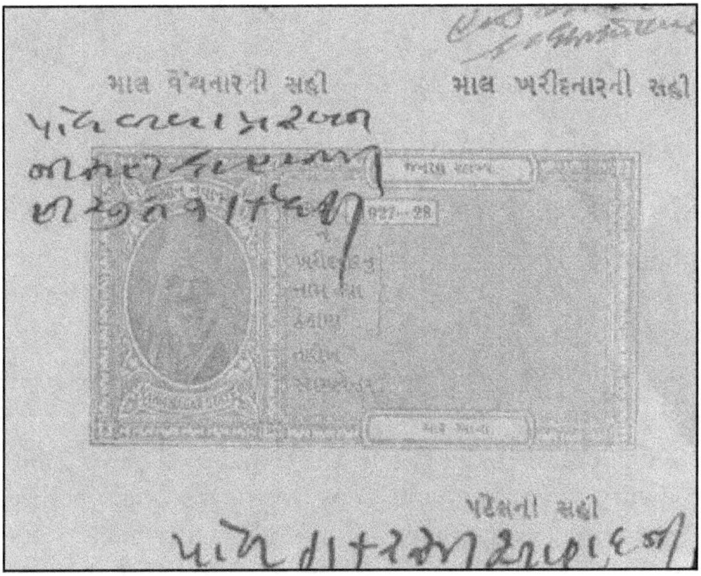
માલ વેચનારની સહી

માલ ખરીદનારની સહી

પટેલના સહી

Putukkottai (State)

புதக்கோட்டை
சமஸ்தானம்

Pudukkottai was a kingdom and later a princely state in British India, which existed from 1680 until 1948.

The Kingdom of Pudukkottai was founded in about 1680 as a feudatory of Ramnad and grew with subsequent additions from Tanjore, Sivaganga and Ramnad. One of the staunch allies of the British East India Company in the Carnatic, Anglo-Mysore and Polygar wars, the kingdom was brought under the Company's protection in 1800 as per the system of Subsidiary. The state was placed under the control of the Madras Presidency from 1800 until 1st October 1923, when the Madras States Agency was abolished, and until 1948 it was under the political control of the Government of India.

Puddukotai Durbar painted by Raja Ravi Varma

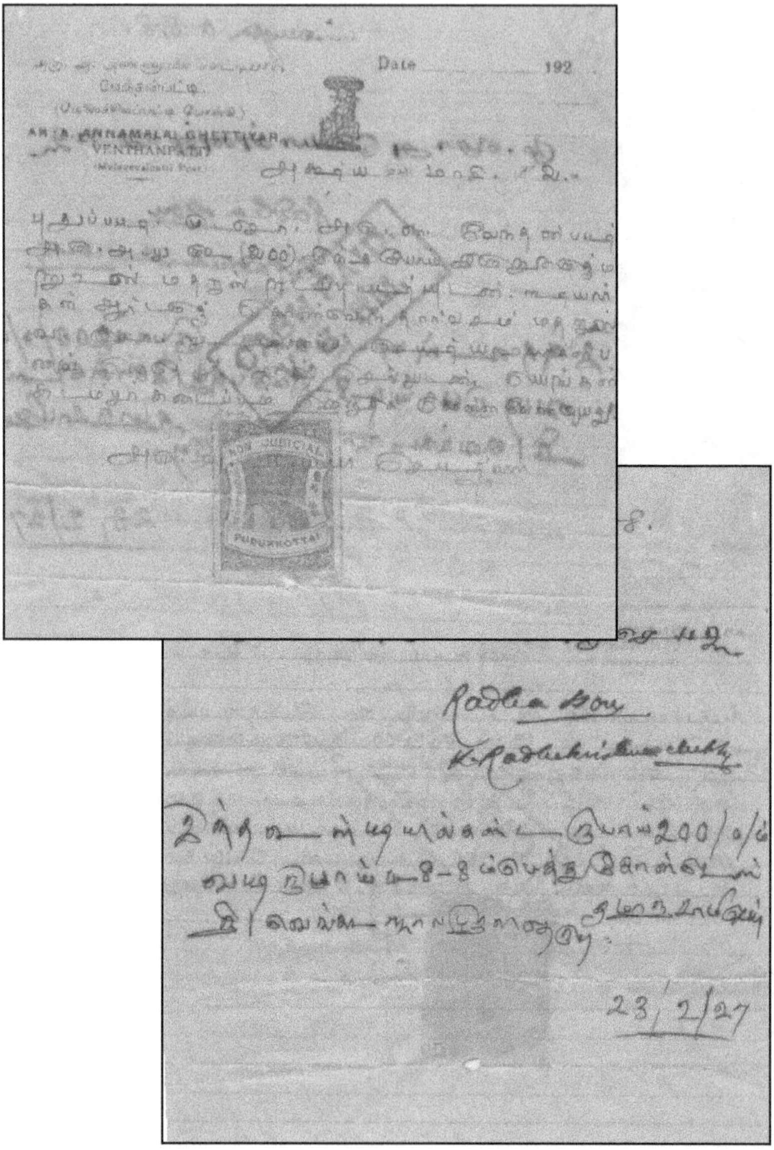
Date 192
ARTA ANNAMALAI CHETTIYAR
VENTHANPATTI
NON-JUDICIAL
PUDUKKOTTAI
23/2/27

Rajkot (State)

રાજકોટ રયિાસત

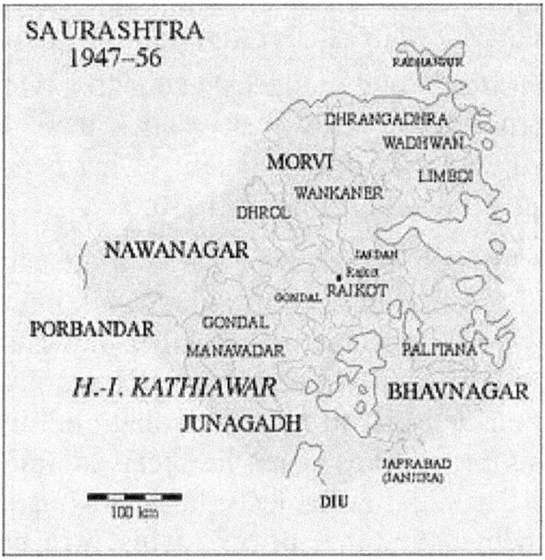

Rajkot State was one of the princely states of India during the period of the British Raj. It was a 9-gun salute state belonging to the Kathiawar Agency of the Bombay Presidency. Its capital was in Rajkot, located in the historical Halar region of Kathiawar on the banks of the Aji River. Nowadays Rajkot is the fourth largest city of Gujarat state.

In 1807 Rajkot State became a British protectorate. His Highness Bavajirajsinhji Mehramanji and his son, Lakhajirajsinhji II Bavajirajsinhji, were model rulers who slowly developed their state into a haven of liberal learning, discourse and intellectual activity. The state became a favourite venue for meetings of various India wide political, cultural and intellectual organisations.

The British constructed many impressive colonial buildings and educational institutions, which are Connaught Hall, Masonic Hall, Lang Library, Watson Museum and The Rajkumar College. Peasant, youth, farmers' and citizens' councils were encouraged and prospered. However, all this changed when His Highness Thakur Saheb Dharmendrasinhji Lakhajiraj succeeded his father in 1930.

Although he received a liberal education and was the first of his line to be sent abroad, his interests and inclinations were the reverse of his father and grandfather. The British authorities restricted him from exercising full powers for a year and placed him on probation, but he gave full vent to his proclivities when he received full powers a year later. He taxed his subjects heavily, hoarded goods then sold them at inflated prices to his own subjects after creating scarcity, then frittered away the proceeds on his own pastimes.

Unlike his father, who lived frugally and spent practically the entire revenue on developing his state, Dharmendrainhji used 50% of the state funds on himself. Not surprisingly, he became the butt of many demonstrations, strikes and boycotts, organised by Congress and other left-wing organisations.

Mahatma Gandhi did fasting to ask to form people's council and liberation of people of Rajkot at Rashtriya Sala in 1939. Thakur Sahib Dharmendrasinhji's early death in 1940 while hunting lions in Sasan Gir, came as relief to his subjects.

His Highness Thakur Saheb Pradyumansinhji Lakhajiraj tried his best to reverse his late brother's failures, but time and circumstances were not on his side.

Although he did manage to improve the lot of his subjects, War conditions hampered progress for several years.

No sooner had the Second World War ended, before the events of partition, independence and merger overtook any plans he had. The state merged with its neighbours to form the United State of Saurashtra in February, 1948 and then after Rajkot became the capital of the State of Saurashtra headed by U. N. Dhebar as chief Minister and Jam Saheb of Navanagar as Raj Pramukh in 1948.

Thakur Lakhajirajsinhji II Bavajirajsinhji of Rajkot

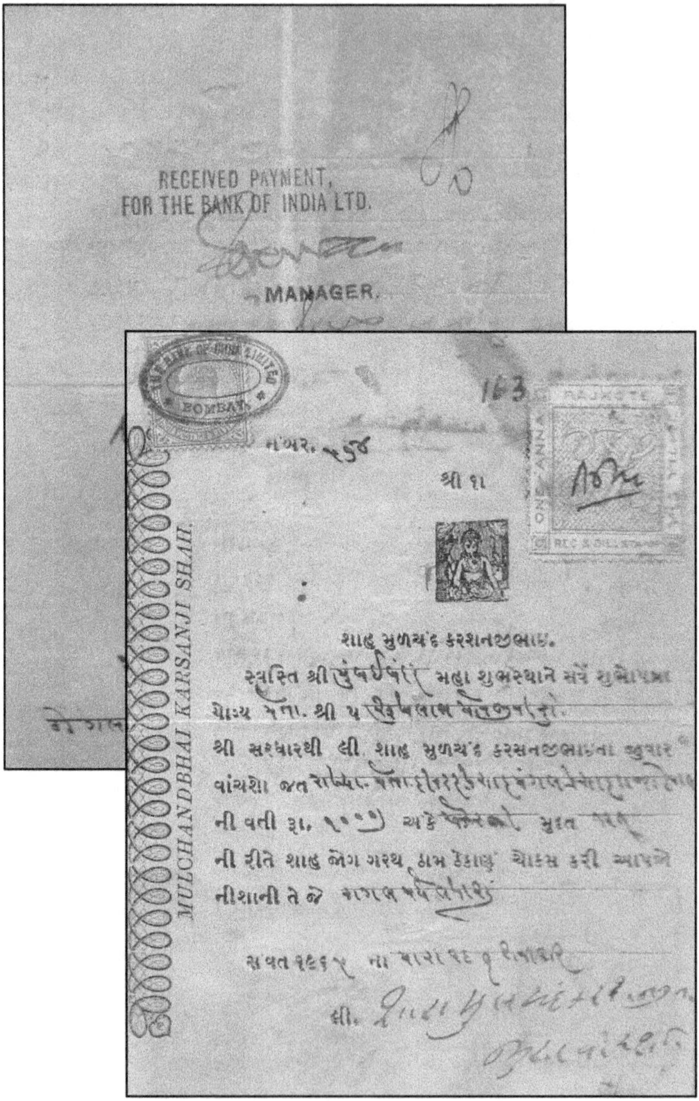

RECEIVED PAYMENT,
FOR THE BANK OF INDIA LTD.

MANAGER.

MULCHANDBHAI KARSANJI SHAH.

નંબર.

શ્રી ૧।

શાહ મુળચંદ કરશનજીભાઈ.

સ્વસ્તિ શ્રી મુંબઈબંદર મહા શુભસ્થાને સર્વે શુભોપમા

યોગ્ય ભાઈ. શ્રી

શ્રી સરધારથી લી. શાહ મુળચંદ કરસનજીભાઈના જુહાર

વાંચશો જત

ની વતી રૂ. ૧૦૦૦) અંકે મુદત

ની રીતે શાહ જોગ ગરથ ઠામ ઠેકાણું ચોકસ કરી આપજો

નીશાની તે જે

સંવત ૧૯૬૨ ના

લી.

Sagwara

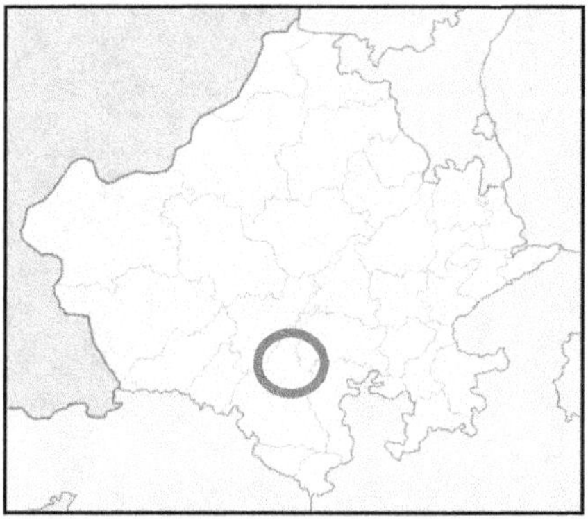

Sagwara is a municipality in Dungarpur district in the Indian state of Rajasthan. It is one of two towns in Sagwara Tehsil, and the administrative centre for the Tehsil.

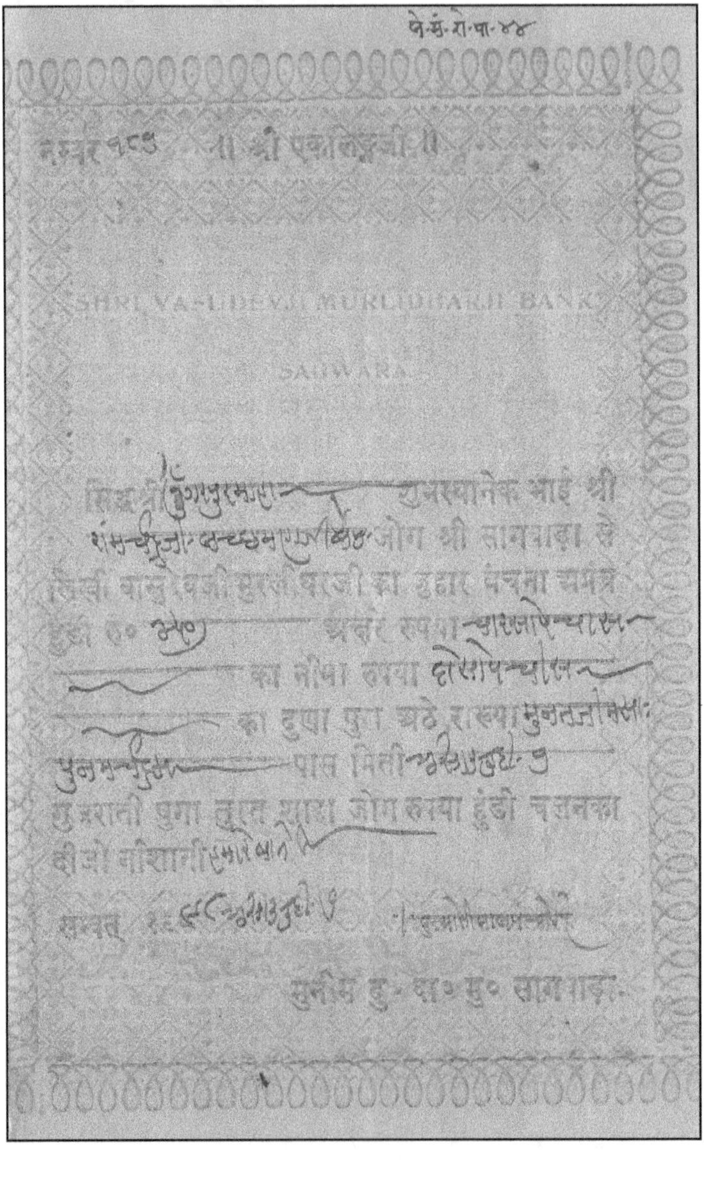
॥ श्री एकलिंगजी ॥
SHRI VASUDEVJI MURLIDHARJI BANK
SAHWARA

Travancore (Kingdom)

തിരുവിതാംകൂ

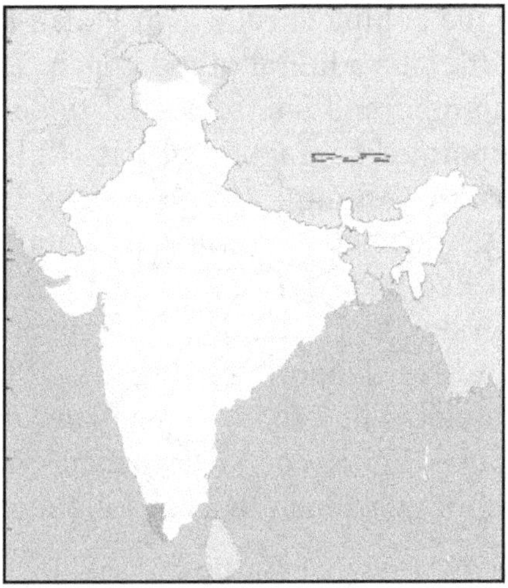

The **Kingdom of Travancore** was an Indian kingdom from 1729 until 1949. It was ruled by the Travancore Royal Family from Padmanabhapuram, and later Thiruvananthapuram.

When the region was once part of the Chera empire, it was known as *Thiruvazhumkode* It was contracted to *Thiruvankode* and anglicised by the English to *Travancore*.

The history of Travancore began with Marthanda Varma, who inherited the kingdom of Venad (Thrippappur), and expanded it into Travancore during his reign (1729–1758).

After defeating a union of feudal lords and establishing internal peace, he expanded the kingdom of Venad through a series of military campaigns from Kanyakumari in the south to the borders of Kochi in the north during his 29-year rule. This led to war between the Dutch East India Company who had been allied to some of these kingdoms and Travancore.

The Travancore-Dutch War (1739–1753) is the earliest example of an Asian state overcoming a European power in war. In 1741, Travancore won the Battle of Colachel against the Dutch East India Company, resulting in the complete eclipse of Dutch power in the region. In this battle, the admiral of the Dutch, Eustachius De Lannoy, was captured and later defected to Travancore. De Lannoy was appointed as Captain of His Highness' body-guard and later Senior Admiral ("Valiya kappittan") and he modernised the Travancore army by introducing firearms and artillery. Travancore became the most dominant state in the Kerala region by defeating the powerful Zamorin of Kozhikode in the battle of Purakkad in 1755. Ramayyan Dalawa, the Prime Minister (1737–1756) of Marthanda Varma, also played an important role in this consolidation and expansion.

At the Battle of Ambalapuzha, Marthanda Varma defeated the union of the kings who had been deposed and the king of the Cochin kingdom.

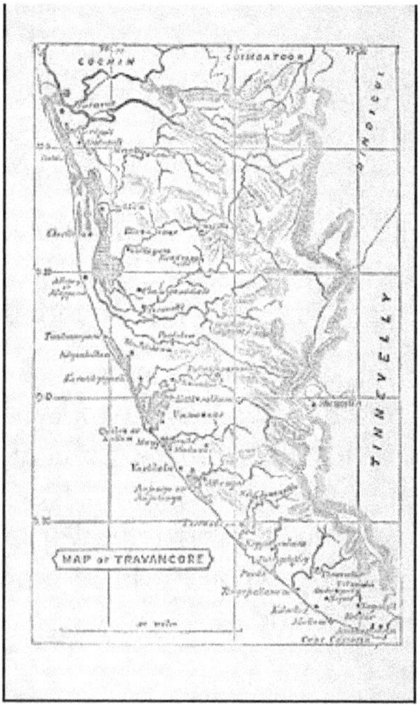

Map of Travancore in 1871

Kowdiar Palace, Trivandrum

Dewan Rajah
Sir T. Madhava Rao
1857-1872

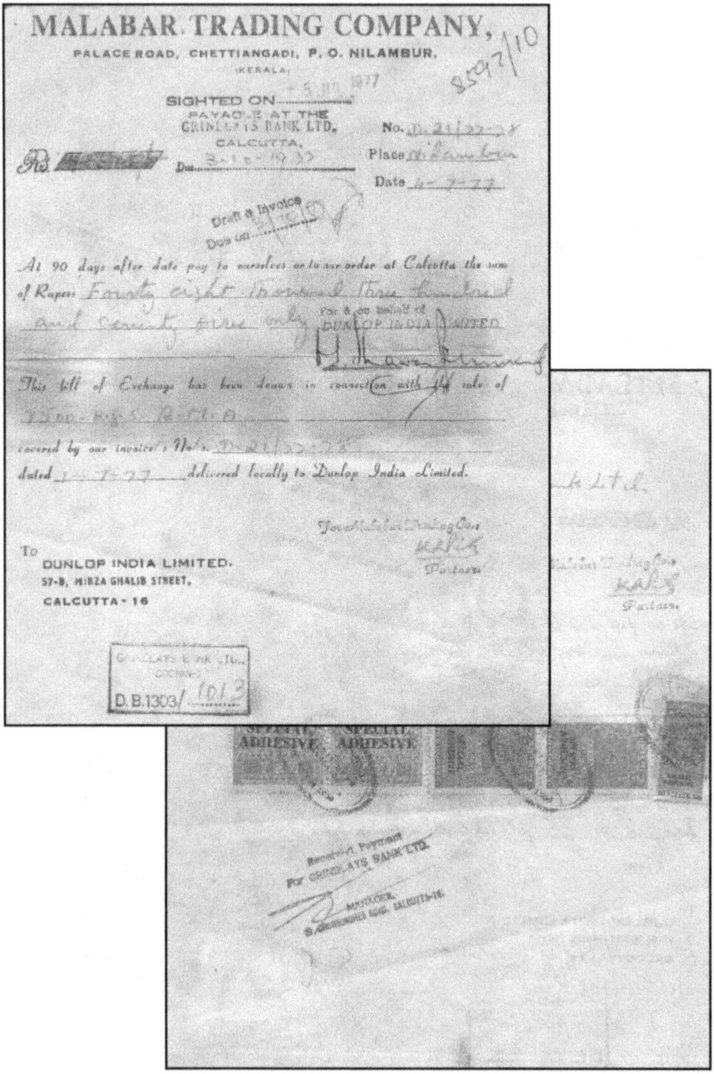

MALABAR TRADING COMPANY,

PALACE ROAD, CHETTIANGADI, P. O. NILAMBUR.

(KERALA)

8597/10

SIGHTED ON 5 JUL 1977

PAYABLE AT THE GRINDLAYS BANK LTD. CALCUTTA.

Rs. [redacted] Due 3-10-1977

No. D-21/77-78

Place Nilambur

Date 4-7-77

Draft & Invoice Due on

At 90 days after date pay to ourselves or to our order at Calcutta the sum of Rupees Fourty eight thousand three hundred and seventy five only

For & on behalf of DUNLOP INDIA LIMITED

This bill of Exchange has been drawn in connection with the sale of 7500 Kgs. RMA

covered by our invoice/s No/s. D-21/77-78

dated 4-7-77 delivered locally to Dunlop India Limited.

For Malabar Trading Co.

Partner

To
DUNLOP INDIA LIMITED.
57-B, MIRZA GHALIB STREET,
CALCUTTA - 16

GRINDLAYS BANK LTD. COCHIN

D.B.1303/1013

SPECIAL ADHESIVE SPECIAL ADHESIVE

Received Payment For GRINDLAYS BANK LTD.

MANAGER.

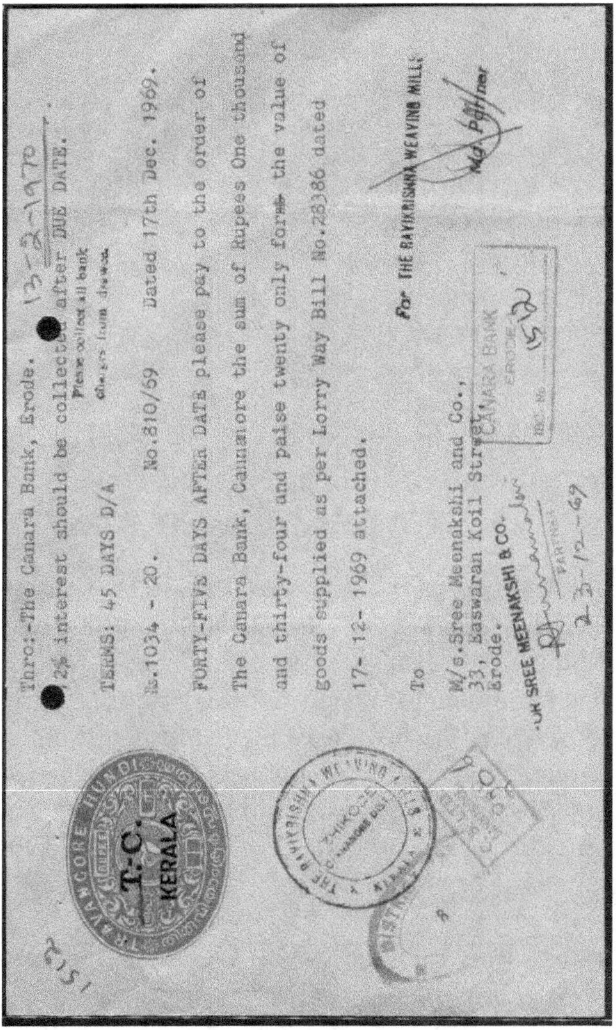
Thro:-The Canara Bank, Erode. 13-2-1970

2% interest should be collected after DUE DATE.

Please collect all bank charges from drawee.

TERMS: 45 DAYS D/A

Rs.1034 - 20. No.810/69 Dated 17th Dec. 1969.

FORTY-FIVE DAYS AFTER DATE please pay to the order of The Canara Bank, Cannanore the sum of Rupees One thousand and thirty-four and paise twenty only for the value of goods supplied as per Lorry Way Bill No.28386 dated 17- 12- 1969 attached.

For THE RAVIKRISHNA WEAVING MILLS

Md. Partner

To

M/s.Sree Meenakshi and Co.,
33, Easwaran Koil Street,
Erode.

Uttar Pradesh (State)
उत्तरप्रदेश
اتر پردیش

Uttar Pradesh is the most populous state in the Republic of India as well as the most populous country subdivision in the world. The state, located in the *Northern Region* of the Indian subcontinent, has over 200 million inhabitants. It was created on 1 April 1937 as the United Provinces during British rule, and was renamed *Uttar Pradesh* in 1950.

In 1920, the capital of the province was shifted from Allahabad to Lucknow. The high court continued to be at Allahabad, but a bench was established at Lucknow. Allahabad continues to be an important administrative base of today's Uttar Pradesh and has several administrative headquarters. Uttar Pradesh continued to be central to Indian politics and was especially important in modern Indian history as a hotbed of the Indian independence movement.

After India's independence, the United Provinces were renamed "*Uttar Pradesh*" in 1950, preserving UP as the acronym. The state has provided eight of India's prime ministers and is the source of the largest number of seats in the *Lok Sabha*.

University of Allahabad

Buland Darwaza

Kashi Vishwanath Temple

Dhamek Stupa, Saranath

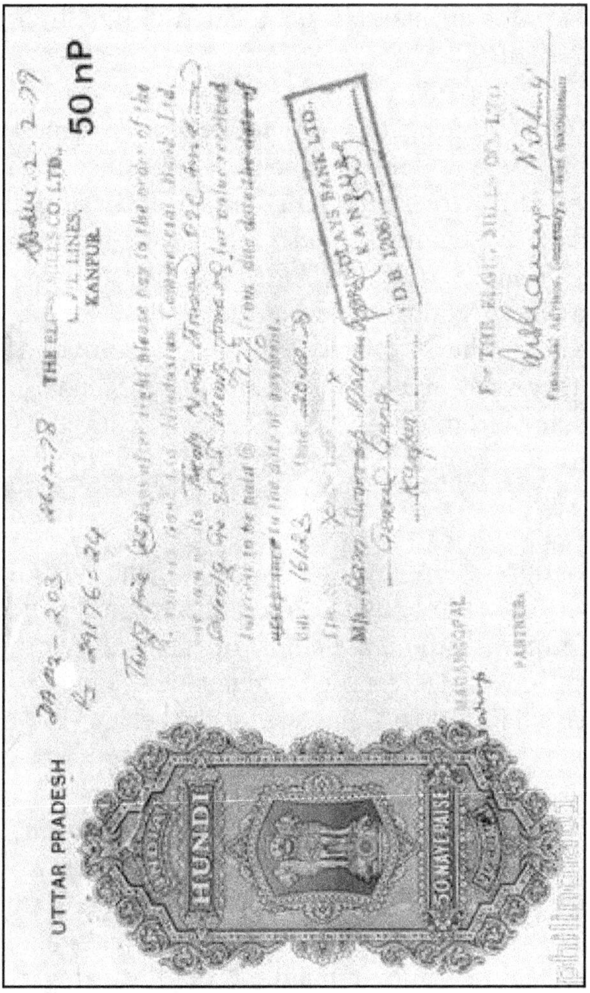
UTTAR PRADESH
50 nP
HUNDI
50 NAYE PAISE

West Bengal (State)

West Bengal is an Indian state, located in East India on the Bay of Bengal.

The kingdom of Magadha was formed in 7th century BCE, consisting of the regions now comprising Bihar and Bengal. It was one of the four main kingdoms of India at the time of the lives of Mahavira, founder of Jainism, and Gautama Buddha, founder of Buddhism. It consisted of several janapadas or kingdoms. Under Ashoka, the Maurya Empire of Magadha in the 3rd century BCE extended over nearly all of South Asia, including Afghanistan and parts of Balochistan. From the 3rd to the 6th centuries CE, the kingdom of Magadha served as the seat of the Gupta Empire.

Two kingdoms – Vanga or Samatata and Gauda – are mentioned in some texts to have appeared after the end of Gupta Empire, although details of their ruling time are uncertain. The first recorded independent king of Bengal was Shashanka, who reigned in the early 7th century. Shashanka is often recorded in Buddhist annals as an intolerant Hindu ruler who is noted for his persecution of the Buddhists. Shashanka murdered Rajyavardhana, the Buddhist King of Thanesar, and is noted for destroying the Bodhi tree at Bodhgaya, and replacing Buddha statues with Shiva lingams. After a period of anarchy, the Pala dynasty ruled the region for four hundred years starting from the eighth century. It was followed by a shorter reign of the Hindu Sena dynasty.

Some areas of Bengal were invaded by Rajendra Chola I of the Chola dynasty between 1021 and 1023. Islam made its first appearance in Bengal during the 12th century when Sufi missionaries arrived Later, occasional Muslim raiders reinforced the process of conversion by building mosques, madrases and khanqahs. Between 1202 and 1206, Muhammad bin Bakhtiyar Khilji, a military commander from the Delhi Sultanate, overran Bihar and Bengal as far east as Rangpur, Bogra and the Brahmaputra River. Although he failed to bring Bengal under his control, the expedition defeated Lakshman Sen. His two sons moved to a place then called Vikramapur (present-day Munshiganj District), where their diminished dominion lasted until the late 13th century.

Tipu Sultan Mosque

Dakshineswar Kali Temple

Adina Mosque

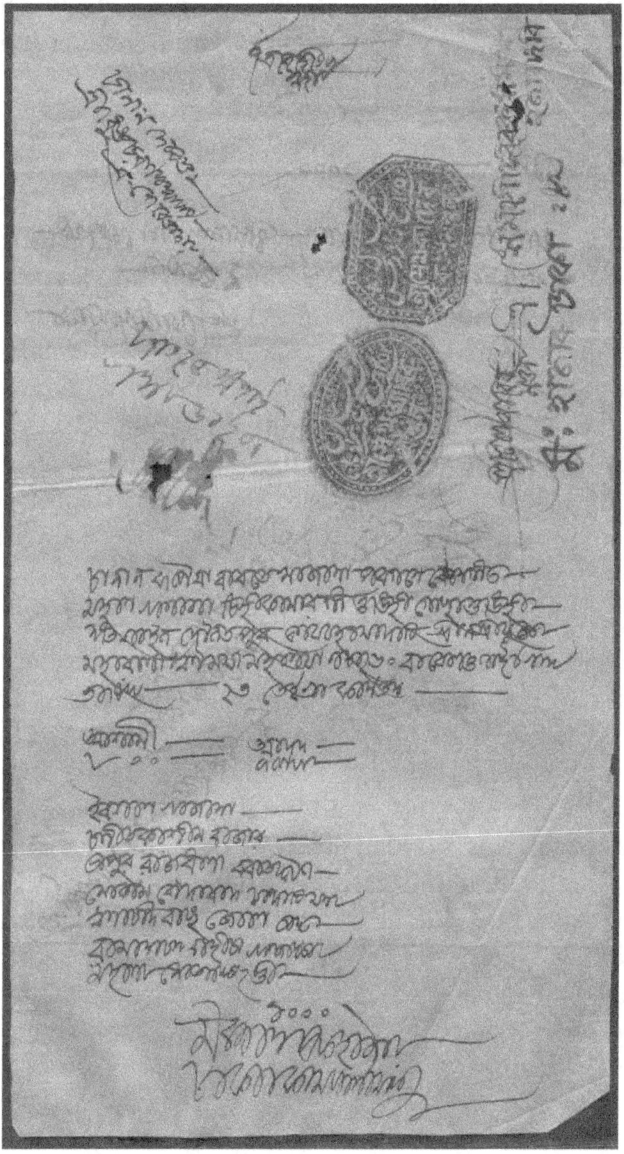

British India

In 1608, the English East India Company established a settlement at Surat (now in the state of Gujarat), and this became the company's first headquarters town.

It was followed in 1611 by a permanent Factory at Machilipatnam on the Coromandel Coast, and in 1612 the company joined other already established European trading companies in Bengal. However, following the decline of the Mughal Empire in 1707 by the hands of the Marathas and after the East India Company's victory at the Battle of Plassey in 1757 and Battle of Buxar, both in Bengal 1764, the Company gradually began to formally expand its dominions and collectively call the area India. By the mid-19th century, and after the three Wars the East India Company had become the paramount political and military power in South Asia, its territory held in trust for the British Crown.

Company rule in Bengal, however, ended with the Government of India Act 1858 following the events of the Bengal Rebellion of 1857. From then known as British India, it was thereafter directly ruled by the British Crown as a colonial possession of the United Kingdom, and India was officially known after 1876 as the *British Indian Empire*. India was divided into *British India*, regions that were directly administered by the British, with Acts established and passed in British Parliament, and the *Princely States*, that were ruled by local rulers of different ethnic backgrounds. These rulers were allowed a measure of internal autonomy in exchange for British suzerainty.

British India constituted a significant portion of India both in area and population; in 1910, for example, it covered approximately 54% of the area and included over 77% of the population, In addition, there were Portuguese and French enclaves in India.

Independence from British rule was achieved in 1947 with the formation of two nations, the Dominions of India and Pakistan, the latter also including East Bengal, present-day Bangladesh.

The term *British India* also applied to Burma for a shorter time period: starting in 1824, a small part of Burma, and by 1886, almost two thirds of Burma had come under *British India*. This arrangement lasted until 1937, when Burma commenced being administered as a separate British colony. *British India* did not apply to other countries in the region, such as Sri Lanka (then Ceylon), which was a British Crown colony, or the Maldive Islands, which were a British protectorate.

At its greatest extent, in the early 20th century, the territory of *British India* extended as far as the frontiers of Persia in the west; Afghanistan in the northwest; Nepal in the north, Tibet in the northeast; and China, French Indo-China and Siam in the east. It also included the Colony of Aden in the Arabian Peninsula.

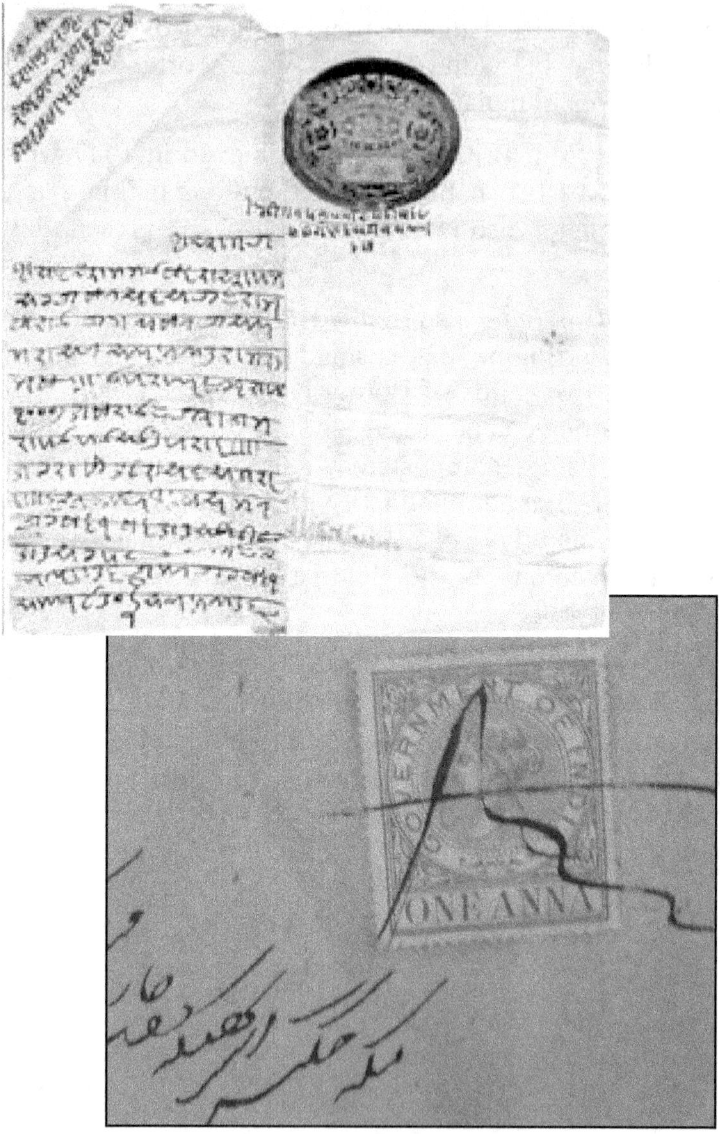

British India Hundi (Obverse and Reverse)
Early Victorian

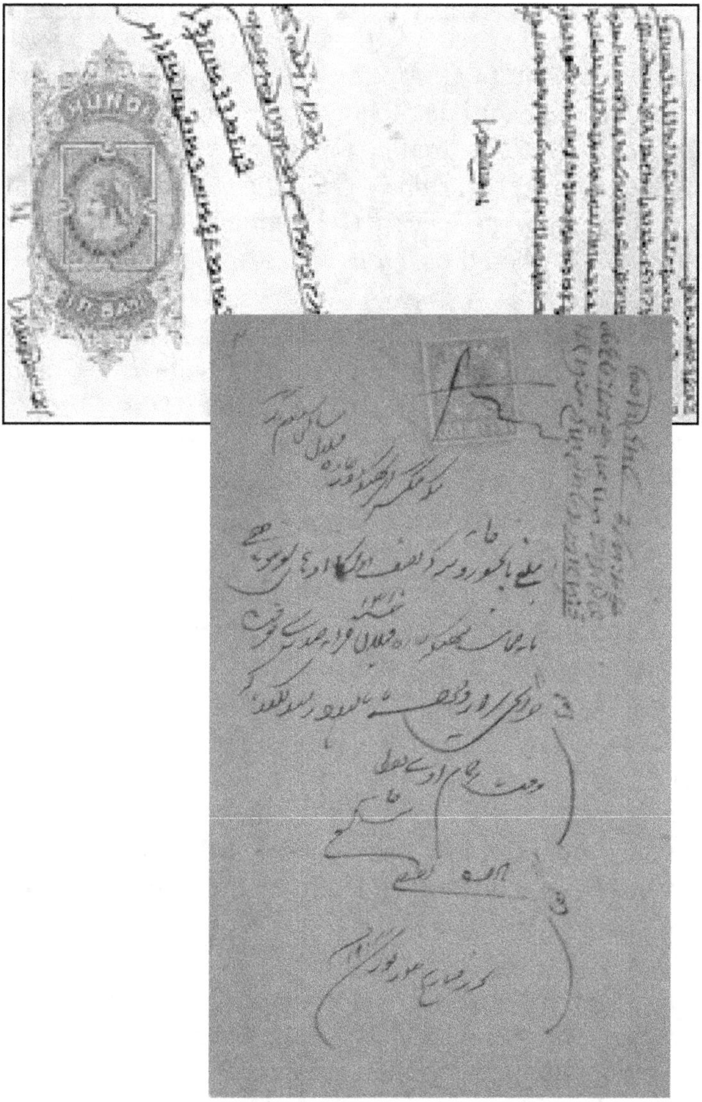

British India Hundi (Obverse and Reverse)
Late Victorian

Opium Hundis

The **British East India Company** was an English company which was formed initially to pursue trade with the East Indies, but ended up trading mainly with the Indian subcontinent and Qing China. The illegal trade of opium with China formally started in 1673. Company rule in India lasted until 1858 when the new British Raj took over.

A form of triangular trade started between British, China and India where in commodities such as silver, tea and opium were bartered between the countries. This form of trade strategy was not uncommon at the time (ie slave trading) but, essentially, this one was designed by the British to gain Company benefits.

During this trade, India was merely an instrument for the British to produce the opium that they intended to sell to China in return for tea and silver which was exported to Britain. China played a major role in this trade as it was the sole producer and consumer of tea and opium involved in the trade.

The British East India Company occupied the Indian states of Bihar and Bengal and expanded trade through the port of Calcutta.

In the 18th century, Britain had a huge trade deficit with Qing dynasty China and so in 1773, the Company created a British monopoly on opium buying in Bengal by prohibiting the licensing of opium farmers and private cultivation.

Despite the Chinese ban on opium imports, reaffirmed in 1799 by the Jiaqing Emperor, the drug was smuggled into China from Bengal by traffickers and agency. The monopoly system established in 1799 continued with minimal changes until 1947.

As the opium trade was illegal in China, Company ships could not carry opium to China. So the opium produced in Bengal was sold in Calcutta on condition that it was sent to China.

The considerable proceeds of the drug-smugglers landing their cargoes in China were paid directly into the Company's factory at Canton and by 1825 most of the money needed to buy tea in China was raised by this illegal opium trade.

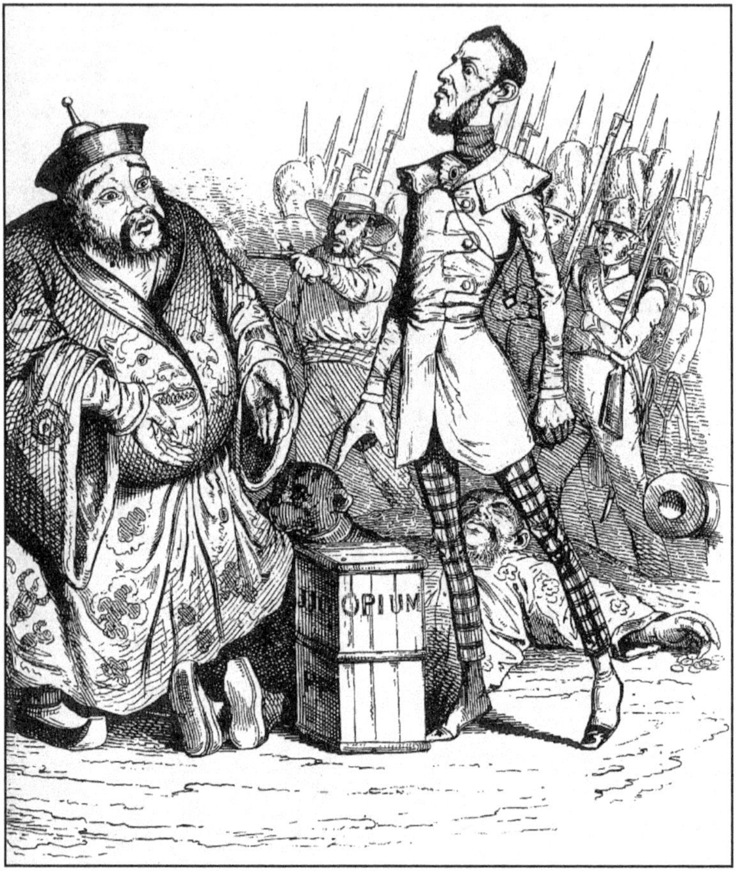

Contemporary Cartoon

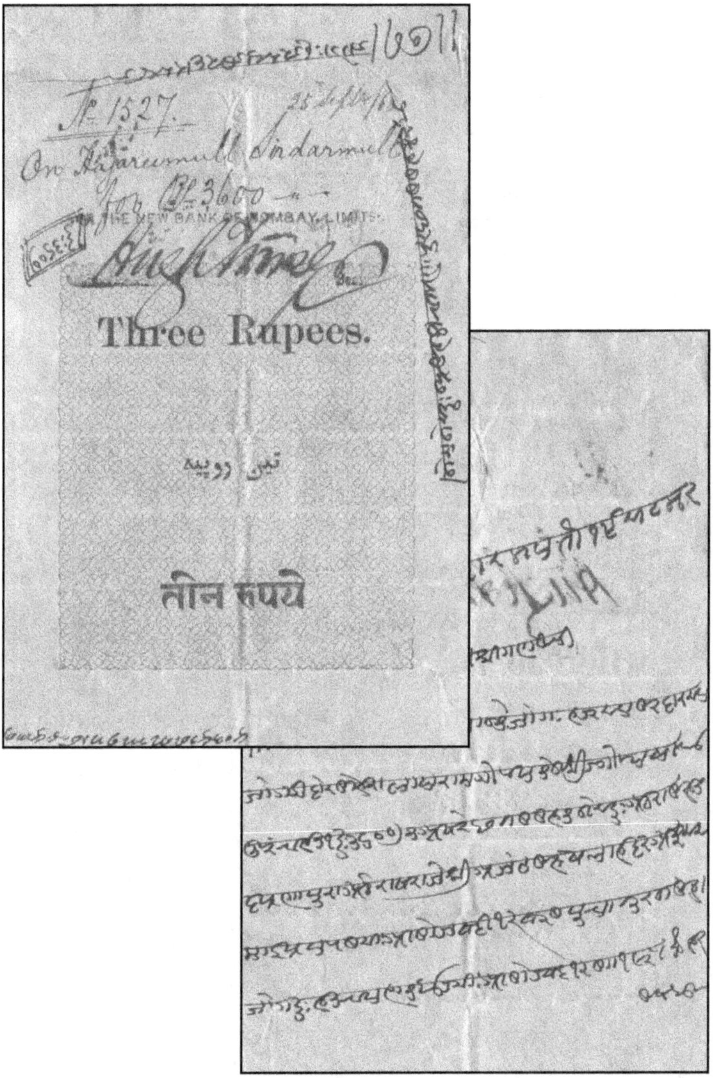

1886 Calcutta Opium Hundi

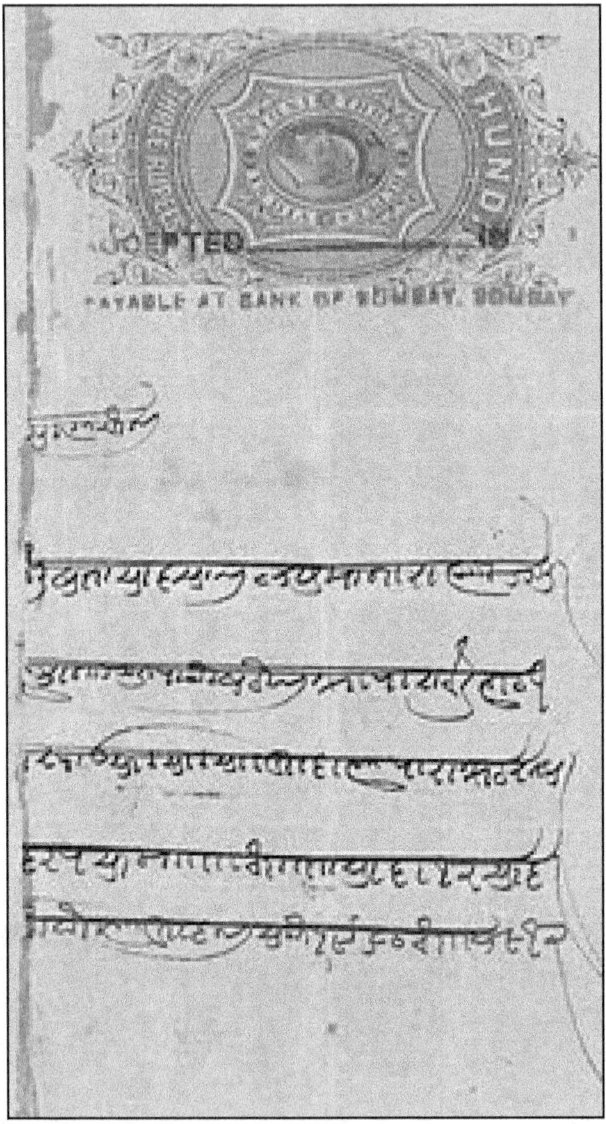

Mandsaur Opium Hundi

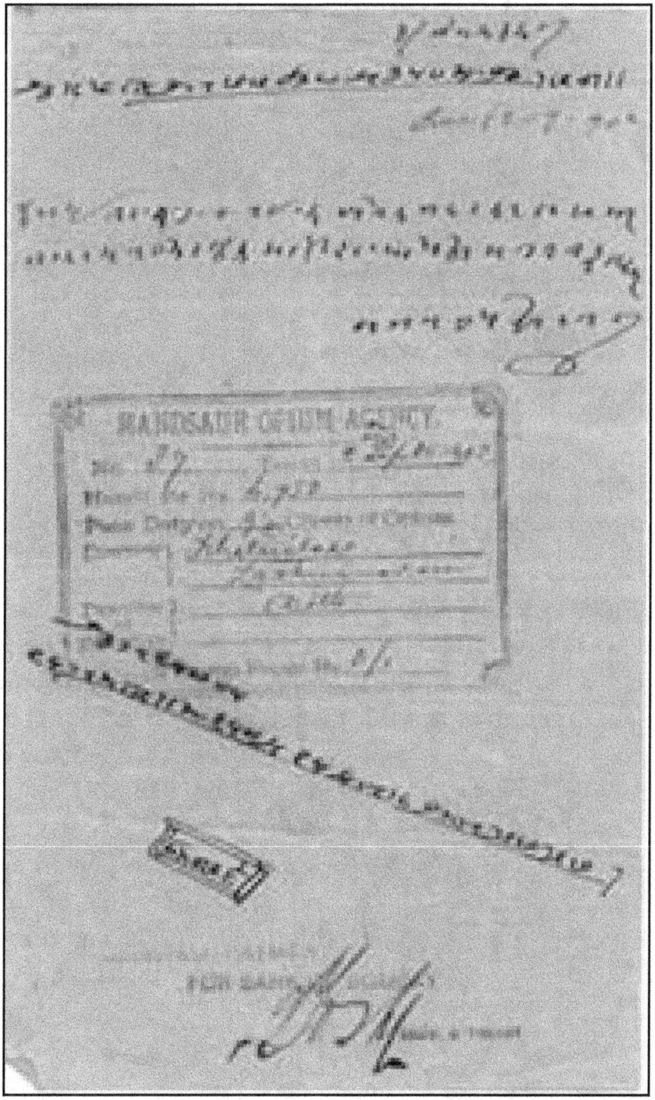
MANDSAUR OPIUM AGENCY

Mandsaur Opium Hundi

Special Khadi Hundi

Khādī is Indian cloth spun and woven by hand. The raw materials may be cotton, silk, or wool, which are spun into threads on a spinning wheel called a charkha

Mahatma Gandhi promoted the spinning of khādī for rural self-employment and self-reliance in 1920's India thus making khadi an integral part and icon of the Swadeshi movement. The freedom struggle revolved around the use of khādī fabrics and the dumping of foreign-made clothes. Thus it symbolized the political ideas and independence itself, and to this day most politicians in India are seen only in khādī clothing. The flag of India is only allowed to be made from this material, although in practice many flag manufacturers, especially those outside of India, ignore this rule. Khadi often associated with Mahatma Gandhi, who advocated the use of Khadi to promote self-reliance instead of using cloth manufactured industrially in Britain.

50 years of Khadi & Village Industries (2007)

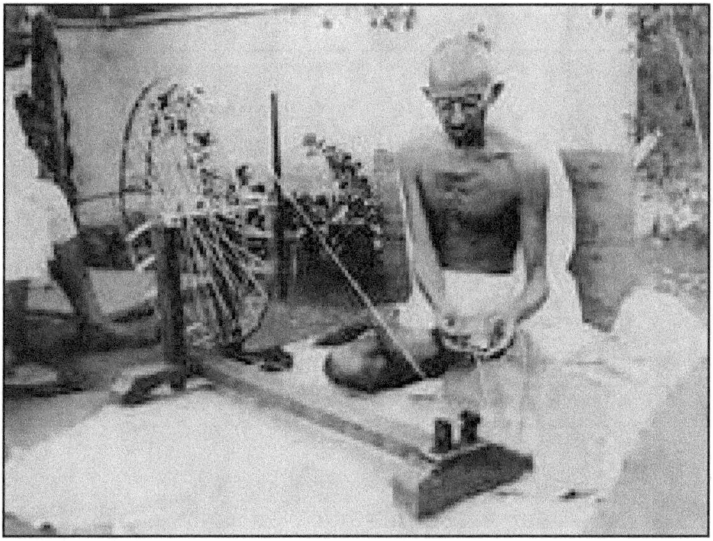

KHADI & VILLAGE INDUSTRIES COMMISSION
TWO RUPEES
CHARKHA JAYANTI
KHADI HUNDI
HUNDI EXCHANGEABLE FOR KHADI AT CERTIFIED BHANDARS.

खादी ग्रामोद्योग कमीशन
दो रुपये
चरखा जयंती
खादी हुंडी
हुंडी के बदले प्रमाणित भंडारों से खादी मिलेगी.

KHADI & VILLAGE INDUSTRIES COMMISSION
TWO RUPEES
CHARKHA JAYANTI
KHADI HUNDI
EXCHANGEABLE FOR KHADI BY ISSUING INSTITUTION.
REDEEMABLE BY ISSUING INSTITUTION
VALID IF SIGNED FOR ONE YEAR FROM THE DATE OF ISSUE

खादी ग्रामोद्योग कमिशन
दो रुपये
चरखा जयंती
खादी हुंडी
हुंडी के बदलेमें प्रमाणित प्रसारक संस्थाद्वारा खादी मिलेगी।

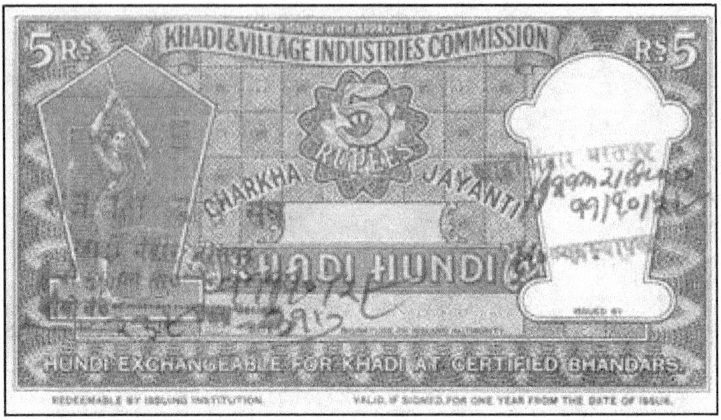
5 Rs
KHADI & VILLAGE INDUSTRIES COMMISSION
Rs 5
5 RUPEES
CHARKHA JAYANTI
KHADI HUNDI
ISSUED BY
HUNDI EXCHANGEABLE FOR KHADI AT CERTIFIED BHANDARS.
REDEEMABLE BY ISSUING INSTITUTION.
VALID, IF SIGNED, FOR ONE YEAR FROM THE DATE OF ISSUE.

खादी ग्रामोद्योग कमिशन
पाँच रुपये
चरखा जयंती
खादी हुंडी
005752
हुंडी के बदले प्रमाणित भंडारों से खादी मिलेगी।

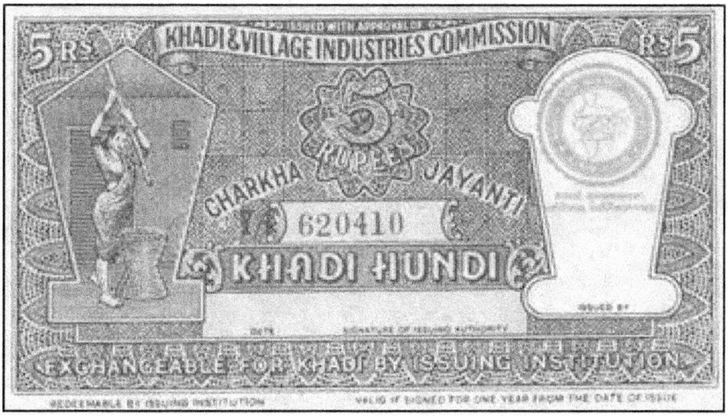
KHADI & VILLAGE INDUSTRIES COMMISSION
5 RS.
RS. 5
5
RUPEES
CHARKHA JAYANTI
620410
KHADI HUNDI
EXCHANGEABLE FOR KHADI BY ISSUING INSTITUTION

खादी ग्रामोद्योग कमिशन
पाँच रुपये
चरखा जयंती
खादी हुंडी

ALL INDIA KHADI & VILLAGE INDUSTRIES BOARD
5
RUPEES
KHADI HUNDI
राजस्थान
AGAINST THIS HUNDI ONLY KHADI CERTIFIED BY
SARVA SEVA SANGH CAN BE PURCHASED IN REGION ISSUING HUNDI
HUNDI WILL LAPSE ON 31-3-55
HUNDI CAN BE EXCHANGED ONLY FOR KHADI.

अखिल भारत खादी और ग्रामोद्योग मंडल
खादी हुंडी
B 600639

KHADI & VILLAGE INDUSTRIES COMMISSION
Rs 10
10
RUPEES
CHARKHA JAYANTI
KHADI HUNDI
EXCHANGEABLE FOR KHADI BY ISSUING INSTITUTION
REDEEMABLE BY ISSUING INSTITUTION
VALID IF SIGNED FOR ONE YEAR FROM THE DATE OF ISSUE

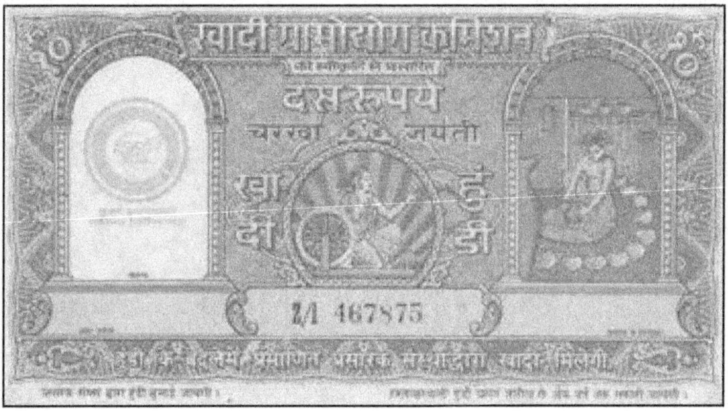
खादी ग्रामोद्योग कमिशन
दस रुपये
चरखा जयंती
खादी
हुंडी
467875

ALL INDIA KHADI & VILLAGE INDUSTRIES BOARD
10
RUPEES
KHADI HUNDI
राजस्थान
AGAINST THIS HUNDI ONLY KHADI CERTIFIED BY
SARVA SEVA SANGH CAN BE PURCHASED IN REGION ISSUING HUNDI
HUNDI WILL LAPSE ON 31-3-55.
HUNDI CAN BE EXCHANGED ONLY FOR KHADI.

अखिल भारत खादी और ग्रामोद्योग मंडळ
चरखा जयंती १९५४
१०
रुपया
खादी हुंडी

Gandhi: Rastriya Smarakh Nidhi

The National Gandhi Memorial Trust, also called the Gandhi Qaumi Yaadgar Fund, is a memorial trust run by the Central Government of India established to commemorate the life of Mahatma Gandhi.

It funds the maintenance of various places associated with Mahatma Gandhi's activities during India's freedom movement, and is also a leading producer of literature on Gandhi and Gandhian thought in India.

The initial public fund raising for the Trust was considered to be very successful, and Dr. Martin Luther King wrote that at $130 million it was "perhaps the largest, spontaneous, mass monetary contribution to the memory of a single individual in the history of the world".

Mani Bhavan, located at 19, Laburnum Road in the Gamdevi precinct of downtown Mumbai, acted as the focal point of Gandhi's political activities in Mumbai between 1917 and 1934.

१
गान्धी
राष्ट्रीय
स्मारक
निधि
AZ — 004200
एक रुपया
1

گاندھی قومی یادگار فنڈ
ज. भ. कृपालानी

Nehru: Smarakh Kosh Hundi

Jawaharlal Nehru was an Indian nationalist leader and statesman and he was the first Prime Minister of Independent India and to date India's longest serving Prime Minister from 1947 – 1964. Born in Allahabad and educated in England at Harrow School and Trinity College in Cambridge. After returning to India, he joined the Indian National Congress in 1919 and was influenced by Mahatma Gandhi's determination for self rule from the British. During the 1920s and 1930's he was imprisoned by the British several times for civil disobedience. He played a key role in negotiating with the British on Indian Independence after the end of World War II. He opposed the partition of India but had to accept partition as a necessity.

On 15th August, 1947 when India became an independent country, Nehru became the first Prime Minister. He held that office until his death on 27th May, 1964. His daughter, Indira Gandhi, was the third Prime Minister of India and her son Rajiv Gandhi served as Prime Minister from 1984-1989. Nehru wrote two well known books: Glimpses of World History and Discovery of India.

These hundis are in the form of uniface fund raising tickets for a Nehru memorial. *Smarak* in Hindi means memorial, and *Kosh* literally means treasury. These fund raising tickets were issued in Jaipur, Rajasthan.

जवाहरलाल नेहरू स्मारक कोष
सौ रुपया

Ganesha

The son of Shiva and Parvati, Ganesha has an elephantine countenance with a curved trunk and big ears, and a huge

pot-bellied body of a human being. He is the Lord of success and destroyer of evils and obstacles. He is also worshiped as the god of education, knowledge, wisdom and wealth. In fact, Ganesha is one of the five prime Hindu deities (Brahma, Vishnu, Shiva and Durga being the other four).

Ganesha's head symbolizes the *Atman* or the soul, which is the ultimate supreme reality of human existence, and his human body signifies *Maya* or the earthly existence of human beings. The elephant head denotes wisdom and its trunk represents Om, the sound symbol of cosmic reality.

Whilst Ganesha is depicted rather differently in the many art designs, there is a common theme that runs through most representations. In his upper right hand, Ganesha is often seen holding a goad, which helps him propel mankind forward on the eternal path and remove obstacles from the way.

The noose that is often seen in Ganesha's left hand is a gentle implement to capture all difficulties.

The broken tusk that Ganesha has is a symbol of sacrifice, which he broke for writing the *Mahabharata*. The rosary in his other hand suggests that the pursuit of knowledge should be continuous. The *laddoo* (sweet) he holds in his trunk indicates that one must discover the sweetness of the *Atman*. His fan-like ears convey that he is all ears to our petition.

The snake that runs round his waist represents energy in all forms. And he is humble enough to ride the lowest of creatures, a mouse.

The most popular story of the birth of this zoomorphic deity, as depicted in the *Shiva Purana*, goes like this: Once goddess Parvati, while bathing, created a boy out of the dirt of her body and assigned him the task of guarding the entrance to her bathroom.

When Shiva, her husband returned, he was surprised to find a stranger denying him access, and struck off the boy's head in rage. Parvati broke down in utter grief and to soothe her, Shiva sent out his squad (*gana*) to fetch the head of any sleeping being that was facing the north. The company found a sleeping elephant and brought back its severed head, which was then attached to the body of the boy. Shiva restored its life and made him the leader (*pati*) of his troops.

Hence his name 'Ganapati'. Shiva also bestowed a boon that people would worship him and invoke his name before undertaking any venture.
ref: Subhamoy Das

There are a number of cases where Ganesha has found himself on the face of Hundis over the years.

One can only surmise that this was an invocation to Ganesha to ensure that the relevant hundi would be transacted successfully and without undue obstacles.

Some examples are shown on the following page.

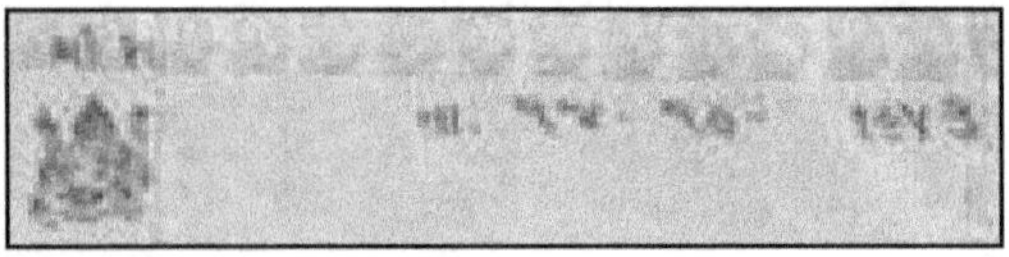

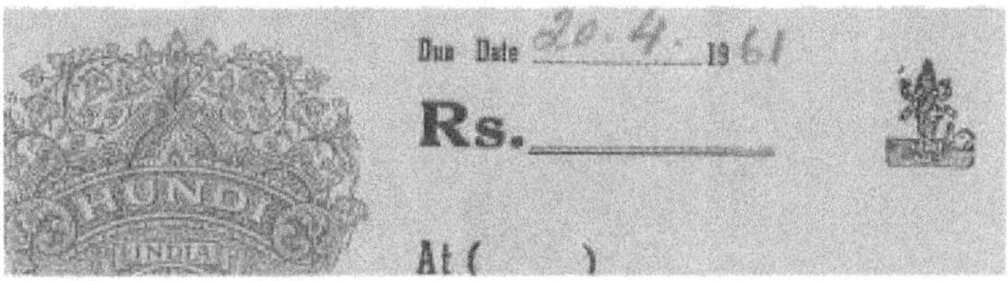
Due Date 20.4. 1961
Rs.
HUNDI
INDIA
At ( )

163
RAJKOTE
ONE ANNA

Revenue Stamps and Seals

Contrary to general assumptions, a Revenue Stamp is not used for the purpose of authentication, but is used to generate revenue. It was first implemented by the British during for the East India Company. Stamp duty was first introduced during the year 1797. In the beginning, it was limited to only a few areas like Bengal, Banaras, Bihar & Orissa.

Revenue Stamps were not only used on Hundis, but were used to collect fees or revenue for maintaining courts. The Indian Stamp Act 1899 was intended to govern the usage of Revenue Stamps. Interestingly, however, this law was amended for 51 times since 1899 to 2004.

Under section 30 of the Act, a payment of more than Rs. 5000/- attracted a Revenue Stamp of Re 1/-. In this case if a payee refused to give a receipt with a Revenue Stamp, then he could be fined Rs. 100/- under section 65.

For every legally permitted transaction a certain amount of revenue was needed to be given to the government. Stamping of receipts or main documents evidencing giving and taking of money also need such revenue and the revenue stamp is affixed in proof of that.

A properly stamped receipt or debt document or note gets a *prima facie* priority as an acceptable legal proof as against a receipt which was not stamped, although those which were not properly stamped could, even so, be rejected depending on many other factors.

Revenue stamps were therefore used by the British India Company, Princely States and, the Indian Government to collect taxes and fees. The purpose of Revenue Stamps was therefore to signify that a one-time tax leviable on the contract had been signed had been paid to the appropriate authority, and that a contract/document is legal and enforceable in a court of law. Instead of a separate document stating that the tax had been paid, the stamp affixed to the paper (or the stamp paper itself) accompanied the contract for ever.

Section 2 of the Indian Stamp Act 1899 made it mandatory to affixing a stamp on any receipt as defined therein above Rs 5000.

2(23) "Receipt" included any note, memorandum or writing:

- whereby any money, or any bill of exchange, cheque or promissory note is acknowledged to have been received, or
- whereby any other movable property is acknowledged to have been received in satisfaction of a debt .....

Stamped Paper

Stamped Paper has been widely used around the world to collect taxes on documents requiring stamping. The papers are bought blank apart from the pre-printed stamp and are available from stationers, lawyers' offices, post offices and courts according to local regulations. The parties to the matter then write their legal business on the paper and lodge it with the court or other interested party. This is an efficient way of collecting taxes and stamping documents without the need to submit them to a separate government stamp office.

The **1765 Stamp Act** required all British colonies in the New World to use stamped paper prepared in London and embossed with a Revenue Stamp. This led to political agitation which has been credited with sowing the seeds of the American Revolution.

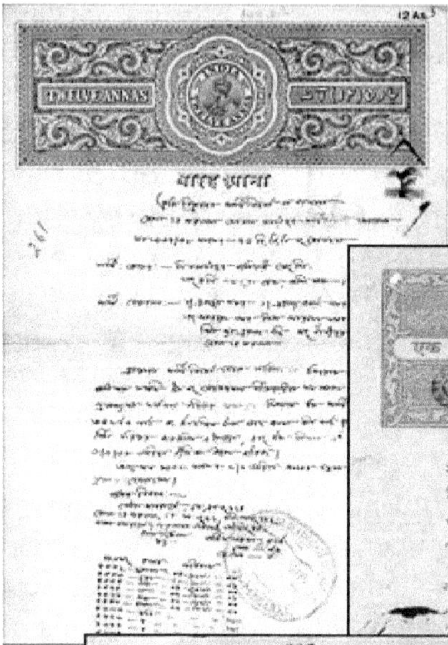

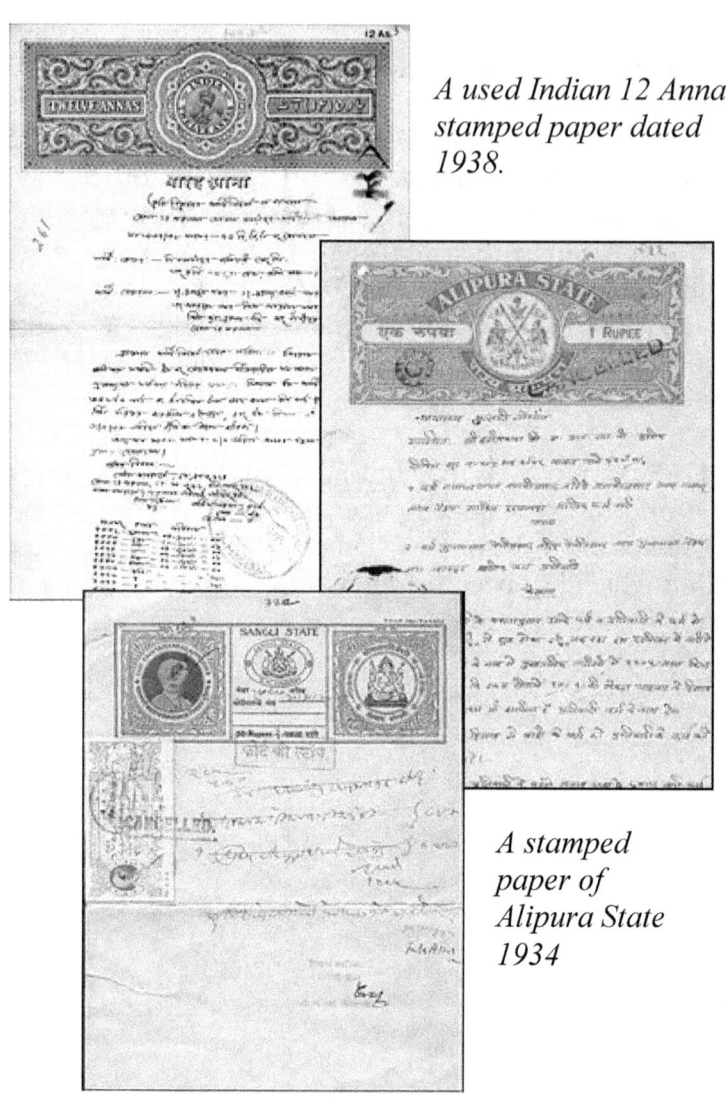

A used Indian 12 Anna stamped paper dated 1938.

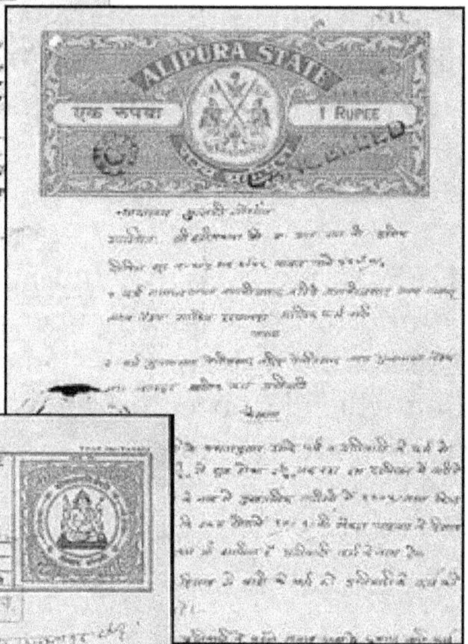

A stamped paper of Alipura State 1934

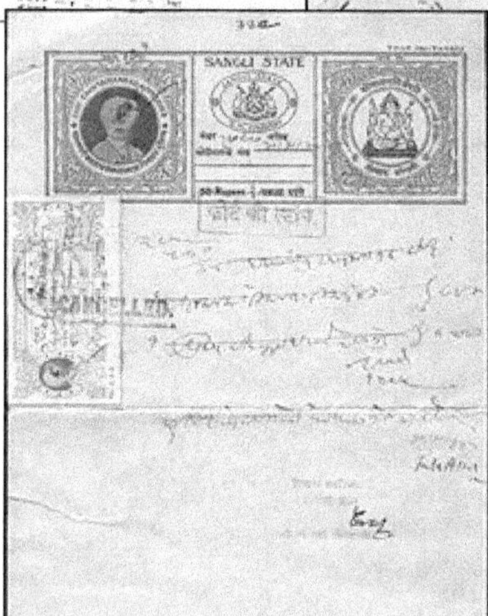

A stamped paper from Sangli State.

A block of 1887 Travancore

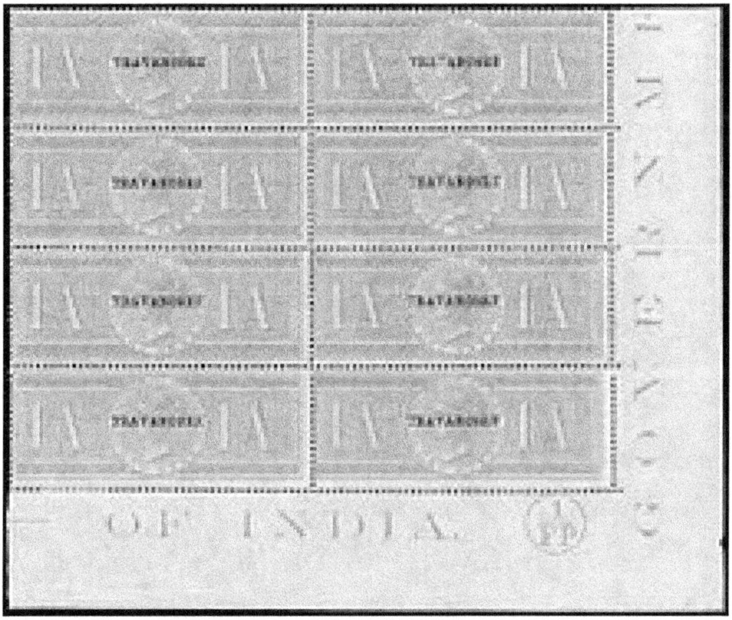

revenues depicting Queen Victoria.

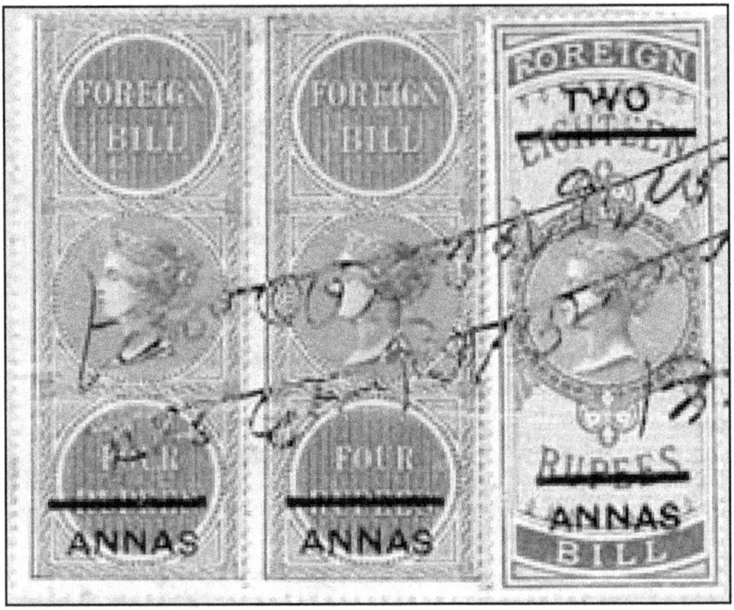

Adhesive Stamps on Private

Adhesive stamps on Commercial Scrip

Embossed Queen Victoria Revenue Seals

British India Revenue Seal

Watermark on Hundi

Revenue Form (King Edward)

Revenue Form (Ashoka Pillar)

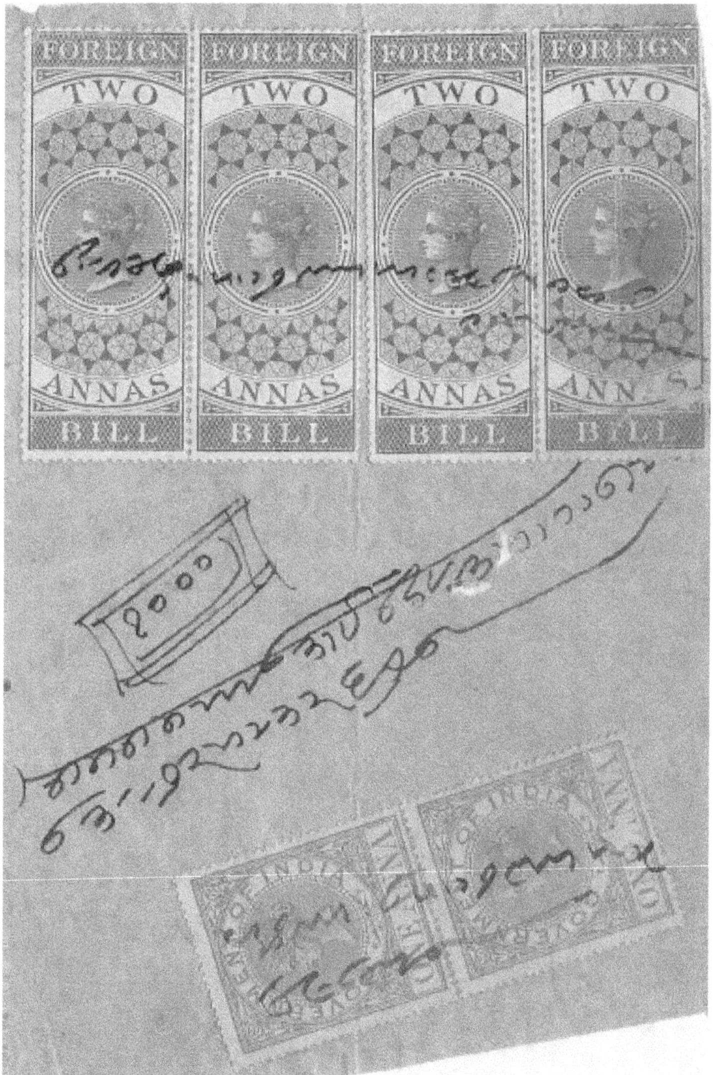

Long Victoria Stamps on Hundi

HUNDI
FOUR ANNAS
INDIA
FOUR ANNAS

Salute States

When the ruler of a princely state arrived at the Indian capital (originally at Calcutta (Kolkata), then at Delhi), he was greeted with a number of gun-firings. The number of these consecutive "gun salutes" changed from time to time, being increased or reduced depending on the degree of honour which the British chose to accord to a given ruler. The number of gun salutes accorded to a ruler was usually a reflection of the state of his relations with the British and/or his perceived degree of political power; a 21-gun salute was considered the highest. The King (or Queen) of the United Kingdom (who until 1948 was also the Emperor of India) was accorded a 101-gun salute, and 31 guns were used to salute the Viceroy of India.

The number of guns in a salute assumed particular importance at the time of holding of the Coronation Durbar in Delhi in the month of December 1911. The Durbar was held to commemorate the Coronation of King George V with guns firing almost all day. At that time there were three Princely States that were given 21 gun salutes. These were:

- H.E.H. The Nizam of Hyderabad
- H.H. The Maharaja Gaekwad of Baroda State
- H.H. The Maharaja of Mysore

In 1917, HH The Maharaja Scindia of Gwalior was upgraded to a permanent and hereditary 21-gun salute, and the Maharaja of Jammu and Kashmir was granted the same in 1921. Both were granted the increased ranks as a result of the meritorious services of their soldiers in the First World War.

Apart from these, no other Princely State received a 21-gun salute. Three of the most prominent princes, however, enjoyed a local salute of 21 guns within the limits of their own state and 19 guns in the rest of India. They were the Nawab (Begum) of Bhopal, the Maharaja Holkar of Indore and the Maharana of Udaipur.

The Nizam, Maharajas, Princes, etc. were all deeply keen on protocol and ensured that it was practised as a matter of faith. Any departure from it was not taken kindly by them. Salute of guns was one such protocol that was strictly adhered to.

At the time of Indian independence and partition in 1947, 118 of the roughly 565 princely states were classified as "salute states."

The rulers of the five premier states - Hyderabad, Mysore, Baroda, Jammu & Kashmir and Gwalior - received 21-gun salutes. The rulers of six others - Bhopal, Indore, Udaipur, Kolhapur, Travancore and Kalat - received 19-gun salutes, with Bhopal, Indore and Udaipur entitled to a local 21-gun salute. Of the remaining 111 rulers of the salute states, 88 were entitled to gun salutes ranging from 17 to 11 guns, with additional gun-salutes granted on a local or personal basis; the remaining 23 received a salute of 9 guns.

Rulers with gun salutes of 11 guns or above, whether the salute was hereditary or local only, were entitled to the style of *Highness*; the Nizam of Hyderabad was granted the unique style of *Exalted Highness* in 1918, in recognition of the state's contributions to the Allied war effort during the First World War.

In 1948, all rulers of nine-gun salute states were also granted the style of *Highness*.

Significant Periods in India's History

East India Company	1612 - 1757
Company rule of India	1757 - 1858
British Raj	1858 - 1947
Partition of India	1947
Princely States	1721 - 1949

Other Hundi Issues

Queen Victoria
King Edward VII
King George V
King George VI

Foreign Bills

Hundis from Queen Victoria period

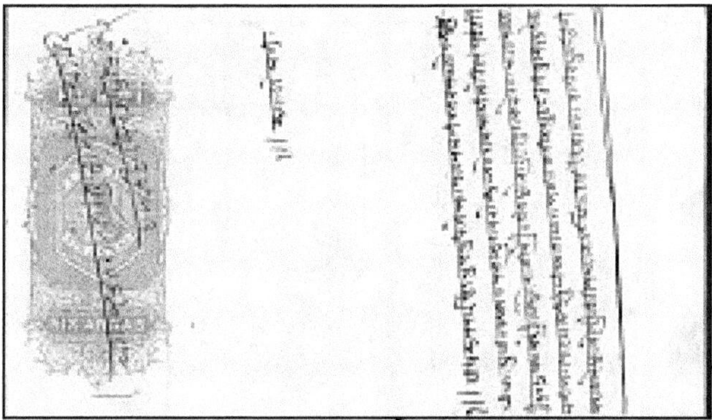

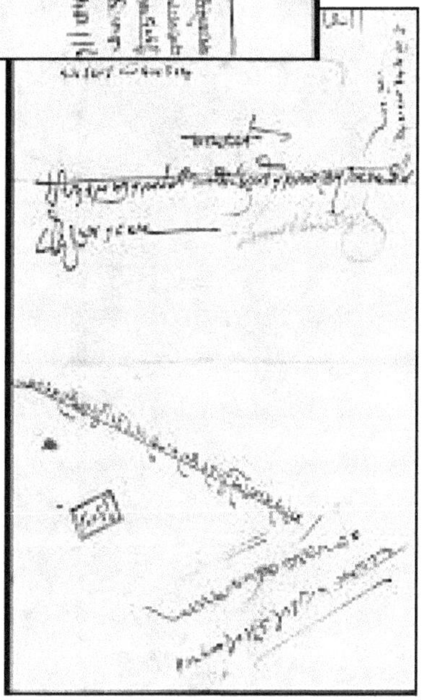

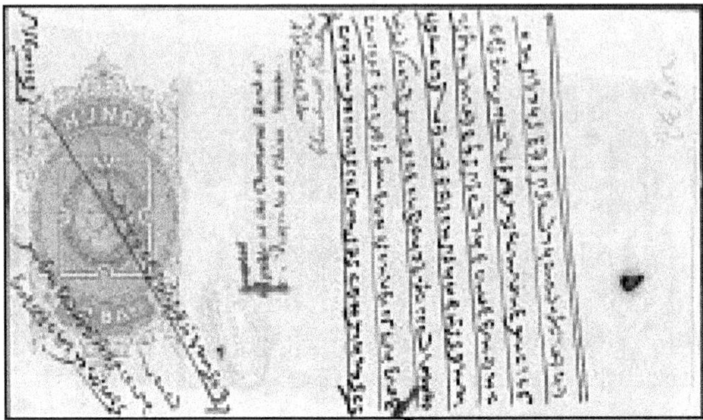

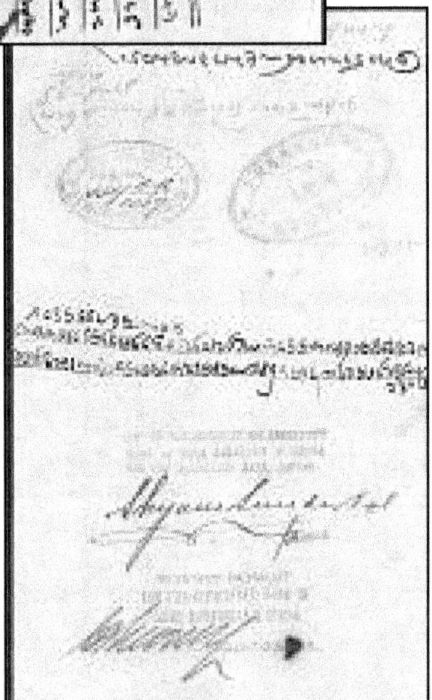

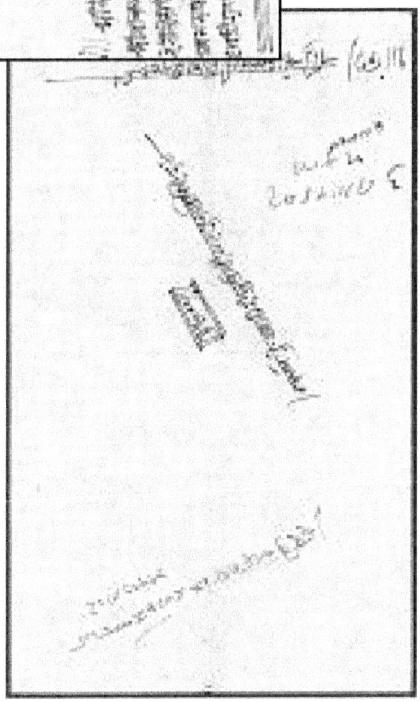

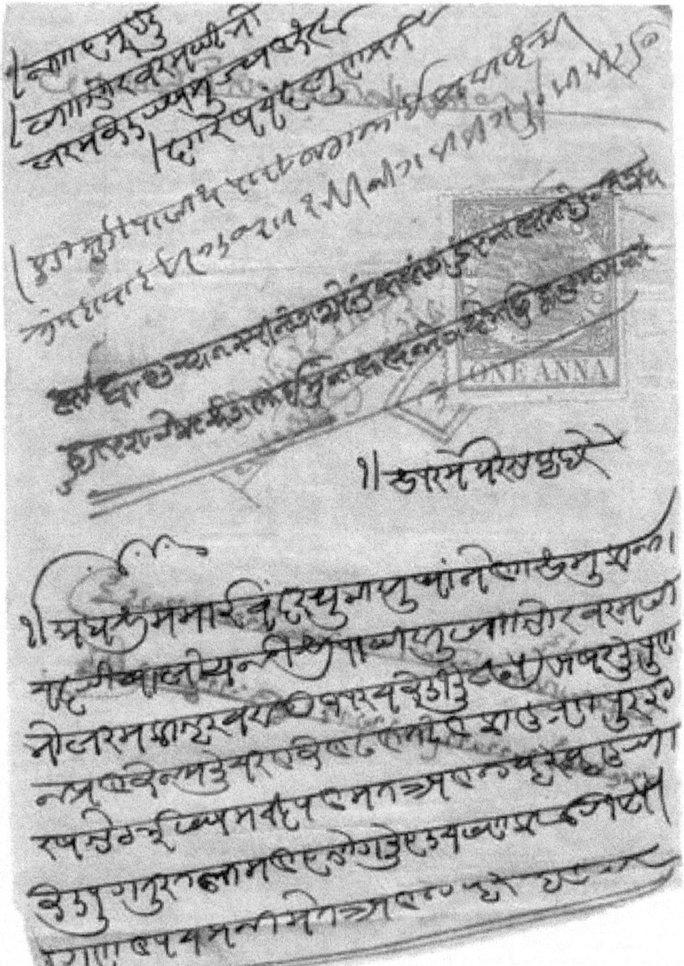

ONE ANNA

FOREIGN
TWO
ANNAS
BILL

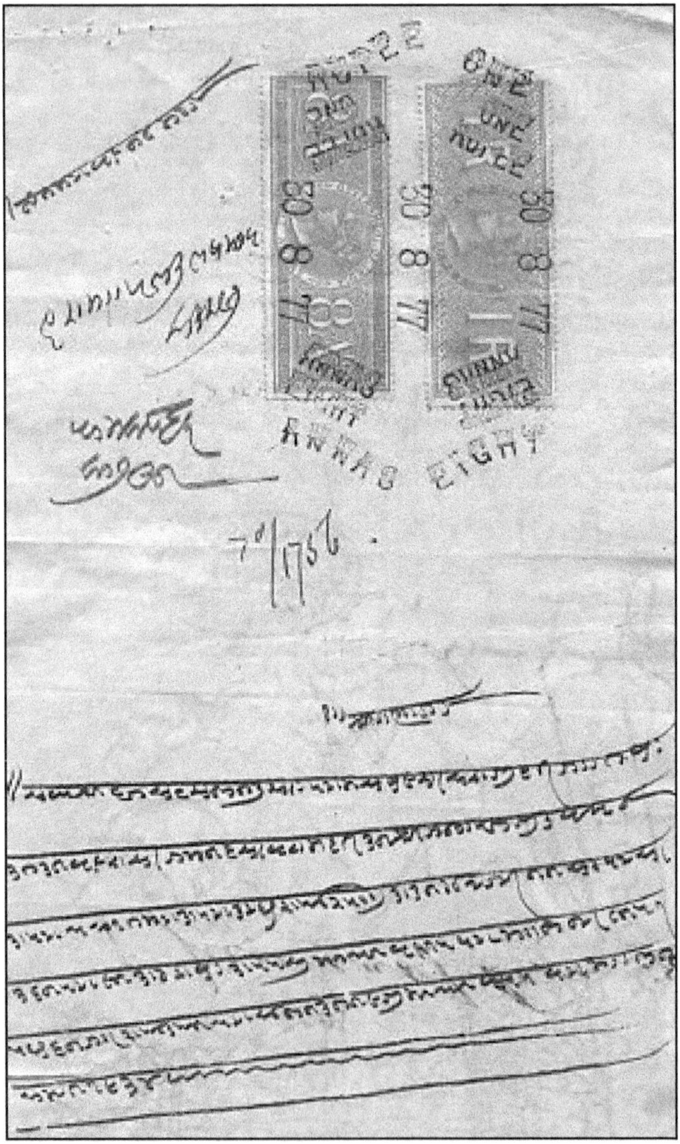
30 8 77
30 8 77
30 8 77
EIGHT

RUPEE ONE
ANNAS EIGHT

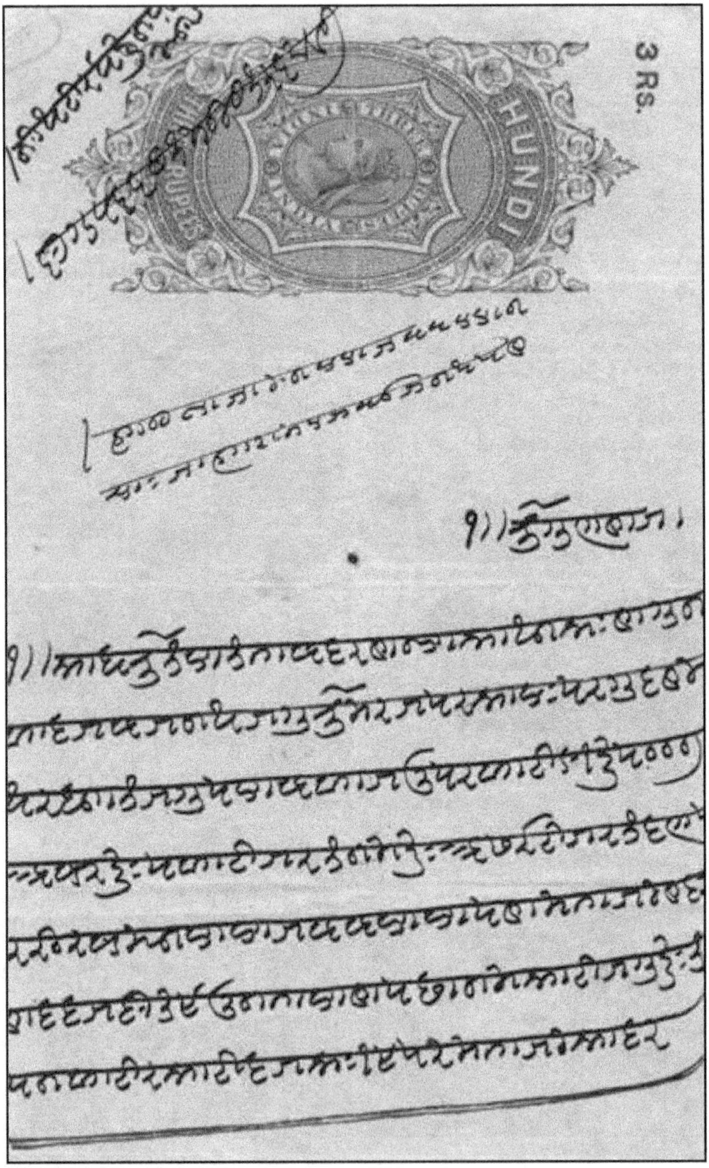
3 RS.
HUNDI

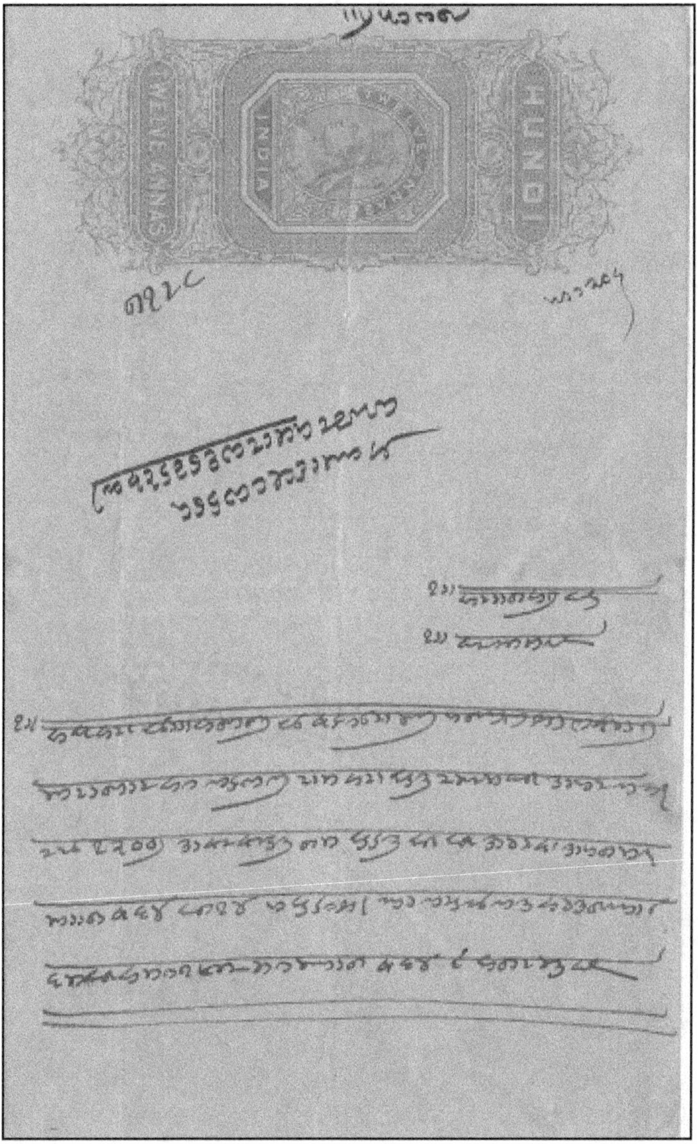
HUNDI
INDIA

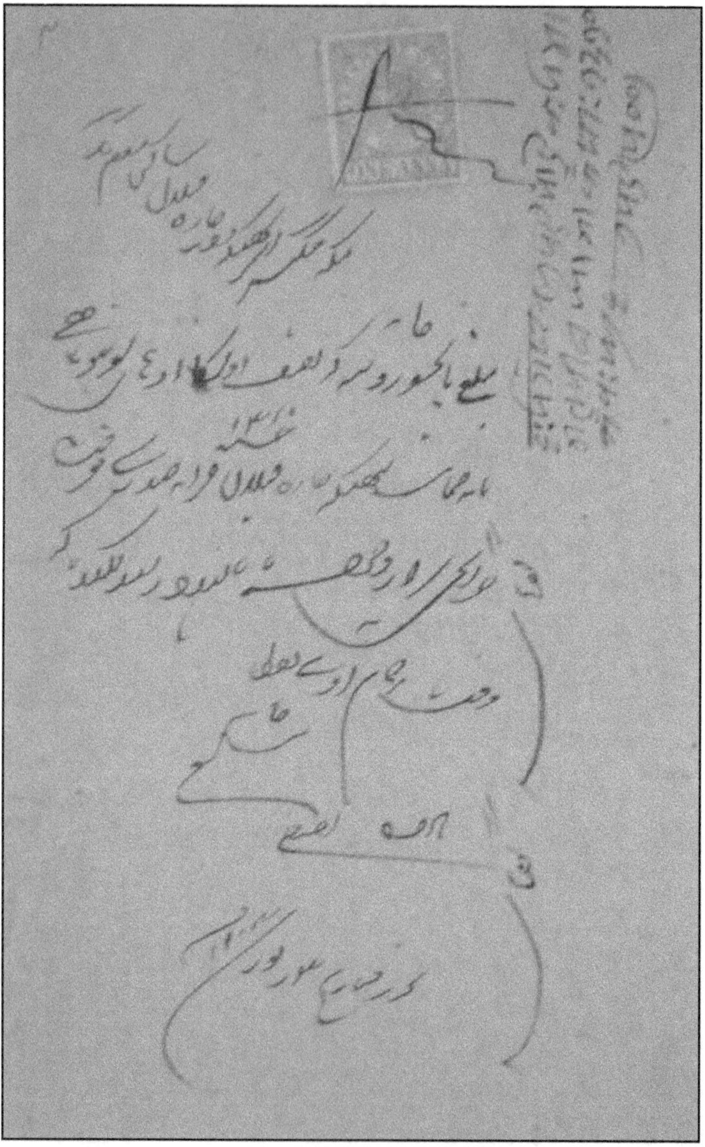

Hundis from King Edward VII period

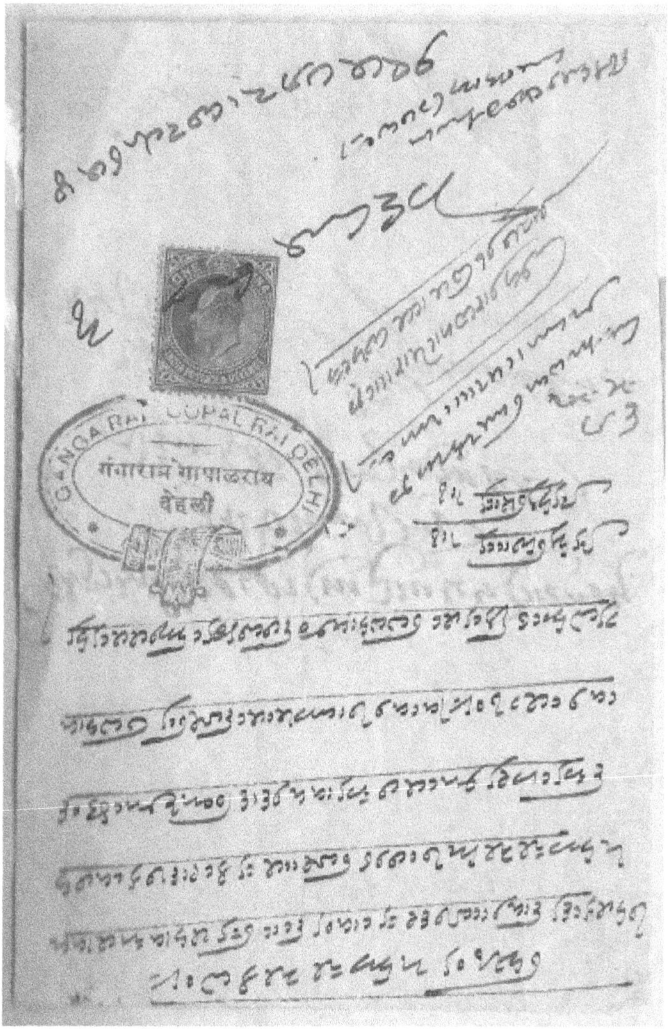

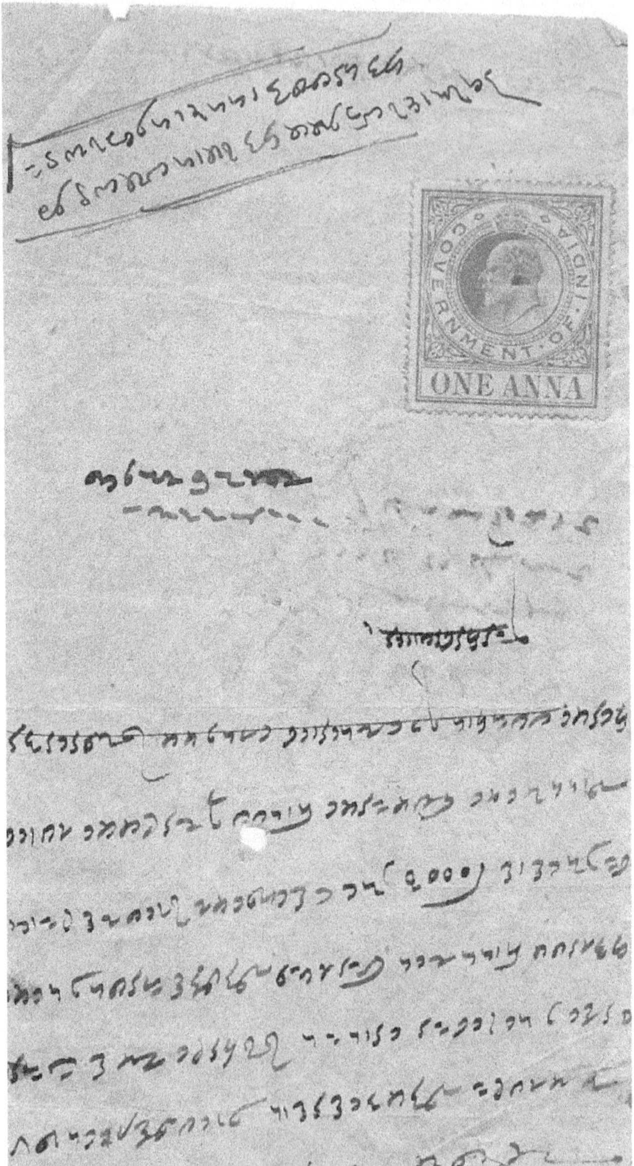
GOVERNMENT OF INDIA
ONE ANNA

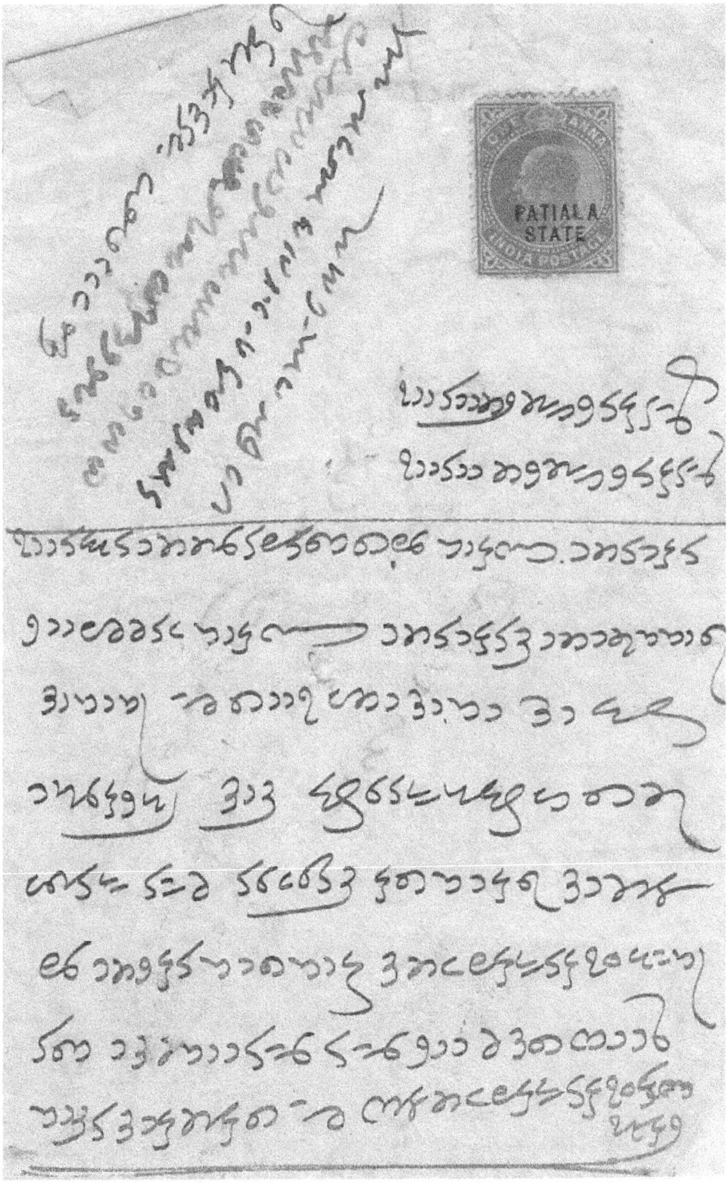
PATIALA
STATE

FOREIGN BILL
FOREIGN BILL
FOREIGN BILL

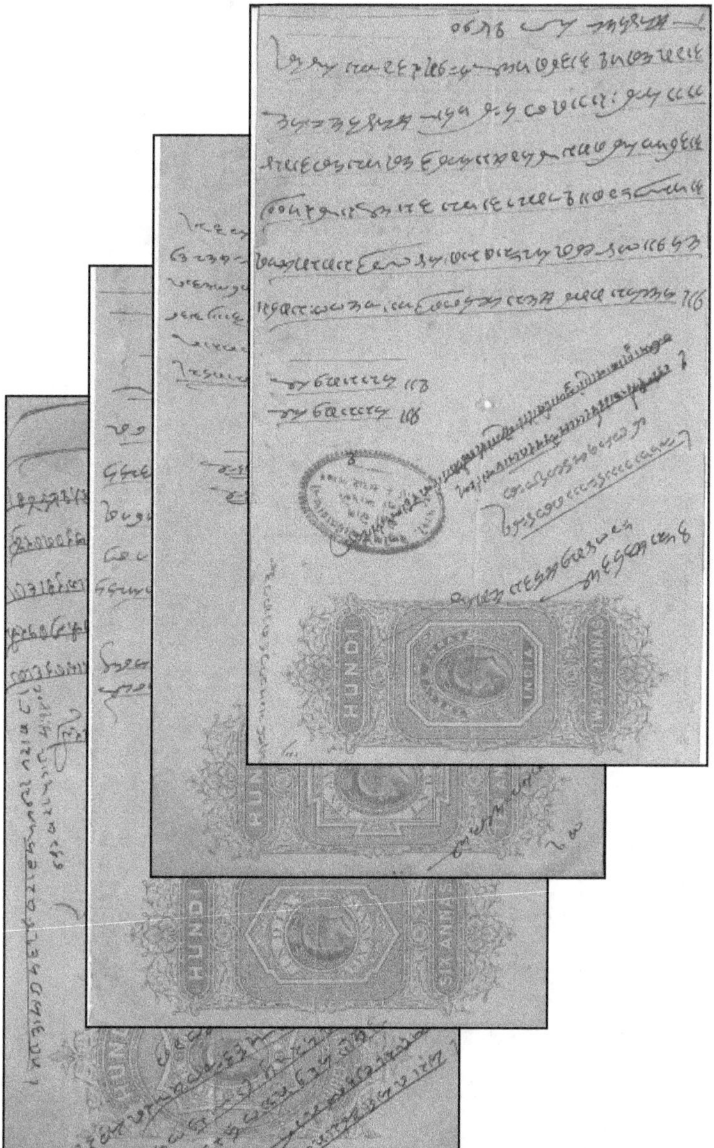

Notice the various revenue stamps on these Hundis

Hundis from King George V period

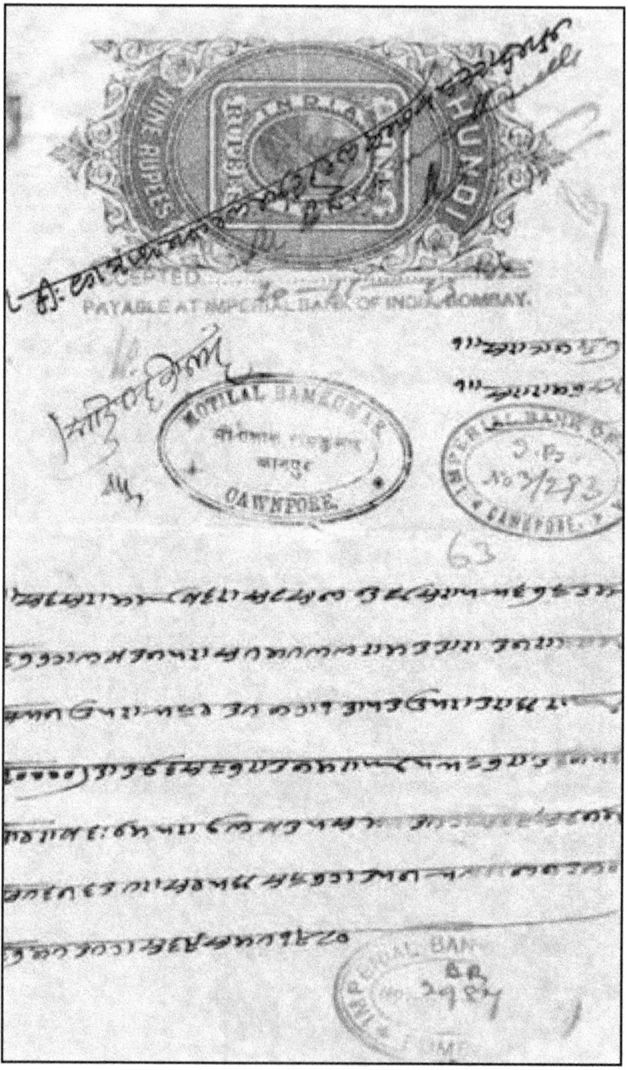

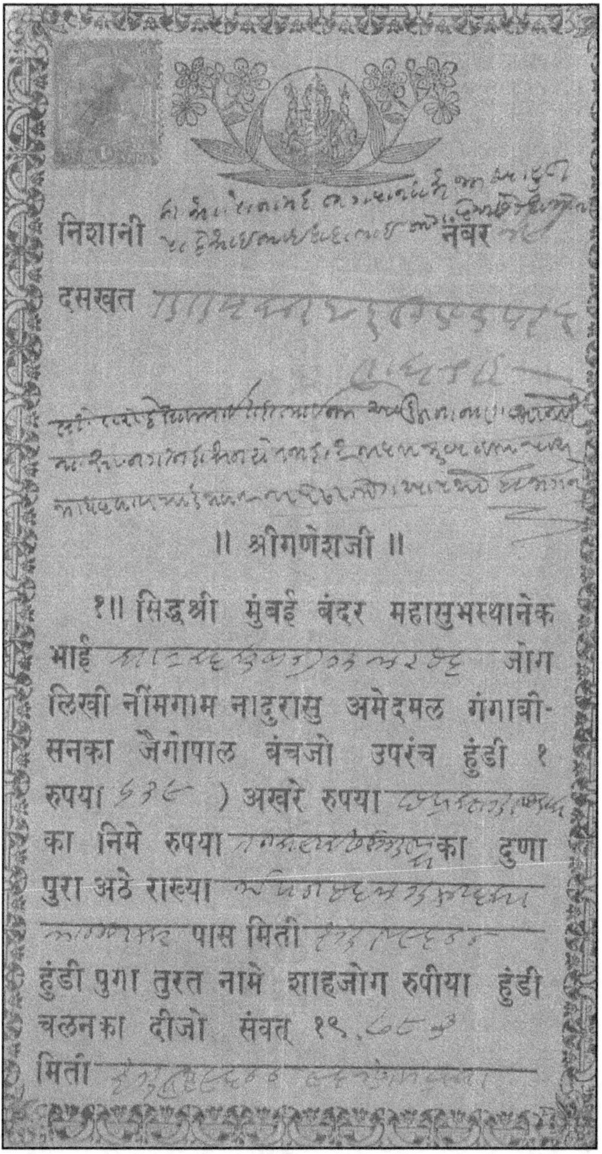

निशानी नंबर

दसखत

|| श्रीगणेशजी ||

१|| सिद्धश्री मुंबई बंदर महासुभस्थानेक
भाई जोग
लिखी नींमगाम नादुरासु अमेदमल गंगावी-
सनका जैगोपाल बंचजो उपरंच हुंडी १
रुपया) अखरे रुपया
का निमे रुपया का दुणा
पुरा अठे राख्या
पास मिती
हुंडी पुगा तुरत नामे शाहजोग रुपीया हुंडी
चलनका दीजो संवत १९
मिती

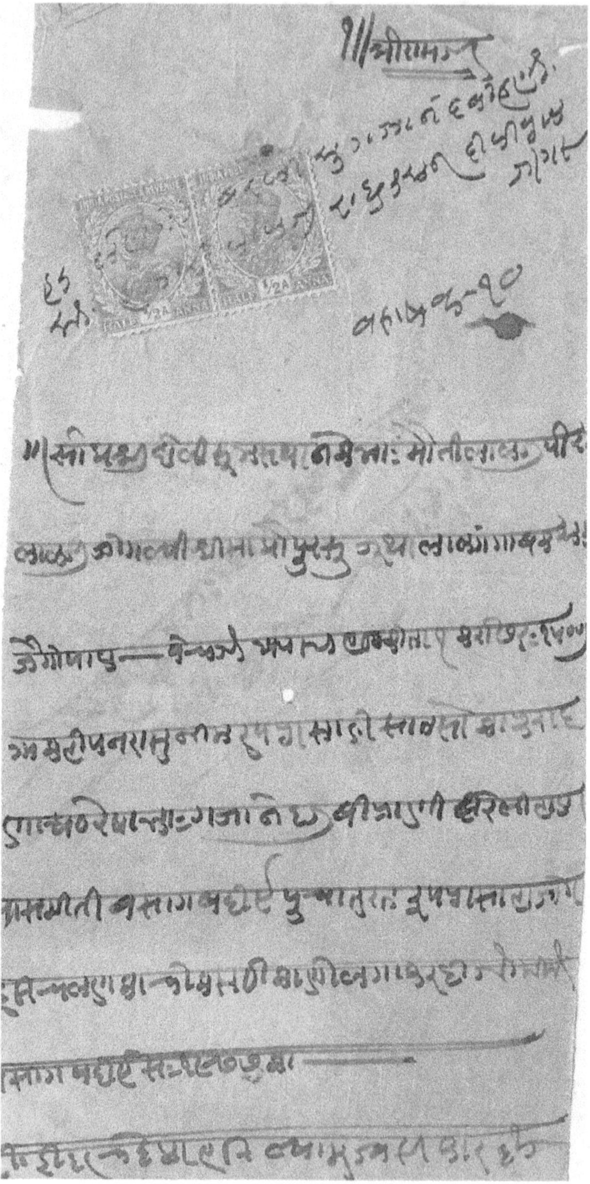

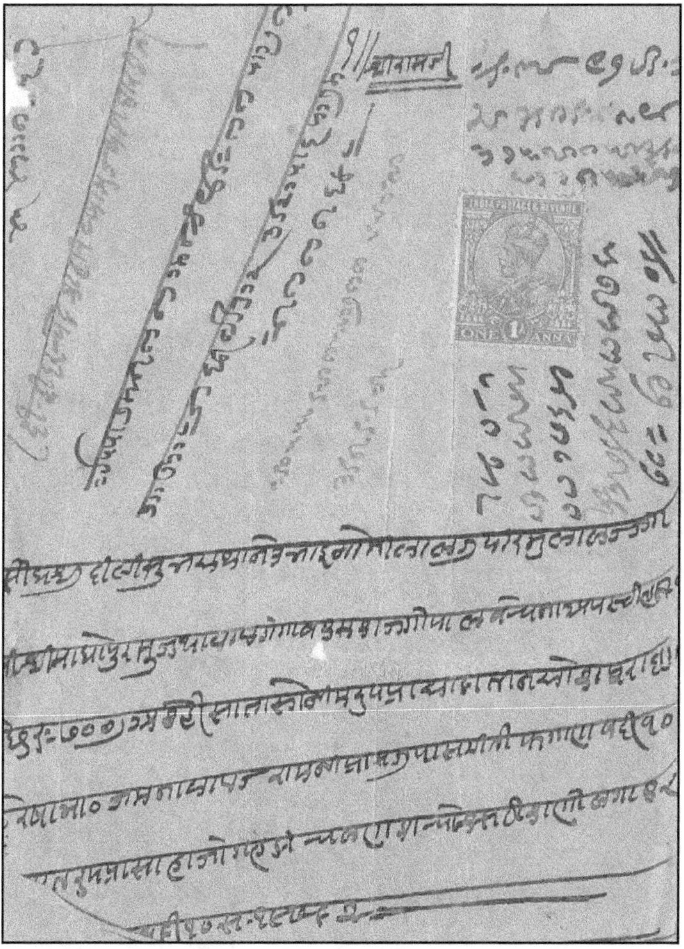

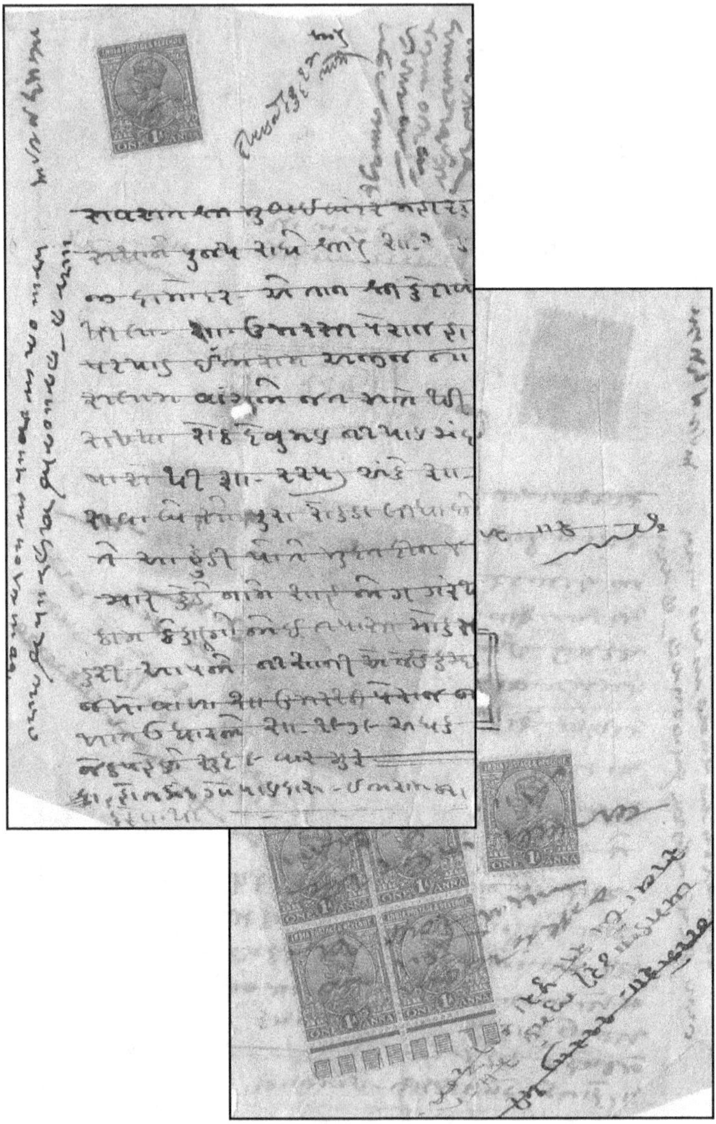

Hundis from King George VI period

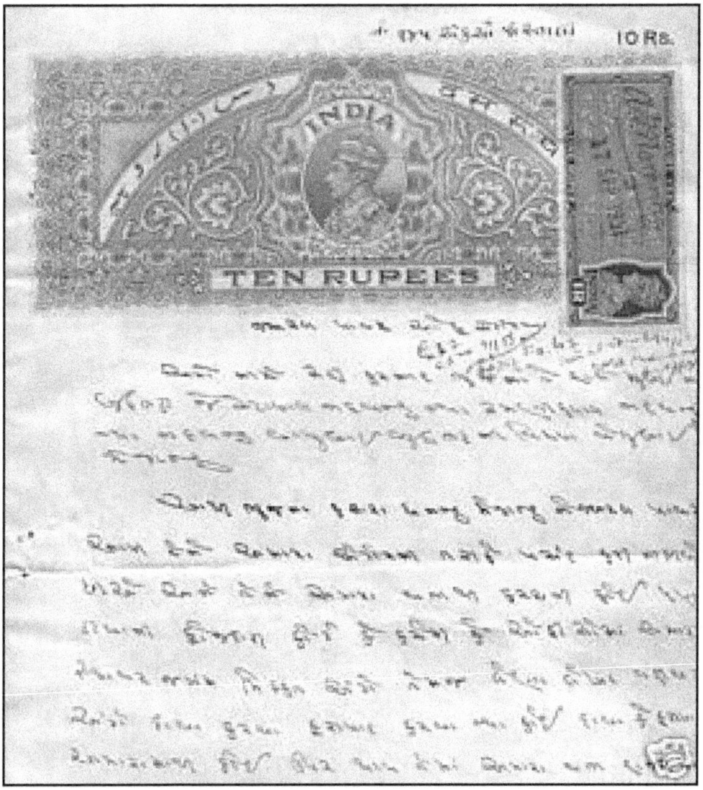

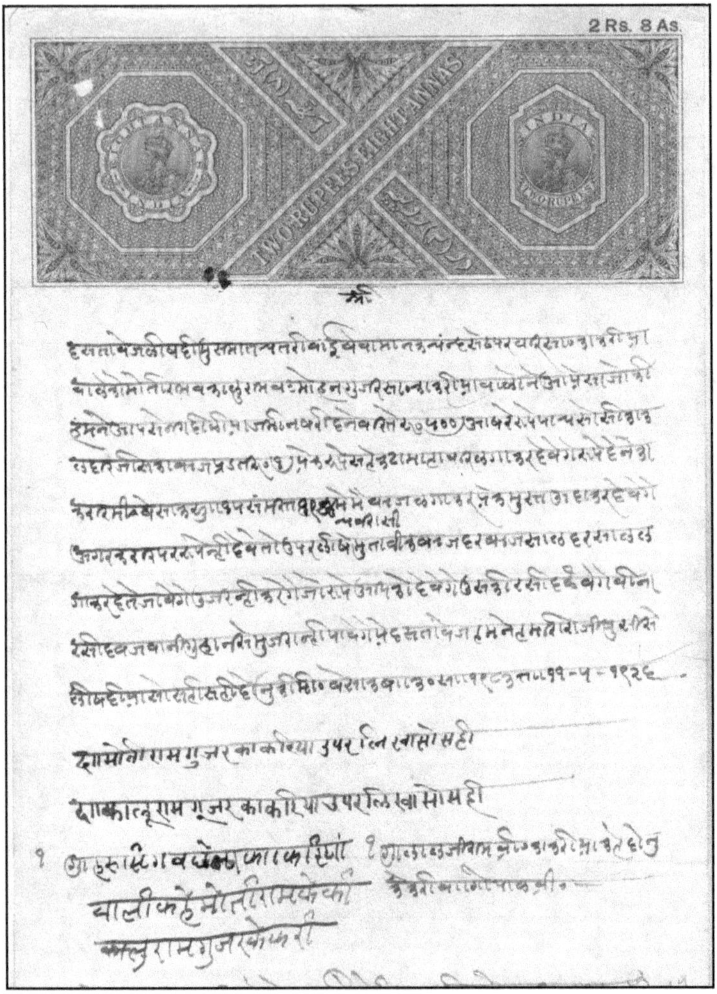
2 Rs. 8 As.
TWO RUPEES EIGHT ANNAS
INDIA
TWO RUPEES

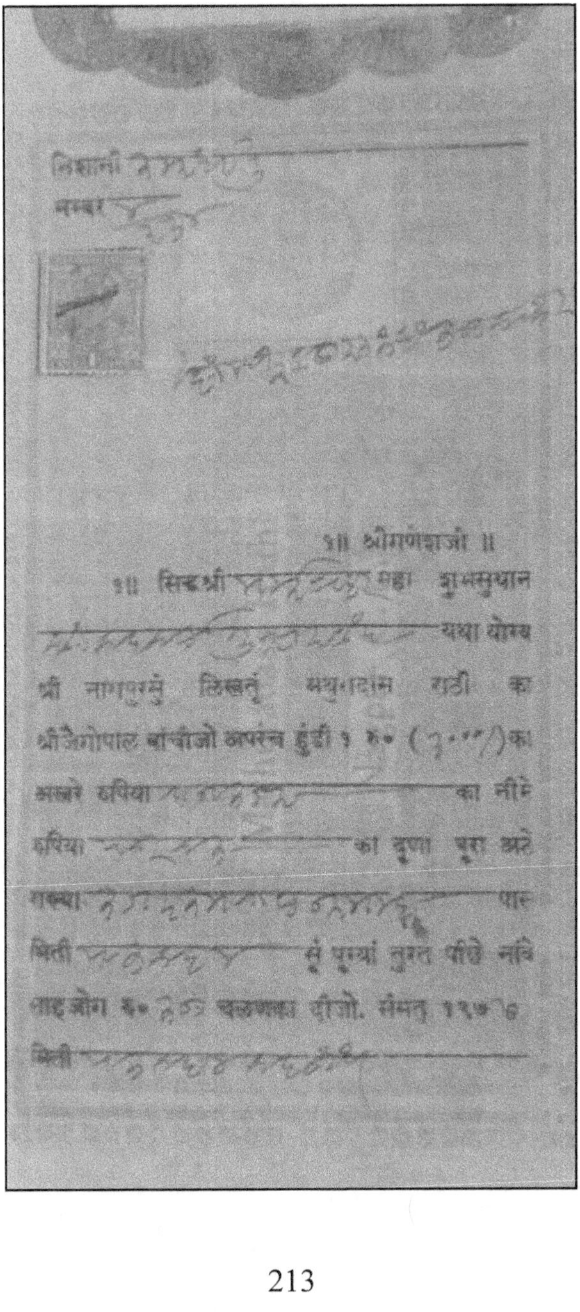

निशानी ___

नम्बर ___

॥ श्रीगणेशजी ॥

॥ सिद्धश्री ___ महा शुभस्थान

___ यथा योग्य

श्री नागपुरसुं लिखतं मथुरादास राठी का

श्रीजैगोपाल बांचीजो अपरंच हुंडी १ रु० (___)का

अखरे रुपिया ___ का नीमे

रुपिया ___ का दुणा पूरा अटे

राख्या ___ पास

मिती ___ सुं पूग्यां तुरत पीछे नवि

शाह जोग रु० ___ चलणका दीजो. संमत् १९७६

मिती ___

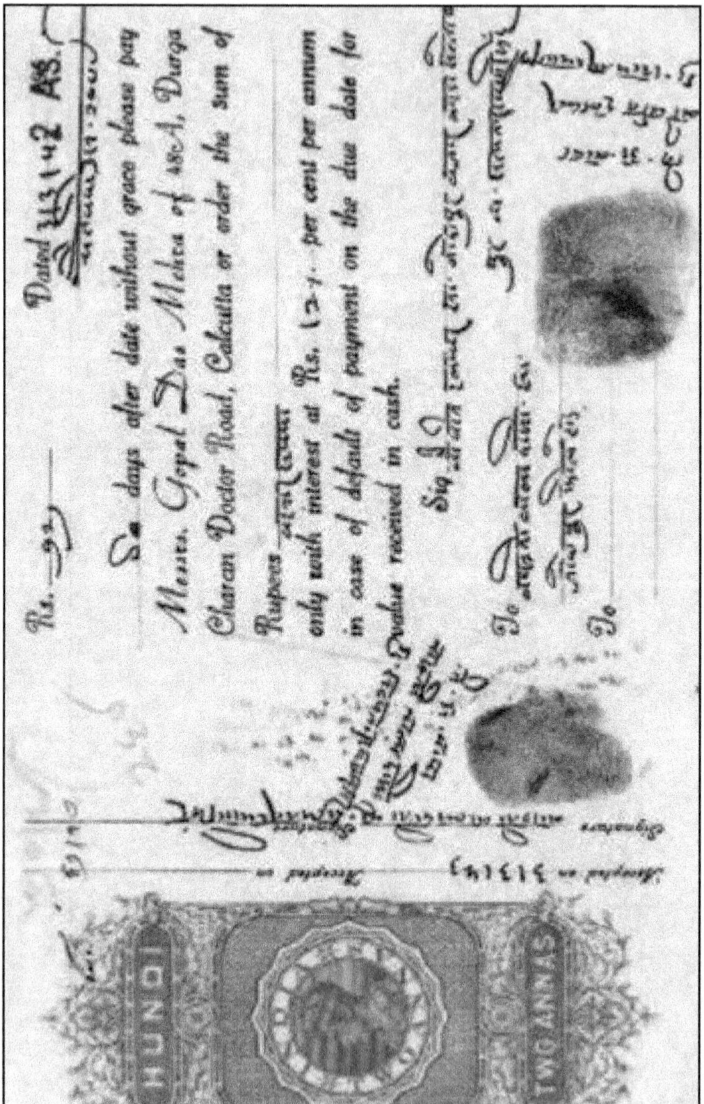
HUNDI

TWO ANNAS

Rs. 92

Dated

days after date without grace please pay Messrs. Gopal Das Mehra of 18A, Durga Charan Doctor Road, Calcutta or order the sum of

Rupees

only with interest at Rs. per cent per annum in case of default of payment on the due date for value received in cash.

Sig.

To

To

Accepted on

Signature

Foreign Bills

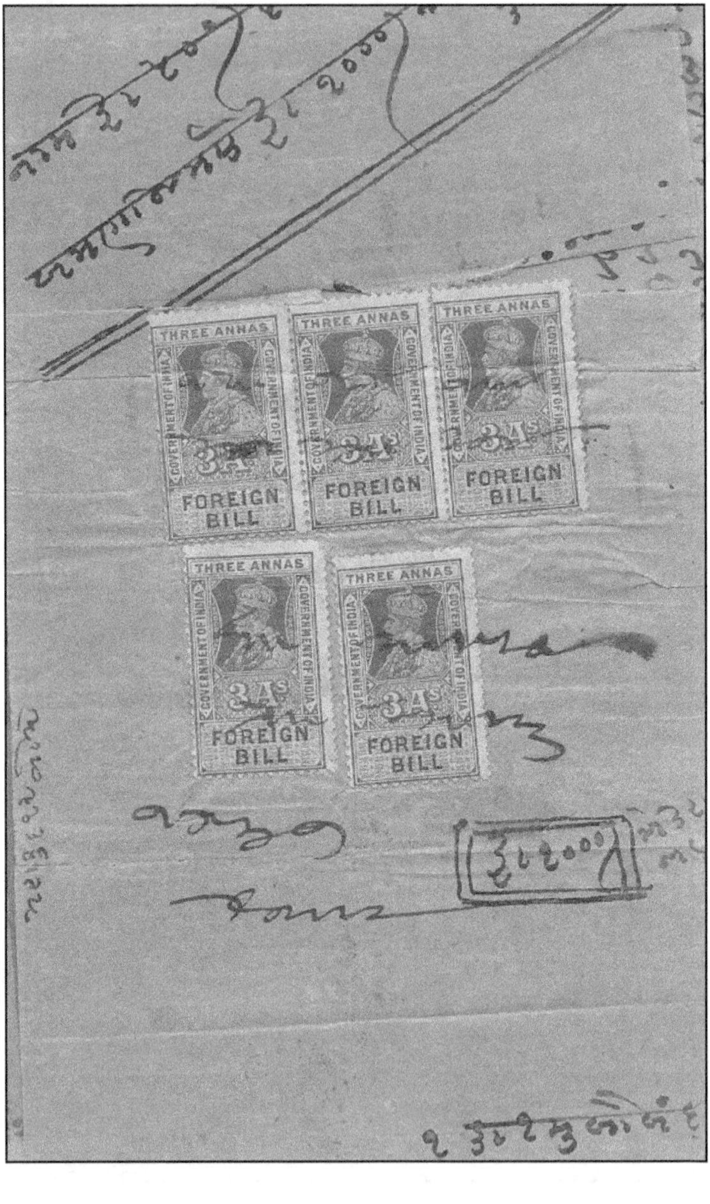
THREE ANNAS
GOVERNMENT OF INDIA
3As
FOREIGN BILL

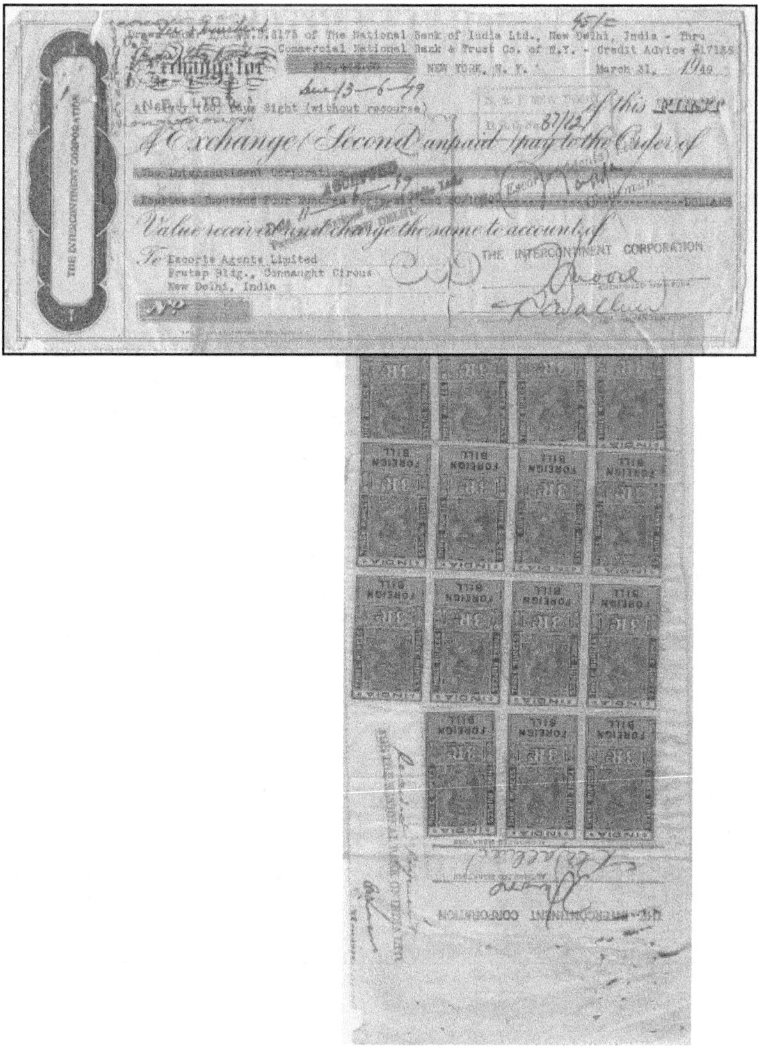

Drawn under [illegible] 3173 of The National Bank of India Ltd., New Delhi, India - Thru Commercial National Bank & Trust Co. of N.Y. - Credit Advice #17155

Exchange for [illegible] NEW YORK, N. Y. March 31, 1949

At Sixty (60) Days Sight (without recourse) of this FIRST

of Exchange (Second unpaid) pay to the Order of

The Intercontinent Corporation

[illegible] Dollars

Value received and charge the same to account of

To Escorts Agents Limited
Pratap Bldg., Connaught Circus
New Delhi, India

No.

THE INTERCONTINENT CORPORATION

FOREIGN BILL

INDIA

THE INTERCONTINENT CORPORATION

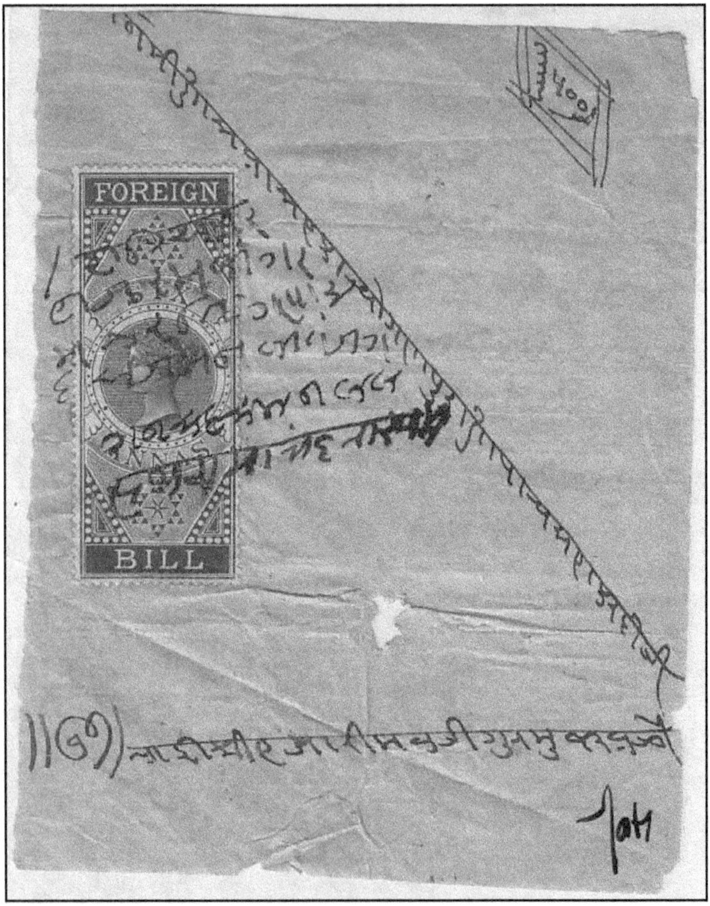
FOREIGN
BILL

FOREIGN
BILL

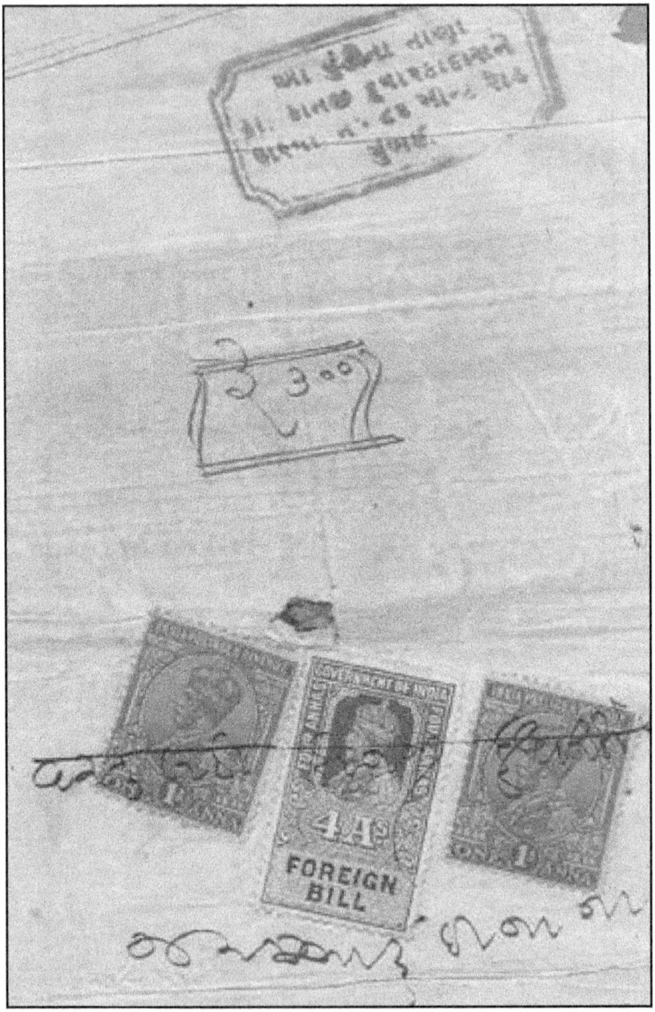
FOREIGN
BILL

Indian Numerals

Modern Devanagari	Hindu–Arabic	Hindi word for the cardinal numeral
०	0	śūnya (शून्य)
१	1	ék (एक)
२	2	do (दो)
३	3	tīn (तीन)
४	4	chaar (चार)
५	5	pāñc (पाँच)
६	6	chaḥ (छः)
७	7	sāt (सात)
८	8	āṭh (आठ)
९	9	nou (नौ)

The table above is a list of the Indian numerals in their modern **Devanagari** form.

This is the form which is used, for the most part, on much of the latter-day Hundi paper.

Hindu-Arabic	0	1	2	3	4	5	6	7	8	9
Arabic-Indic	٠	١	٢	٣	٤	٥	٦	٧	٨	٩
Bengali-Assamese	০	১	২	৩	৪	৫	৬	৭	৮	৯
Gujarati	૦	૧	૨	૩	૪	૫	૬	૭	૮	૯
Gurmukhi	੦	੧	੨	੩	੪	੫	੬	੭	੮	੯
Odia	୦	୧	୨	୩	୪	୫	୬	୭	୮	୯
Lepcha	᱀	᱁	᱂	᱃	᱄	᱅	᱆	᱇	᱈	᱉

The five Indian languages (Hindi, Marathi, Konkani, Nepali and Sanskrit itself) that have adapted the Devanagari script to their use also naturally employ the numeral symbols as a base. The table above presents a listing of the symbols used in various modern Indian scripts in comparison to Hindu-Arabic and Eastern Arabic-Indic numerals for the numbers from zero to nine. These numeric symbols can often be seen in older Hundi.

Telugu	౦	౧	౨	౩	౪	౫	౬	౭	౮	౯
Kannada	೦	೧	೨	೩	೪	೫	೬	೭	೮	೯
Tamil		௧	௨	௩	௪	௫	௬	௭	௮	௯
Malayalam	൦	൧	൨	൩	൪	൫	൬	൭	൮	൯

The Dravidian languages are a language family spoken mainly in southern India and parts of eastern and central India, as well as in northeastern Sri Lanka with small pockets in southwestern Pakistan, southern Afghanistan, Nepal, Bangladesh and Bhutan, and overseas in other countries such as Malaysia and Singapore.

The Dravidian languages with the most speakers are Telugu, Kannada, Tamil, and Malayalam. Hundis from these four geographical groups have often displayed the above numerical symbols.

There are also small groups of Dravidian-speaking scheduled tribes, who live beyond the mainstream communities, such as the Kurukh and Gond tribes.

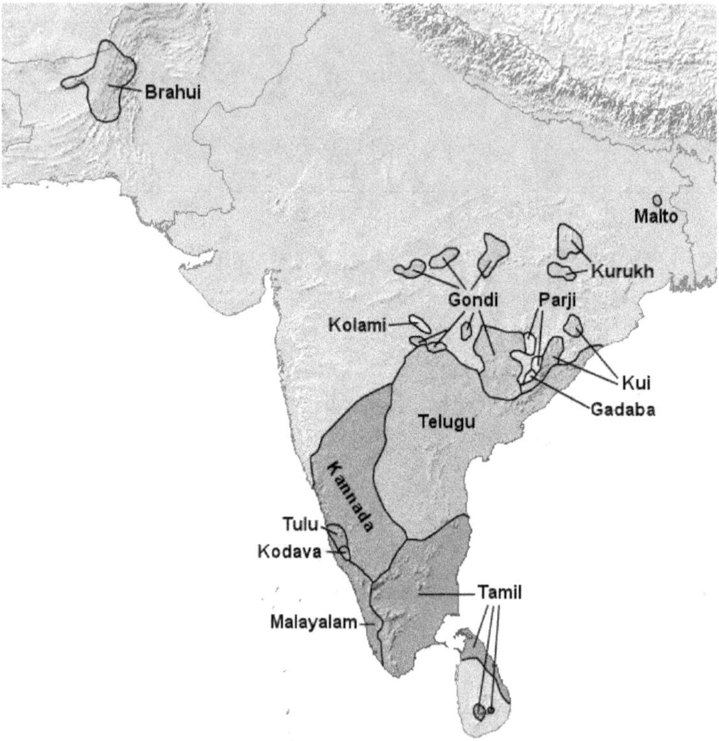

The distribution of the ***Dravidian languages*** *throughout southern India.*

States of India

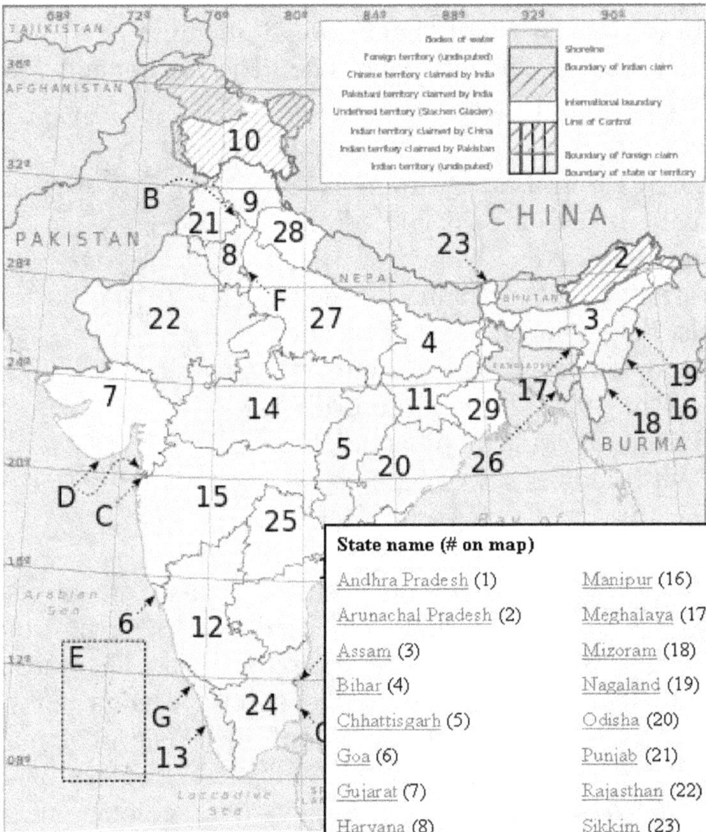

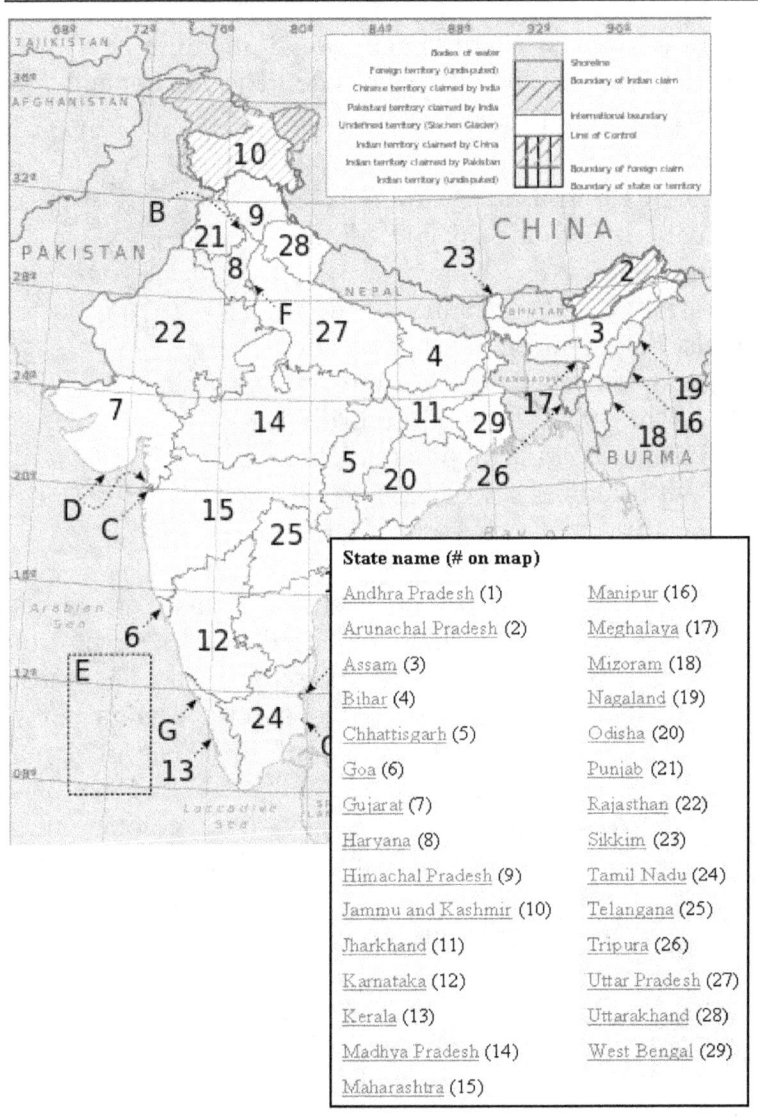

State name (# on map)	
Andhra Pradesh (1)	Manipur (16)
Arunachal Pradesh (2)	Meghalaya (17)
Assam (3)	Mizoram (18)
Bihar (4)	Nagaland (19)
Chhattisgarh (5)	Odisha (20)
Goa (6)	Punjab (21)
Gujarat (7)	Rajasthan (22)
Haryana (8)	Sikkim (23)
Himachal Pradesh (9)	Tamil Nadu (24)
Jammu and Kashmir (10)	Telangana (25)
Jharkhand (11)	Tripura (26)
Karnataka (12)	Uttar Pradesh (27)
Kerala (13)	Uttarakhand (28)
Madhya Pradesh (14)	West Bengal (29)
Maharashtra (15)	

Recent Official Issues

Modern official issues of Hundis are all identifiable by the Revenue Seal on the left hand side. The all contain the official Emblem of India.

सत्यमेव जयते

The **Lion Capital of Ashoka** is a sculpture of four Asiatic lions standing back to back, on an elaborate base that includes other animals. A graphic representation of it was adopted as the official Emblem of India in 1950. It was originally placed atop the Aśoka pillar at the important Buddhist site of Sarnath by the Emperor Ashoka, in about 250 BCE.

The wheel "Ashoka Chakra" from its base has been placed onto the centre of the National Flag of India. The most visible use of the Ashoka Chakra today is at the centre of the Flag of India (adopted on 22nd July 1947), where it is rendered in a navy-blue colour on a white background, replacing the symbol of *charkha* (spinning wheel) of the pre-independence versions of the flag.

A similar four "Indian lion" Lion Capital of Ashoka nwar Chiang Mai, Thailand showing another larger Ashoka Chakra atop the four lions.

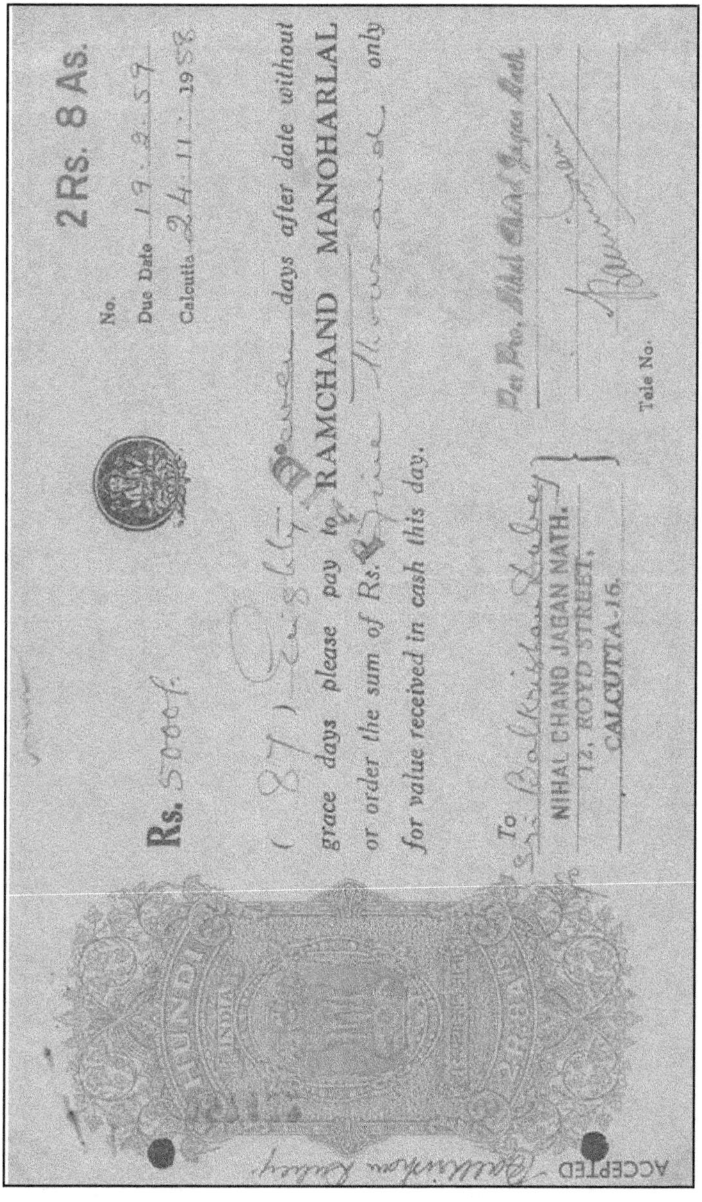
2Rs. 8As.

No.

Due Date 19.2.59

Calcutta 24.11.1958

Rs. 5000/-

(87) Eighty seven days after date without grace days please pay to RAMCHAND MANOHARLAL or order the sum of Rs. Five thousand only for value received in cash this day.

To Sri Balkishan Dubey
NIHAL CHAND JAGAN NATH.
12, ROYD STREET,
CALCUTTA-16.

For Pro. Nihal Chand Jagan Nath

Tele No.

ACCEPTED Balkishan Dubey

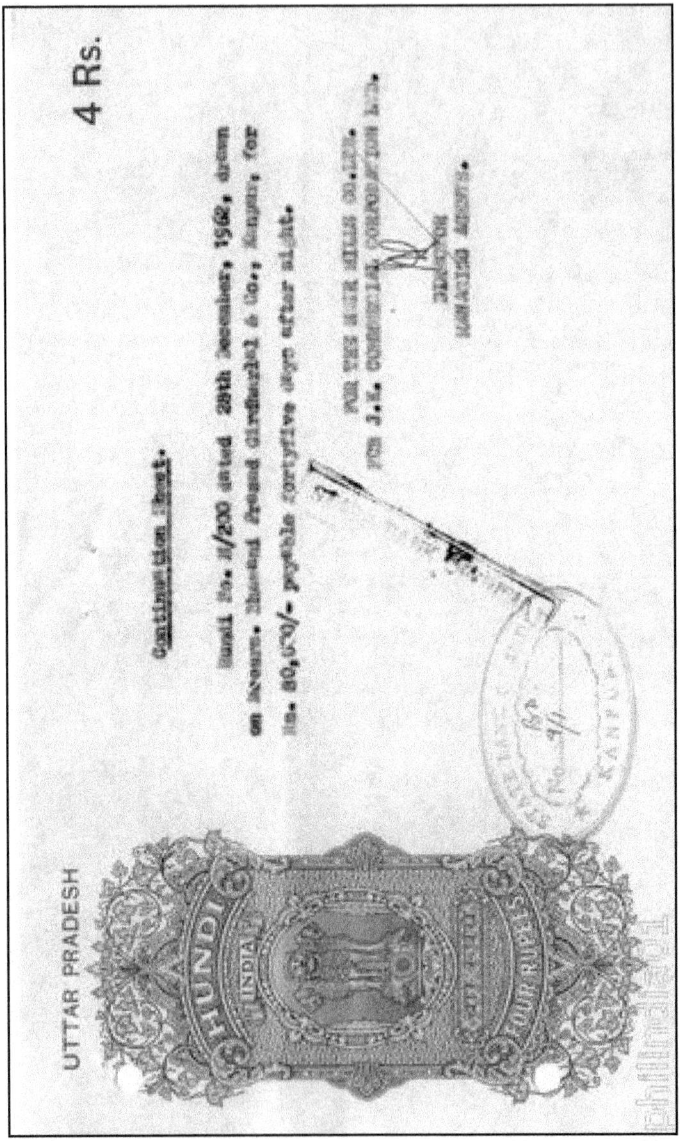
UTTAR PRADESH

4 Rs.

HUNDI

INDIA

FOUR RUPEES

Continuation Sheet.

Hundi No. H/200 dated 28th December, 1962, drawn on Messrs. [illegible] Prasad Girdharilal & Co., Kanpur, for Rs. 80,000/- payable fortyfive days after sight.

FOR THE [illegible] MILLS CO.LTD.
FOR J.K. COMMERCIAL CORPORATION LTD.

DIRECTOR
MANAGING AGENTS.

STATE BANK
No.
KANPUR

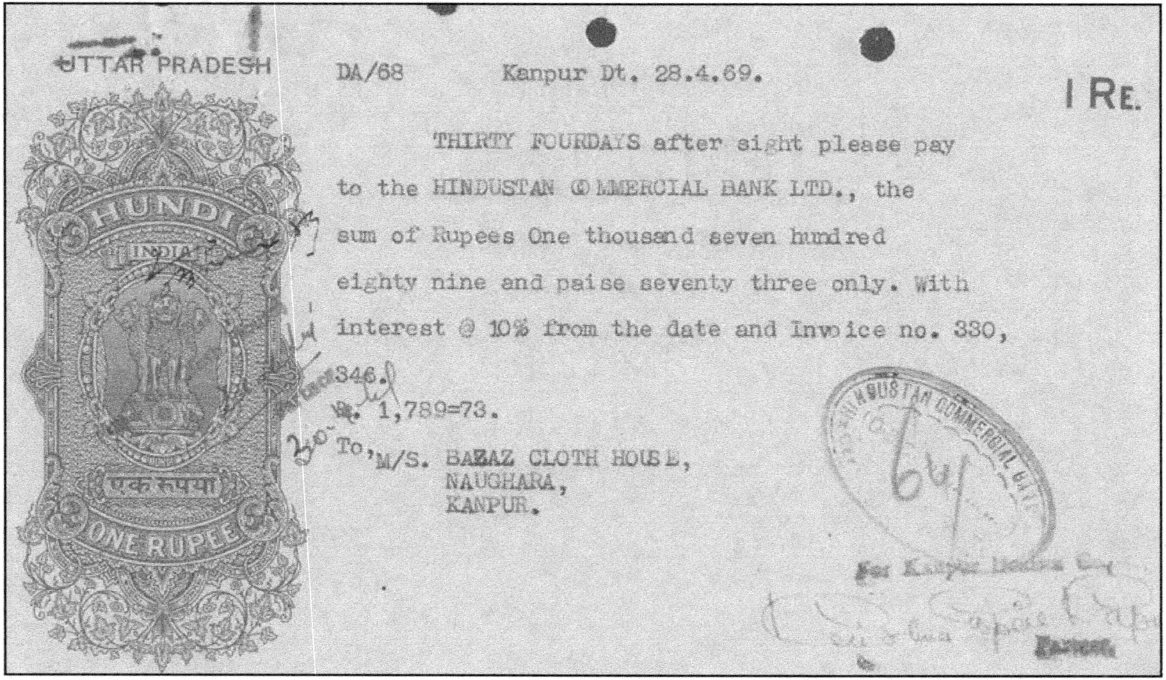

UTTAR PRADESH

HUNDI

INDIA

एक रुपया

ONE RUPEE

DA/68 Kanpur Dt. 28.4.69.

1 RE.

THIRTY FOURDAYS after sight please pay to the HINDUSTAN COMMERCIAL BANK LTD., the sum of Rupees One thousand seven hundred eighty nine and paise seventy three only. With interest @ 10% from the date and Invoice no. 330, 346.

Rs. 1,789=73.

To, M/S. BAZAZ CLOTH HOUSE,
NAUGHARA,
KANPUR.

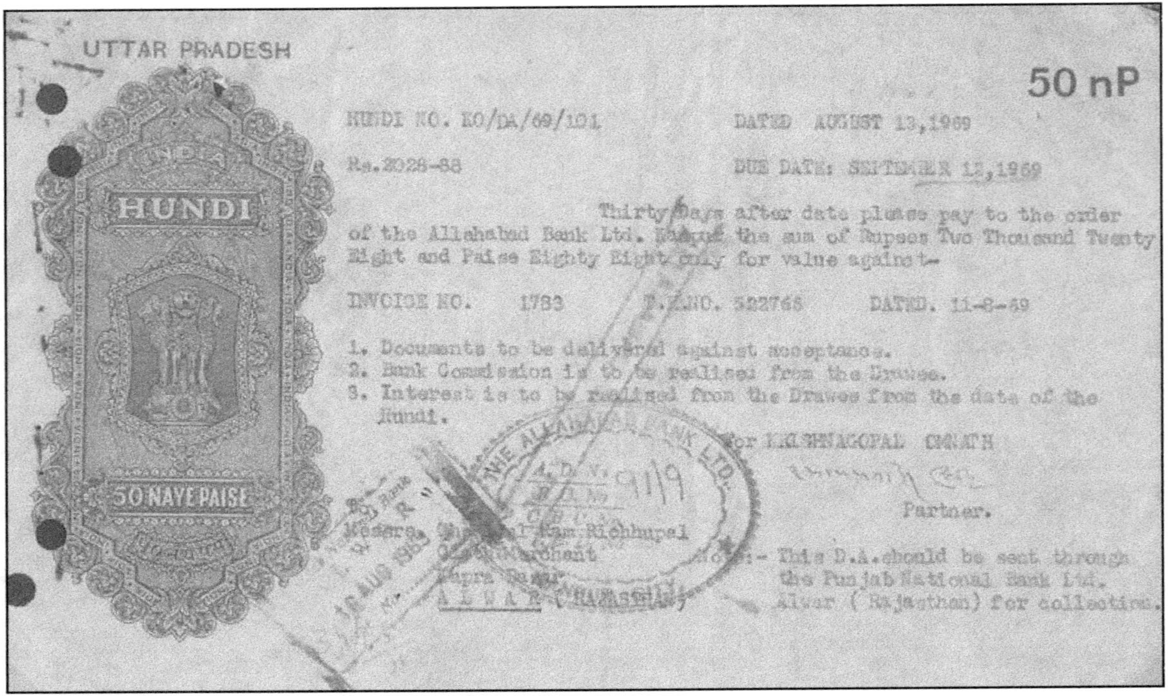

UTTAR PRADESH

HUNDI

50 NAYE PAISE

50 nP

HUNDI NO. KO/DA/69/101 DATED AUGUST 13,1969

Rs.2028-88 DUE DATE: SEPTEMBER 12,1969

Thirty Days after date please pay to the order of the Allahabad Bank Ltd. ... the sum of Rupees Two Thousand Twenty Eight and Paise Eighty Eight only for value against-

INVOICE NO. 1783 R.R.NO. 522768 DATED. 11-8-69

1. Documents to be delivered against acceptance.
2. Bank Commission is to be realised from the Drawee.
3. Interest is to be realised from the Drawee from the date of the Hundi.

For KRISHNAGOPAL OMNATH

Partner.

Messrs. ... Ram Richhupal

... Merchant

... Bazar

ALWAR (RAJASTHAN)

Note:- This D.A.should be sent through the Punjab National Bank Ltd. Alwar (Rajasthan) for collection.

THE ALLAHABAD BANK LTD.

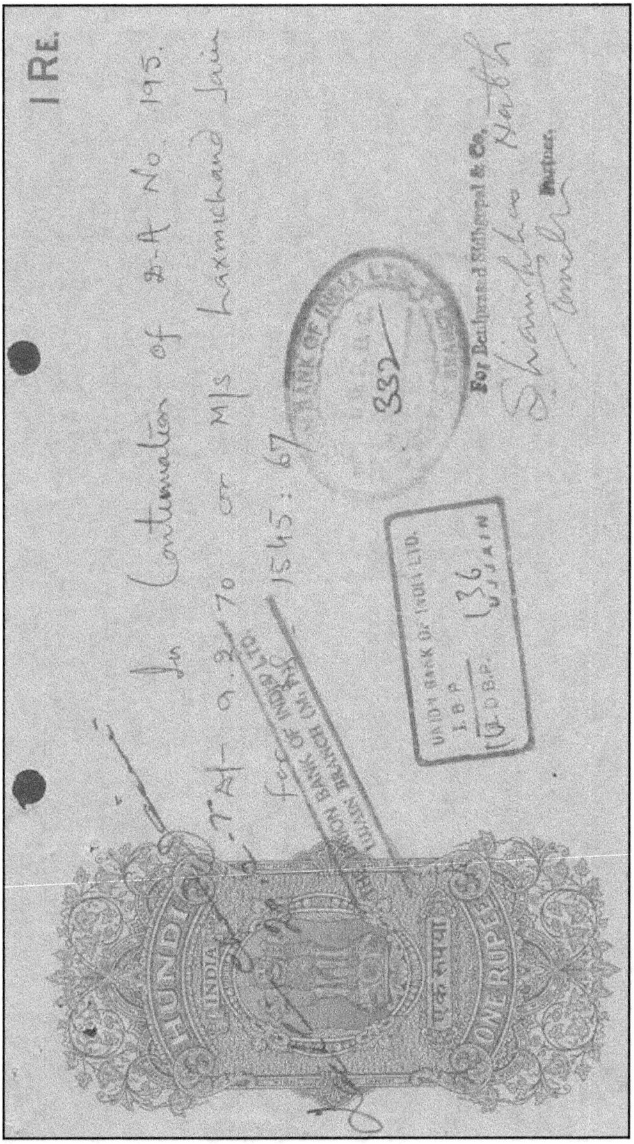
I RE.
HUNDI
INDIA
एक रुपया
ONE RUPEE
In Continuation of D.A No. 195.
Dt- 9.2.70 or M/s Laxmichand Jain
1545 : 67
UNION BANK OF INDIA LTD.
UJJAIN BRANCH
332
UNION BANK OF INDIA LTD.
I.B.P.
D.B.P.
136
UJJAIN
Partner.

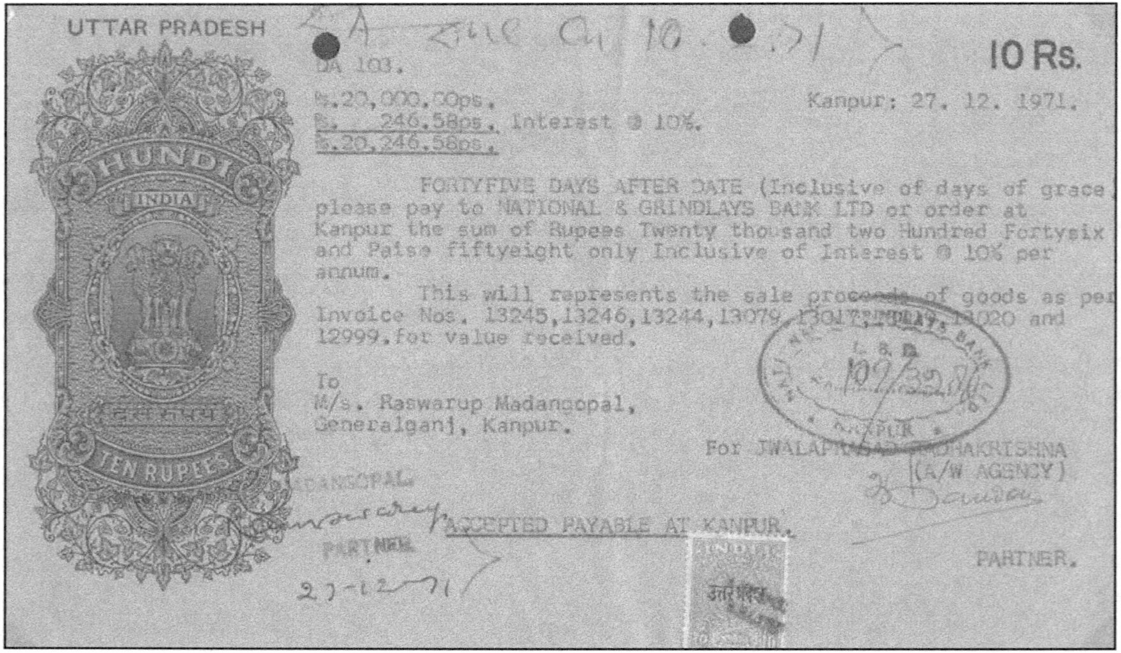

UTTAR PRADESH

10 Rs.

DA 103.

Rs.20,000.00ps.
Rs. 246.58ps. Interest @ 10%.
Rs.20,246.58ps.

Kanpur: 27. 12. 1971.

FORTYFIVE DAYS AFTER DATE (Inclusive of days of grace) please pay to NATIONAL & GRINDLAYS BANK LTD or order at Kanpur the sum of Rupees Twenty thousand two Hundred Fortysix and Paise fiftyeight only Inclusive of Interest @ 10% per annum.

This will represents the sale proceeds of goods as per Invoice Nos. 13245,13246,13244,13079,13017, [illegible] 020 and 12999.for value received.

To
M/s. Raswarup Madangopal,
Generalganj, Kanpur.

For JWALAPRASAD RADHAKRISHNA
(A/W AGENCY)

PARTNER.

MADANGOPAL

ACCEPTED PAYABLE AT KANPUR.

PARTNER.

27-12-71

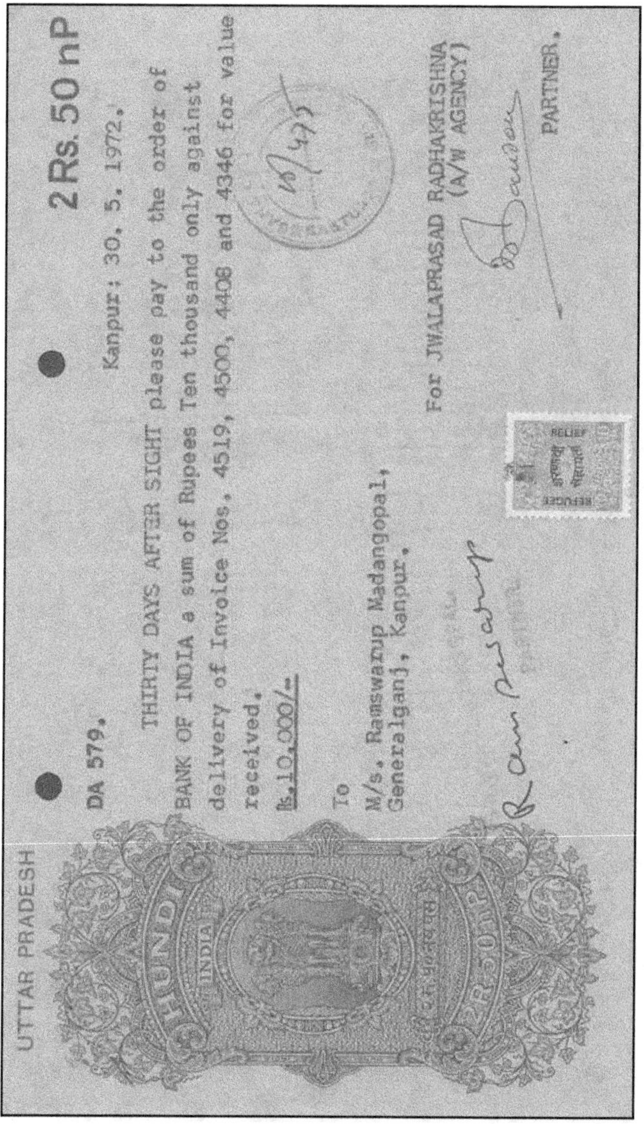

UTTAR PRADESH

HUNDI INDIA

2 Rs. 50 nP

DA 579.

Kanpur: 30. 5. 1972.

THIRTY DAYS AFTER SIGHT please pay to the order of BANK OF INDIA a sum of Rupees Ten thousand only against delivery of Invoice Nos. 4519, 4500, 4408 and 4346 for value received.

Rs.10,000/-

To
M/s. Ramswarup Madangopal,
Generalganj, Kanpur.

For JWALAPRASAD RADHAKRISHNA
(A/W AGENCY)

PARTNER.

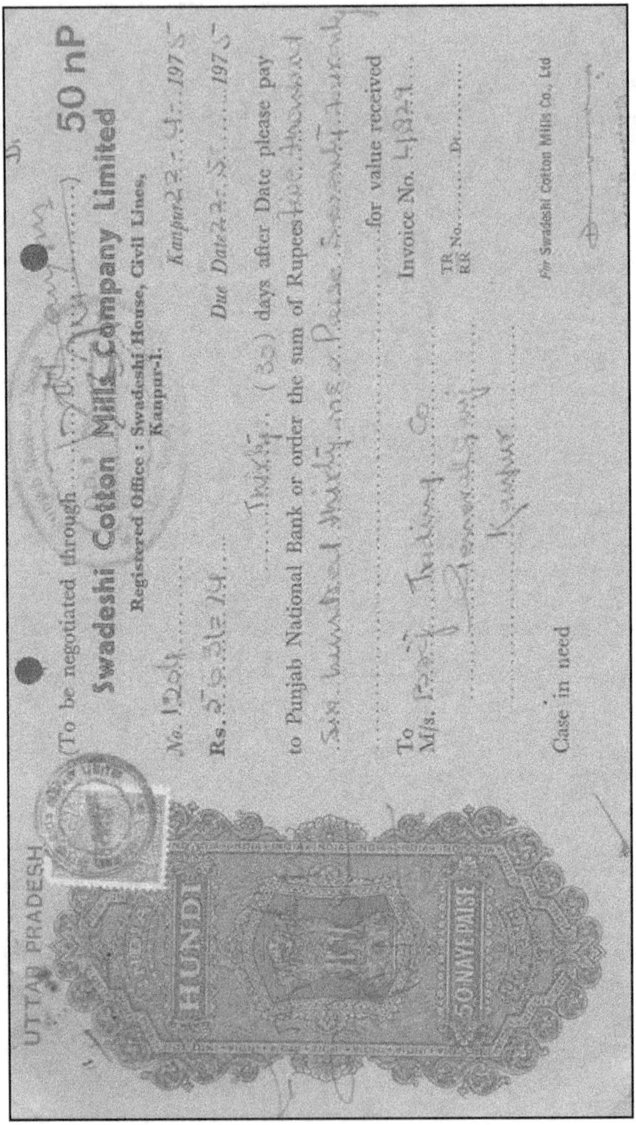
UTTAR PRADESH
HUNDI
50 NAYE PAISE
(To be negotiated through ....)
50 nP
Swadeshi Cotton Mills Company Limited
Registered Office : Swadeshi House, Civil Lines, Kanpur-1.
No. .... Kanpur 197
Rs. .... Due Date 197
.... days after Date please pay
to Punjab National Bank or order the sum of Rupees
.... for value received
To M/s. .... Invoice No. ....
TR/RR No. .... Dt. ....
Case in need
For Swadeshi Cotton Mills Co., Ltd

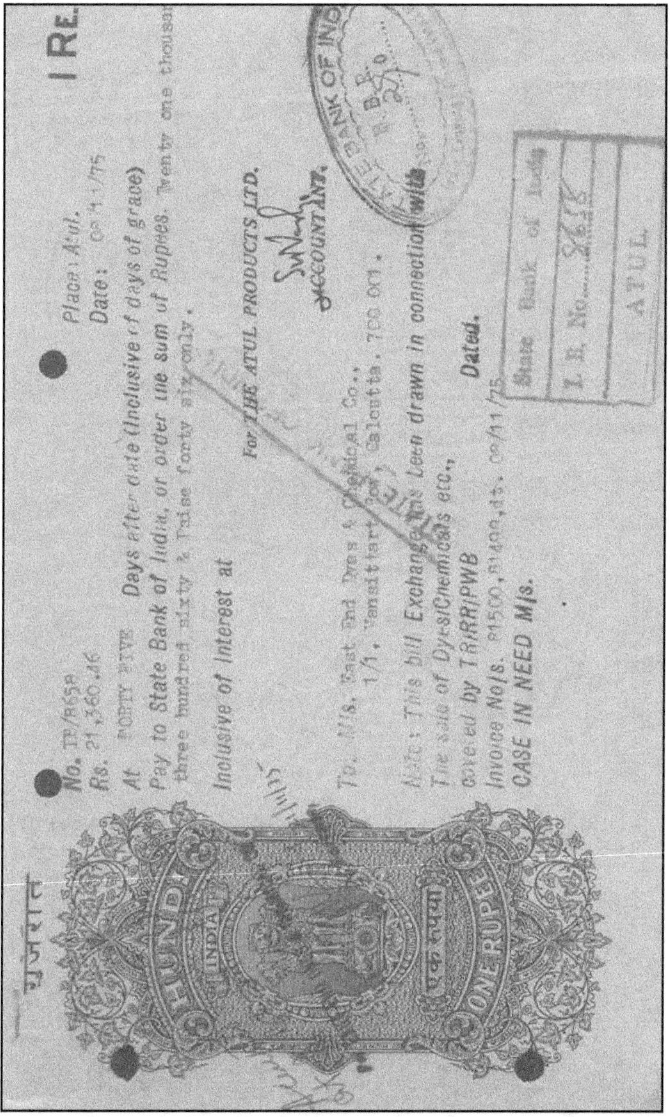

ગુજરાત

HUNDI INDIA एक रुपया ONE RUPEE

I RE.

No. TP/8658
Rs. 21,360.46

Place: Atul.
Date: 08/11/75

At FORTY FIVE Days after date (Inclusive of days of grace)
Pay to State Bank of India, or order the sum of Rupees. Twenty one thousand three hundred sixty & Paise forty six only.

Inclusive of Interest at

For THE ATUL PRODUCTS LTD.

ACCOUNTANT.

To. M/s. East End Dyes & Chemical Co.,
1/1, Vansittart Row, Calcutta. 700 001.

Note: This bill Exchange has been drawn in connection with
The sale of Dyes/Chemicals etc.,
covered by TR/RR/PWB Dated.
Invoice No/s. 81500,81499,dt. 08/11/75
CASE IN NEED M/s.

State Bank of India
I. B. No. 8655
ATUL

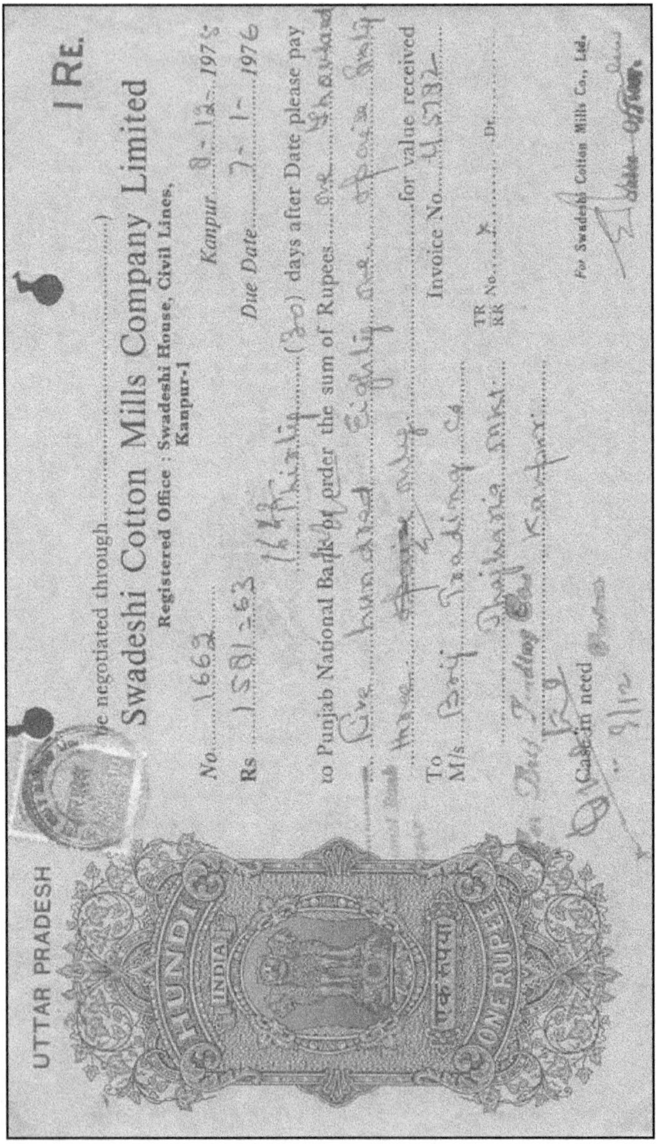
UTTAR PRADESH

I RE.

HUNDI INDIA

एक रुपया ONE RUPEE

To be negotiated through..............................

Swadeshi Cotton Mills Company Limited

Registered Office : Swadeshi House, Civil Lines, Kanpur-1

No. 1663 *Kanpur* 8-12-1975

Rs 1581-63 *Due Date* 7-1-1976

Thirty (30) days after Date please pay

to Punjab National Bank or order the sum of Rupees one thousand five hundred eighty one & paise sixty three only for value received

To M/s Brij Trading Co. Jhijharia Mkt. Kanpur Invoice No. U 5782

TR/RR No. X Dr.

Case in need

For Swadeshi Cotton Mills Co., Ltd.

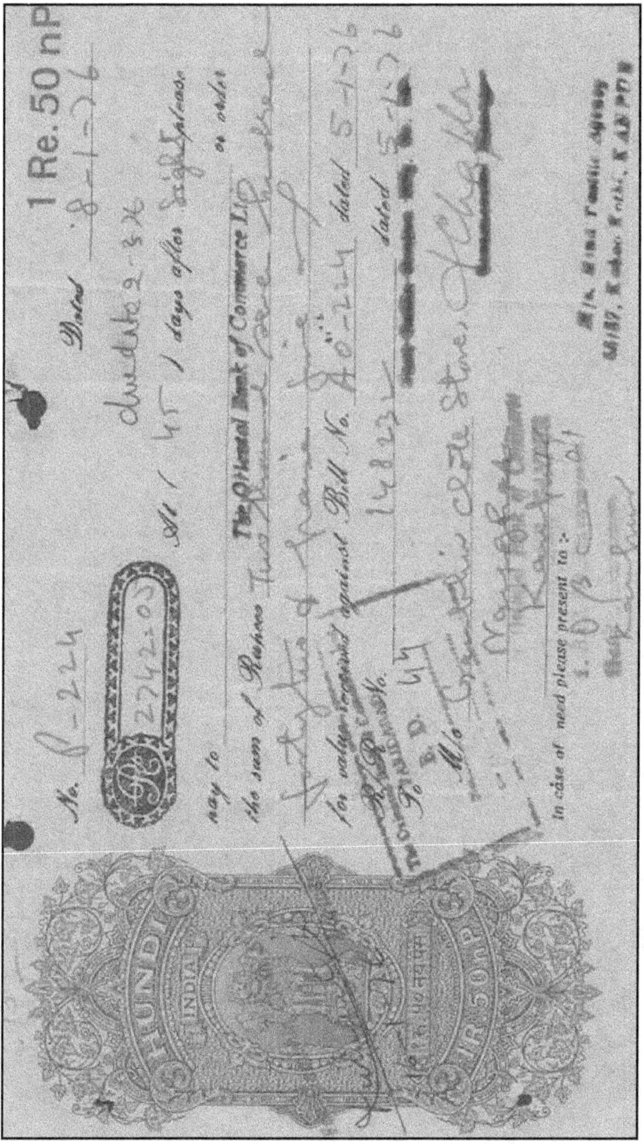

HUNDI INDIA 1R. 50nP

1 Re. 50 nP

No. B-224

Dated 8-1-76

due date 2-3-76

At 45 / days after sight please

pay to The Oriental Bank of Commerce Ltd or order

the sum of Rupees

for value received against Bill No. B-224 dated 5-1-76

dated 5-1-76

In case of need please present to :-

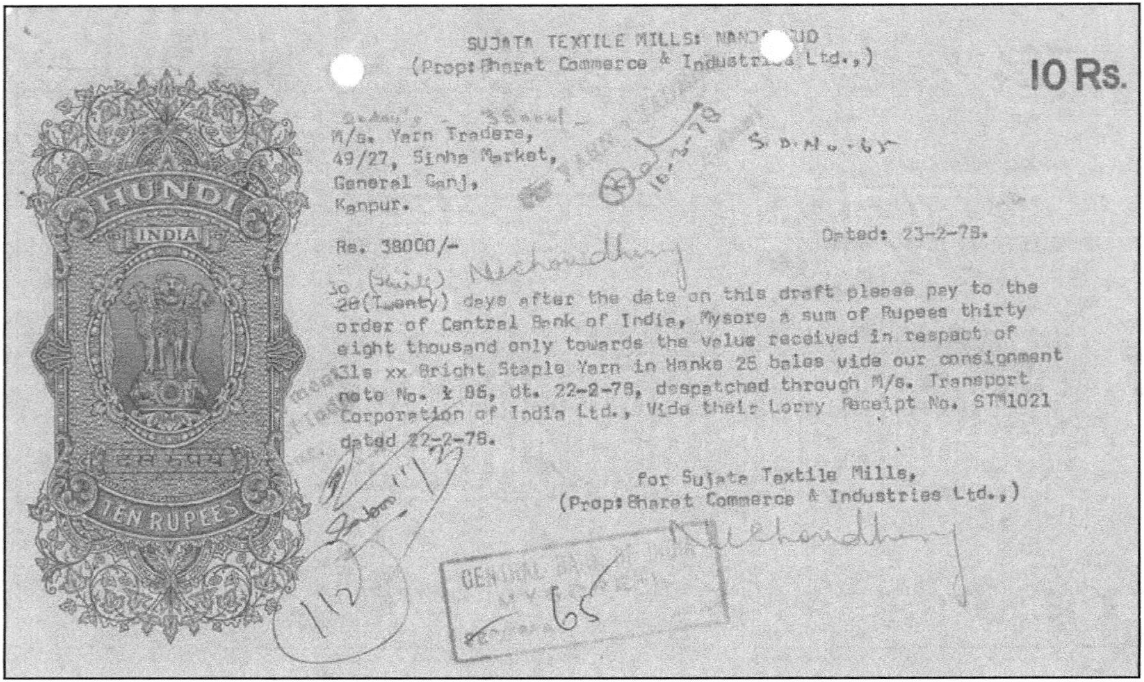

10 Rs.

SUJATA TEXTILE MILLS: NANJANGUD
(Prop: Bharat Commerce & Industries Ltd.,)

M/s. Yarn Traders,
49/27, Sinha Market,
General Ganj,
Kanpur.

S. D. No. 65

Rs. 38000/-

Dated: 23-2-78.

30 (thirty) 20 (Twenty) days after the date on this draft please pay to the order of Central Bank of India, Mysore a sum of Rupees thirty eight thousand only towards the value received in respect of 31s xx Bright Staple Yarn in Hanks 25 bales vide our consignment note No. 86, dt. 22-2-78, despatched through M/s. Transport Corporation of India Ltd., Vide their Lorry Receipt No. STM1021 dated 22-2-78.

For Sujata Textile Mills,
(Prop: Bharat Commerce & Industries Ltd.,)

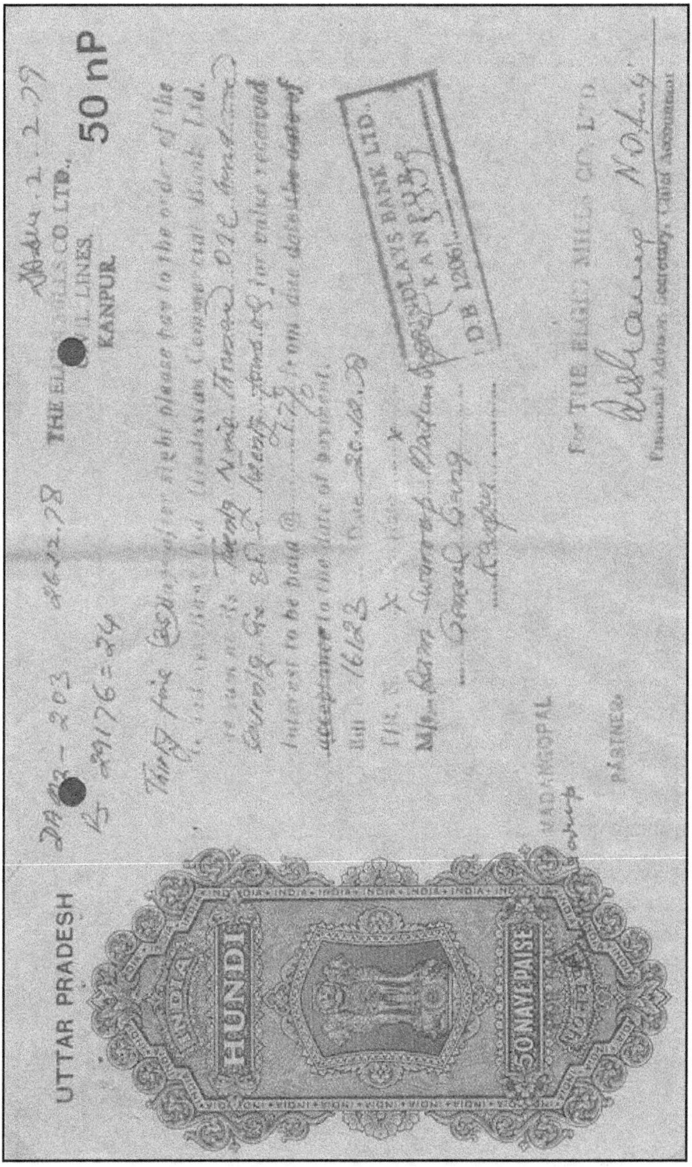
UTTAR PRADESH
HUNDI
50 NAYE PAISE
50 nP
THE ELGIN MILLS CO. LTD.
KANPUR
GRINDLAYS BANK LTD.
KANPUR
For THE ELGIN MILLS CO. LTD.
Financial Adviser, Secretary, Chief Accountant

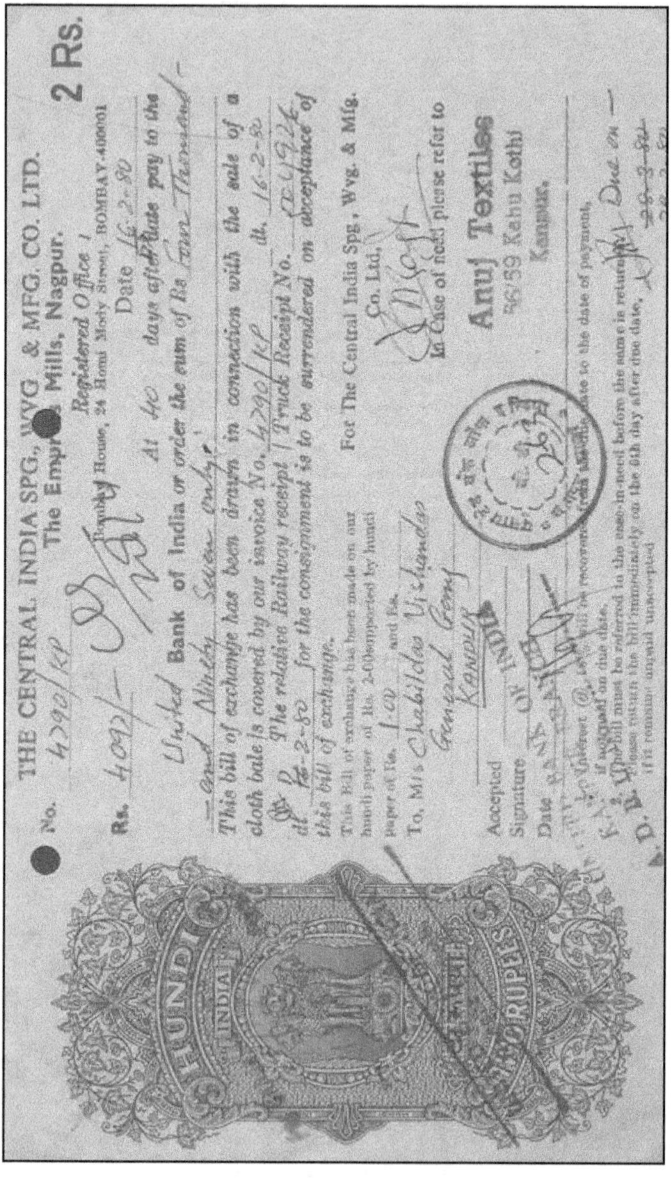

THE CENTRAL INDIA SPG., WVG & MFG. CO. LTD.
The Empress Mills, Nagpur.
Registered Office :
Bombay House, 24 Homi Mody Street, BOMBAY-400001

2 Rs.

No. 4790/KP

Rs. 4097/-

Date 16-2-80

At 40 days after date pay to the United Bank of India or order the sum of Rs Four Thousand and Ninety Seven only.

This bill of exchange has been drawn in connection with the sale of a cloth bale/s covered by our invoice No. 4790/KP dt. 16-2-80

The relative Railway receipt / Truck Receipt No. 004926 dt 16-2-80 for the consignment is to be surrendered on acceptance of this bill of exchange.

This Bill of exchange has been made on our hundi paper of Rs. 2-00 supported by hundi paper of Rs. 1-00 and Rs.

To, M/s Chabildas Vishandas
General Ganj
KANPUR

For The Central India Spg., Wvg. & Mfg. Co. Ltd.,

In Case of need please refer to
Anuj Textiles
56/59 Kahu Kothi
Kanpur.

Accepted
Signature
Date

1. Interest @ ...% will be recovered from the due date to the date of payment, if not paid on due date.
2. The bill must be referred to the case-in-need before the same is returned. Please return the bill immediately on the 6th day after due date, if it remains unpaid unaccepted

Due on — 28-3-80

HUNDI
INDIA
RUPEES

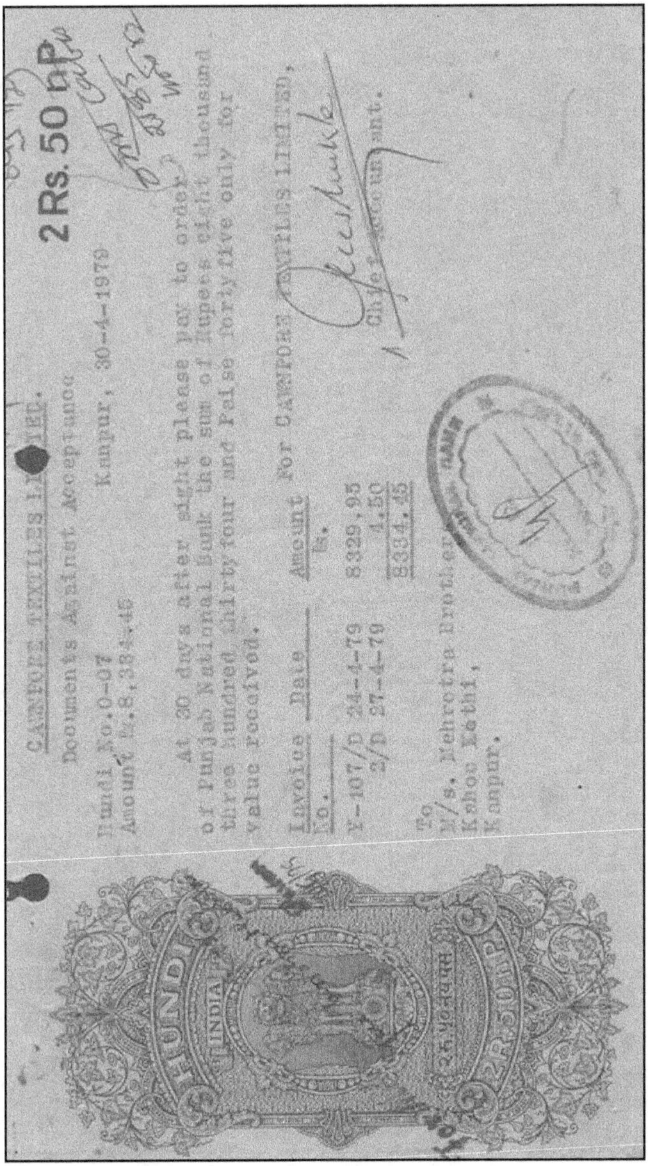

CAWNPORE TEXTILES LIMITED.

Documents Against Acceptance

Hundi No.0-07 Kanpur, 30-4-1979

Amount Rs.8,384.45

At 30 days after sight please pay to order of Punjab National Bank the sum of Rupees eight thousand three hundred thirtyfour and Paise fortyfive only for value received.

2 Rs. 50 nP.

Invoice No.	Date	Amount Rs.
Y-107/D	24-4-79	8329.95
2/D	27-4-79	4.50
		8334.45

For CAWNPORE TEXTILES LIMITED,

Chief Accountant.

To
M/s. Mehrotra Brothers,
Kshoo Kathi,
Kanpur.

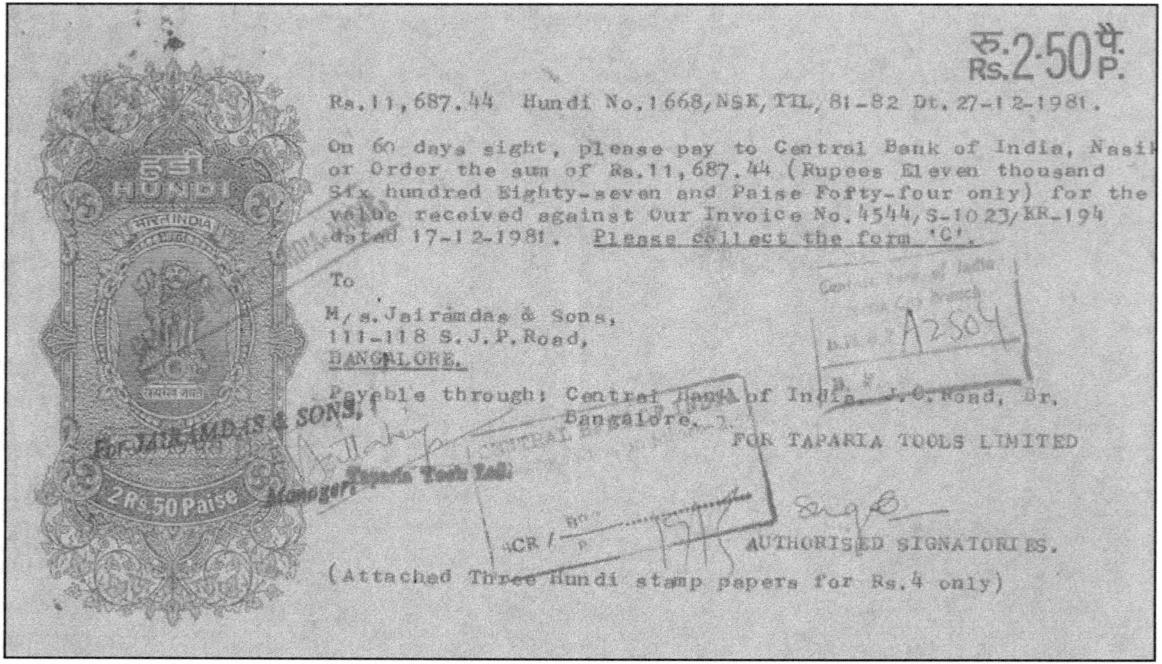

रु. 2·50 पै.
Rs. 2·50 P.

Rs.11,687.44 Hundi No.1668,NSK,TTL,81-82 Dt.27-12-1981.

On 60 days sight, please pay to Central Bank of India, Nasik or Order the sum of Rs.11,687.44 (Rupees Eleven thousand Six hundred Eighty-seven and Paise Fofty-four only) for the value received against Our Invoice No.4544,S-1023/KR-194 dated 17-12-1981. Please collect the form 'C'.

To

M/s.Jairamdas & Sons,
111-118 S.J.P.Road,
BANGALORE.

Payable through: Central Bank of India, J.C.Road, Br.
Bangalore.

FOR TAPARIA TOOLS LIMITED

AUTHORISED SIGNATORIES.

(Attached Three Hundi stamp papers for Rs.4 only)

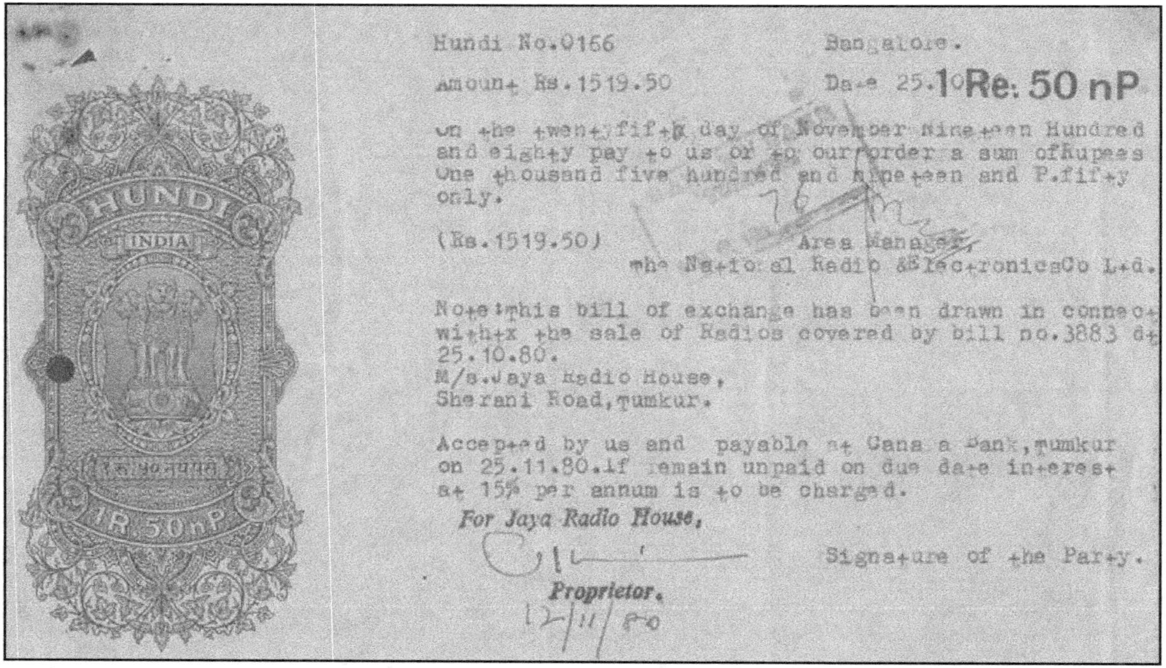

Hundi No.0166 Bangalore.

Amount Rs.1519.50 Date 25.1 Re. 50 nP

On the twentyfifth day of November Nineteen Hundred and eighty pay to us or to our order a sum of Rupees One thousand five hundred and nineteen and P.fifty only.

(Rs.1519.50) Area Manager,
The National Radio & Electronics Co Ltd.

Note: This bill of exchange has been drawn in connect with the sale of Radios covered by bill no.3883 dt 25.10.80.
M/s.Jaya Radio House,
Sharani Road, Tumkur.

Accepted by us and payable at Canara Bank, Tumkur on 25.11.80. If remain unpaid on due date interest at 15% per annum is to be charged.

For Jaya Radio House,

Proprietor.
12/11/80

Signature of the Party.

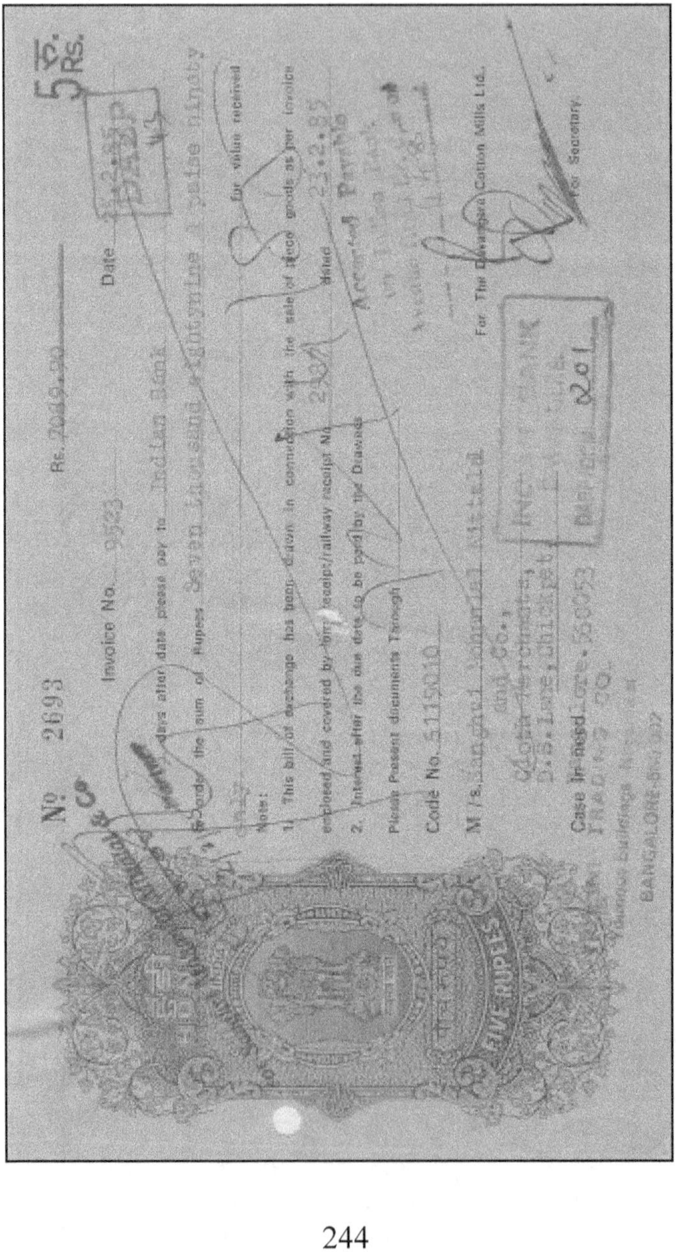
Nº 2693 Rs. 7089.90 5 Rs.

Invoice No. 9523 Date 23.2.85

days after date please pay to Indian Bank

or order the sum of Rupees Seven thousand eightynine & paise ninety only for value received

Note:

1. This bill of exchange has been drawn in connection with the sale of piece goods as per invoice enclosed and covered by lorry receipt/railway receipt No. 2387 dated 23.2.85

2. Interest after the due date to be paid by the Drawees

Please Present documents Through

Code No. 5119010

M/s. Sanghvi Mohanlal Kittalal and Co., Cloth Merchants, D.S. Lane, Chickpet, Bangalore-560053

Case in need

For The Davangere Cotton Mills Ltd.

For Secretary.

HUNDI
25 PAISE
SPECIAL ADHESIVE
Authorised Signatory

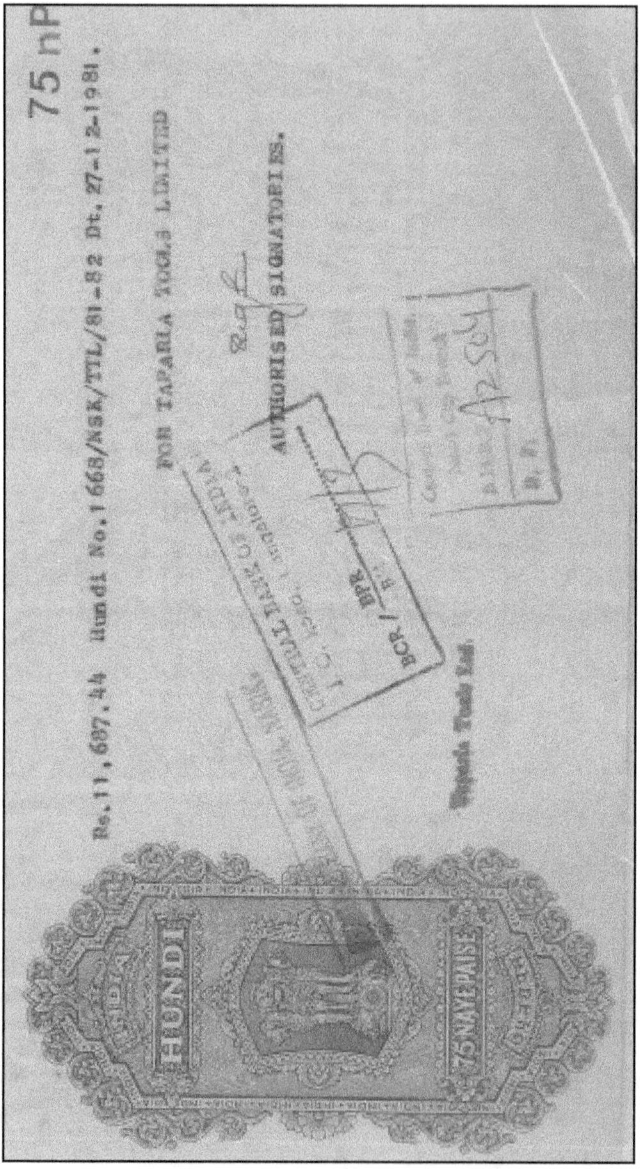
75 nP

Rs.11,687.44 Hundi No.1668/NSK/TTL/81-82 Dt. 27-12-1981.

FOR TAPARIA TOOLS LIMITED

AUTHORISED SIGNATORIES.

CENTRAL BANK OF INDIA

BCR / BPR / B

INDIA HUNDI 75 NAYE PAISE

Also available from the same author:

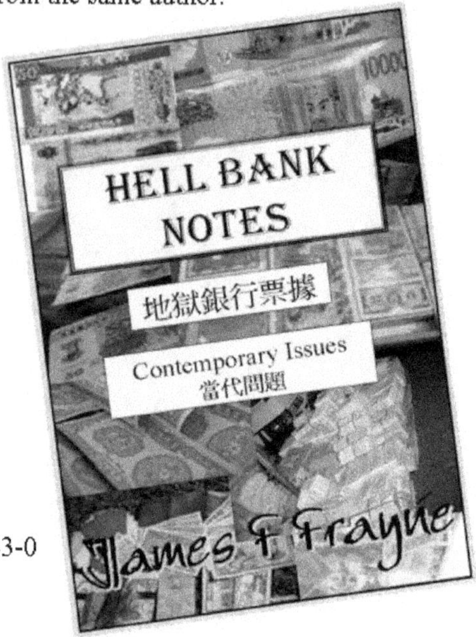

ISBN:
978-1-326-30443-0

The sole intended purpose of these ***faux notes*** is to be offered as burnt-offerings to the deceased as often practiced by the Chinese and several East Asian cultures, their specific purpose being to be burnt in strict accordance with Taoist tradition.

Available through all major book sellers including Amazon as a paper-back in black & white or Kindle in full colour.

Also available from the same author:

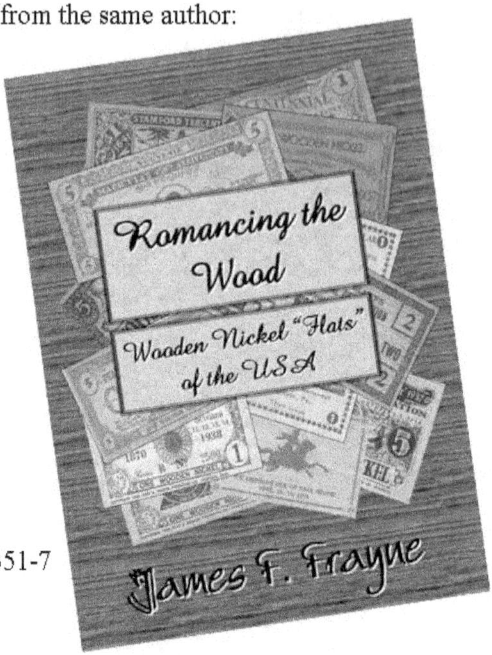

ISBN:
978-1-326-79351-7

This book represents a mere selection of the Wooden Nickel 'Flats' that have been issued since the late 1930s. Even just this small selection, though, uncovers a wealth of local history. Yet to uncover all this information nation-wide would mean volume after volume of incredible history.

Available through all major book sellers including Amazon as a paper-back in black & white or Kindle in full colour.

Also available from the same author:

ISBN:
978-0-244-60232-1

The note that gave the game away for a fleeing monarch; notes that were printed with a child's John Bull printing set; notes that were issued during times of siege; the Government that was involved in gun-boat diplomacy, forgery and illegal drug smuggling. The notes involved and many more, together with the illuminating stories behind them, are all in this publication.

Available through all major book sellers including Amazon as a paper-back in black & white or Kindle in full colour.

www.ingramcontent.com/pod-product-compliance
Lightning Source LLC
Chambersburg PA
CBHW060453290526
45791CB00001B/93
* 9 7 8 1 3 2 6 8 7 0 7 7 5 *